What Happens to Truth

in an Age of Delusion?

What Happens to Truth

in an Age of Delusion?

Harry Antonides

Nsmpress

Contents

Foreword

Some shoes seem too big to fill, so there's no point in even trying. I don't know what size Harry Antonides' shoes are, but I prefer just to sit at his feet and listen to what he has to say. Readers of this book have that opportunity, to sit at his feet and to learn.

The beautiful thing about books is that they give voice to ideas that do not fade, and their words reach an audience with whom the author may not otherwise have had an opportunity to connect.

Harry Antonides has been a leader in the Christian and Reformed community for many years, working originally for the Christian Labour Association of Canada, and later for an associated think tank called the Work Research Foundation (now Cardus). He has utilized his talents and intellectual abilities in service to the community and to this his Father's world, a lot of his time spent reading, researching, writing and speaking.

The point of it all was to discern truth from falsehood, never an easy task, when so many ideas are competing for attention. That task seems much more difficult today when there are the elements of "fake news," mis-information and propaganda spinning about from all sides. Given the milieu that this generation has chosen to adopt – that of relativism – this is no solid foundation, but one of shifting sand. So as we write these words, our culture is very much adrift and uncertain, and revolutionary changes are occurring at breakneck speed.

Each generation has its challenges. Harry Antonides provides us with insight and perspective from a high vantage point, while standing on solid rock, to see the lay of the land; to discern the world of ideas through Gospel vision; to recognize that there is still such a thing as the true truth; he helps us identify the dangers in the terrain, and leads those who wish to follow, with those good feet, to a better way forward.

From this compelling and cohesive compilation of essays and reviews, addressing events of the late 20th and early 21st centuries, we can learn much for today from someone with keen insights who has earned our trust and respect.

As for those big shoes, let's fill the shoes we have been given with the same zeal and dedication to the truth, for God's glory.

John Van Dyk
Editor
Christian Renewal Magazine

Introduction

The United States government has betrayed its own citizens. The betrayal began many years ago, as diverse strands of deceitful intent gained in influence, coalescing under certain key players and movements, gaining in strength and power to become a formidable enemy within.

Certain figures stand out in their deceptiveness, some of who would openly and proudly proclaim it. Saul Alinksky, in his Rules for Radicals, would openly describe the more brazen tactics of deceit to his followers, instructing them on how to undermine and ruin the existing political system. Others would advocate strangling the government with unsustainable and costly programs (Cloward and Piven), defeating the powers that be through legalized warfare (Lawfare), or fomenting dissension with public displays of peaceful protest (the Occupy movement), or not so peaceful, (the Weather Underground, and more recently, Antifa).

This is clearly a strategy of internal warfare that relies more on subversion and deceit than it does on bombs and bullets, the latter having been proven to be less effective, and more costly to undertake.

In this asymmetrical warfare, the enemies within are opportunistic in their common cause. They readily form powerful alliances in government, industry, and the media. They quickly align with other movements when it serves their purposes. Enter Islam – similar, not exactly the same, but close enough. In its 1400-year history, the Qur'an has told a perfectly consistent story, its warlike character modernly displayed and confirmed by 9/11. In this common cause of overthrow, it has its supporters.

Islam has made significant inroads into the cultural and political fabric of North America. The 44th president of the United States, Barack Obama, was entirely sympathetic to the cause of Islam, even to its more radical adherents in Iran, or in the Muslim Brotherhood. Obama could soft peddle his support, as he did shortly after his inauguration in 2008. Addressing the Muslim leadership at the Cairo University in Egypt, Obama told his audience what they wanted to hear including this statement – that he considered it part of his responsibility as president of the United States to fight against negative stereotypes of Islam wherever they appear. Or, Obama could be more forceful in his support, evidenced by the generous loan of $1.7 billion in cash to Iran's totalitarian regime.

This cozying up to agencies like the Muslim Brotherhood is striking when it is considered that the Muslim Brotherhood seeks to turn America into a sharia-based country. More ominous yet, its creed is, "Allah is our objective. The Prophet is our leader. The Qur'an is our law. Jihad is our way. Dying in the way of Allah is our highest hope." The plan is to eliminate western civilization from within, sabotaging its miserable house so that it is eliminated, and Allah's religion is made victorious over all other religions.

These may be rather startling and contentious terms to introduce a book of essays. However, they emphasize the important issues that have concerned me. Part II of this book takes a closer look at various people who have found an appetite and delight for undermining the truth and our cherished institutions, our way of life and our freedoms. I call these the Deceivers. In Part III of this book I contrast them to the signs of hope in the form of Truth-Tellers. The truth shall keep you free, and it is the Truth-Tellers who are the modern-day heroes here. They deserve to be celebrated.

Part I: Truth Under Siege

1 A World in Turmoil

In a sense, God – the personal omnipotent deity of Christendom– has been dying for centuries. His lordship over the world has been threatened by every scientist who discovered a new natural law of organic growth, by every invention of man that safeguarded him against "act of God" disaster, by every new medicine that tamed a disease and solved another mystery of life. But it is the 20th century, the age of technological miracle, that has seen the triumph of the Enlightenment and the apparent banishment of God from the universe – even, thanks to Freud, from the human soul.[1]

When men choose not to believe in God, they do not thereafter believe in nothing, they then become capable of believing in anything (G.K. Chesterton).

If you reject absolute truth absolutely, you are not only incoherent but in danger of becoming the worst kind of dogmatist.[2]

Western civilization is beset by an overwhelming series of seemingly insoluble problems and difficulties. All of them involve the very core of who we are as humans. What is

---

[1] *Time*, December 25, 1964.

[2] "Obama and the End of Liberalism?" Interview Charles Kesler, NRO, January 16, 2013.

the purpose of our lives? How do we know how to live? How do we discern right from wrong? Where do we find the answers to the most burning questions about nationhood in a world of turmoil, violence and warfare? What are the principles that can guide us in structuring government to secure peace and justice for all? Furthermore, how can we distinguish between the public and private sectors of society, so that all the "mediating structures" in society, such as the family, education, media, business, science and untold numbers of voluntary associations, are able to function freely in keeping with their unique character and purpose?

WAR AND RUMORS OF WAR

Looking back over the past century, we are not encouraged to think that these questions have ready and easy answers. In the second decade of the 20th century, Europe was torn apart by a murderous war (World War I) that cut short the lives of an estimated 20 million people.

In revulsion against so much slaughter, people became wary of all militarism and vowed to never again get involved in such barbarity. The result was that just two decades later, Europe was unprepared to stop Hitler's military machine from conquering most of Europe. It took five years of brutal warfare that razed entire German cities, destroyed its industrial infrastructure, and resulted in the death of an estimated 60 million soldiers and civilians, before Western Europe was liberated. (Many more millions were wounded in body and soul in both world wars.) In the meantime, Eastern Europe was left to suffer nearly four more decades of Soviet tyranny.

In 1989 the Cold War came to an end with the unraveling of the Soviet Union, raising the hopes and prospects of a more peaceful world. Yet the world was and is still a dangerous place with new sources of conflict and war festering.

Since World War II, radical Islam has spread its tentacles across many countries, not only in the Middle East, but also into Africa, Asia, and even into the West. Osama bin Laden spoke for millions of Muslims when he declared war on the West, notably the United States, and Israel, the only country in the Middle East with a vibrant culture and freedom of religion.

The treacherous 9/11 attack on America, and subsequent terrorist attacks in European countries, notably in Spain and the U.K., were shocking reminders that we are still living in a violent and dangerous world. These events leave no doubt that hatred of the West is deeply embedded in the hearts of a significant segment of radicalized Muslim believers who are convinced that they are called to establish the caliphate world-wide by violence and stealth.

THE REMAKING OF EUROPE

In the 1950s, millions of Muslim immigrants began to stream into Western countries, since Europe needed workers for its industries. The work often involved menial tasks. Originally these immigrants were expected to serve as guest workers, temporary laborers who would eventually return to their home countries. Instead, many decided to stay and were accorded full citizenship. Their numbers swelled quickly. In the process many began to form separate enclaves in the largest cities. (The total number of Muslim newcomers into Europe according to a 2010 Pew survey was estimated at 44.1 million, with a projection for 58.2 million by 2030.)

Initially the European countries, steeped in the ideology of multi-culturalism, facilitated this development without a program of integration for the newcomers. Meanwhile, many Muslim leaders told their followers to consider the West alien territory and instructed them not to integrate. This is in line with the Muslim doctrine that mankind is divided into a world of peace (Islamic) versus that of war (non-Islamic/infidel). In 2008 the Turkish Prime Minister Recep Tayyip Erdogan told a large crowd of Turkish immigrants in Germany that "assimilation is a crime against humanity."

This growing dissonance between the host countries and large numbers of Muslim immigrants eventually led to severe conflicts and even riots, especially in France. Several countries experienced first-hand the violent wrath of radicalized believers in their duty to spread the rule of Allah. Holland was shaken when the outspoken politician/professor Pim Fortuyn was brutally murdered in May 2002, followed in November 2004 by the murder of Theo van Gogh. Both men had been blunt in their criticism of Dutch immigration policies that allowed radical Islamism to freely take root in that country.

Muslim terrorists attacked Madrid in March 2004 killing nearly 200 and wounding some 2000 victims. In July 2005, a similar attack on the London public transit system killed 56 people and wounded many more. These and other killings of defenseless people sent shock waves through all of the free world. Many began to have serious doubts about the growth in their midst of a separatist Muslim culture in the name of multiculturalism.

THE END OF MULTICULTURALISM?

Both former French President Nicolas Sarkozy and German Chancellor Angela Merkel, have publicly stated that they no longer believe that multiculturalism can lead to peaceful coexistence. Sarkozy, speaking after the killing of seven people in Toulouse by an Al Qaeda-trained Muslim on March 23, 2012, said that there are "too many foreigners on our territory."[3]

Chancellor Merkel was far more direct, leaving no doubt about her views, presumably shared by many Germans. She understands that the problem is not at the surface but reaches down to a people's deepest convictions. Last year Merkel stated that Germany's roots are Judeo-Christian. She said: "Now we obviously have Muslims in Germany. But it is important in regard to Islam that the values represented by Islam must correspond to our constitution. What applies here is the constitution, not Sharia law."

At a meeting of her Christian Democratic Union (CDU) party in October 2011, the Chancellor said that at the beginning of the 1960s

---

[3] *Toronto Star*, March 24, 2012.

Germany welcomed Muslim guest workers, expecting that they eventually would return to their home countries. But that did not happen, so for a while it was believed that Muslims and other Germans could live side-by-side in harmony with each other. This turned out be a multicultural pipe dream, or as Merkel said, this approach has "failed utterly."

At another CDU meeting she said that the debate about immigration, "especially by those of the Muslim faith," was an opportunity for her party to stand up for its convictions. She explained:

> We do not have too much Islam; we have too little Christianity. We have too few discussions about the Christian view of mankind.... We feel bound to the Christian image of humanity – that's what defines us. Those who do not accept this are in the wrong place here.[4]

With that, the Chancellor threw wide open a discussion that until now is mostly avoided in public, especially among the political leadership. Their attitude is one of deference mixed with fear of offending Muslim supremacists who are adept at using the freedom in the West to advance their cause. They have managed to infiltrate and influence every major institution from the media, the universities and the government to advance their cause, while being quick to intimidate and silence anyone who raises a critical voice.

Think of author Salman Rushdie, or the case in Canada against Maclean's magazine, Mark Steyn and Ezra Levant, a few years ago. Such threats and harassment send a chill among public figures who will think twice before they write and speak about what they really think. At the time of this writing the Obama administration is in negotiations with the Organization of Islamic Cooperation to make any

---

[4] Soeren Kern, "Islam in Germany: 'Germany Does Away with Itself,' June 16, 2012.

criticism of Islam a criminal offence. The Secretary of State Hillary Clinton played a major role in these discussions.

A TWO-FOLD CHALLENGE

As anyone knows who follows the daily news, ours is a violent and chaotic world. Most of the Western economies are in trouble, some very seriously so; politically, most governments are struggling to keep the extensive welfare states from collapsing; militarily, many countries in the Middle East and Africa are at war or are fearing the outbreak of war. This is especially acute because of Iran's determination to obtain nuclear weapons and to destroy Israel. What are we to do? What should Christians do?

In summary, we face two serious threats as citizens of the Western nations. The first one is internal, that is the radical secularization of life, so well-expressed in the three quotations at the beginning of this chapter. To be sure, the West was never totally Christian in the sense that it was completely unified as one religious community. But it was Christian in the sense that it was profoundly influenced by the Christian faith. This meant that there was a largely shared belief in God as the Creator of the world, the source of goodness and truth, and of the moral law that enables us to distinguish between right and wrong.

Such shared belief is now gone, and the consequences of that change are not trivial, but go to the core of human existence. Most importantly, it means that we are in the dark about truth; we can no longer distinguish between good and evil or right and wrong. In other words, we live in a world of delusion – as expressed in the title of this book.

The second threat comes from the outside, and is directly related to the first. It concerns the large flood of Muslim immigrants into the West. Among them are many moderates who are happy to escape the Islam-ruled countries mired in poverty and tyranny. The problem lies with those Muslim immigrants whose minds are shaped by leaders who preach a supremacist version of Islam, and who are adept at using the freedom they enjoy in the West to expand their Islamic ideology.

They have been very successful in intimidating anyone who criticizes Islam.

The result is silence or denial about what has rightly been called the creeping Islamization of the West. This is the second major problem to understand and confront, which is made more difficult because it comes at a time when the West is spiritually disarmed. In other words, the West's spiritual emptiness combined with an openness to other influences makes it vulnerable to the inroads of a radicalized Islam that is aggressively spreading its influence all over the world.

The secularism of the West is providing an open door for the jihadists – and they know it. This brings to mind Jesus' words in Matthew 12. He tells the story of a house that is cleared of one evil spirit, which is then taken over by seven even worse evil spirits.

2 The Countercultural Revolution Lives On

This, so I have argued, is the primary project of our counter culture: to proclaim a new heaven and a new earth....[5]

You will not certainly die," the serpent said to the woman. "For God knows that when you eat from it your eyes will be opened, and you will be like God, knowing good and evil (Genesis 3: 4-5).

When the foundations are being destroyed, what can the righteous do? (Psalm 11: 3).

Sometimes it seems as if the world we live in has gone mad. Who can make sense of all the conflicting messages that bombard us every day? A lot of the news is about human ignorance, corruption, incompetence and creeping lawlessness in the Western democracies. Farther out in the rest of the world, dozens of minor and

---

[5] Theodore Roszak, *The Making of a Counter Culture: Reflections on the Technocratic Society and Its Youthful Opposition* (New York: Double1day & Co., Inc., 1969).

major wars are being fought, resulting in bloodshed, starvation and soul-destroying deprivation. North Korea, a cruel and murderous dictatorship, has managed to become a nuclear armed state. Meanwhile, radical Islamists have declared war on the free West, and Islamic Iran is moving closer to obtaining nuclear weapons while threatening to destroy the state of Israel. Some people no longer want to watch the news or read the newspapers because they are too depressing. Most of us can empathize. But is withdrawal from society to live in the comfort of our own small world a valid option for those in the free West? Christians should know the answer to this question.

This chapter will address the movement that has had a revolutionary effect on the Western world, especially on the United States. We are facing radical changes in the way people believe and behave. From a Christian point of view, that is most visible in the way the culture has become de-Christianized. The whole world of "values" and habits has been turned on its head. The term "revolution" captures the spirit of the times, because it involves a determined rejection of long-standing traditions, beliefs and habits.

THE SEEDS OF DESTRUCTION

To understand what is happening, let's take a careful look at the happenings in the U.S. during the wild and riotous 1960s. The Sixties was the decade when the seeds of radical change were sown with far-reaching repercussions. That was the time when the existing culture (the "Establishment") was declared to be oppressive and anti-human, and in need of being dispatched to the junkyard of history.

Whoever lived through that decade will still have vivid memories of the huge protest marches in the major cities. Some of those were peaceful. They called for an end to the injustice suffered by black Americans. Martin Luther King, a clergyman and leader in the African-American Civil Rights Movement, insisted that protests be peaceful. His fearless and eloquent leadership did much to end racial segregation, at least in law if not always in practice. He became famous for his 1963 "I Have a Dream" speech, a riveting plea for justice and brotherhood.

Other leaders in the 1960s revolution took a different tack and chose the way of violence and intimidation. The Black Panthers, Students for a Democratic Society, and the Weather Underground were violent and criminal organizations. A short list of the upheavals and calls for radical change included: many student protests involving strikes and occupation of university buildings; the sexual revolution, with its devastating impact on the family; increasing drug use; anti-Vietnam war protests; riots, looting and burning cities; the Woodstock youth festival in the summer of 1969.

The Beatles, a four-man rock band, burst on to the world stage in the early 1960s, benefiting from and contributing to the cultural revolution then underway. They became an international sensation, attracting huge, adoring crowds to their many performances. One of the band members, John Lennon, boasted to a British reporter: "Christianity will go…. It will vanish and shrink…. We're more popular than Jesus now; I don't know which will go first, rock 'n' roll or Christianity."

Three of the most terrifying and unforgettable crimes were the assassinations of President John F. Kennedy in 1963, that of his brother Robert, and of Martin Luther King in 1968.

It seemed to many that the curse of chaos and lawlessness would never end. But gradually life settled into a less chaotic routine, and the revolution seemed to have spent all its energy. But it hadn't. It merely went underground where the foundation blocks of society were replaced with inferior sandy imitations. That was accomplished by many rebels of the 1960s who ended up as university professors, leaders in education, the arts, the media and entertainment.

The 1960s call to revolution was not superficial but affected the very foundations of society, that is, religion, morality and the many social institutions. The late Irving Kristol (1920-2009) in 1994 wrote an essay entitled "Countercultures" in which he stated that the 1960s counterculture was "certainly one of the most significant events in the last half century of Western civilization. It is reshaping our educational systems, our arts, our forms of entertainment, our sexual conventions, our moral codes."

Kristol pointed out that this movement is against culture; not one that wants to reform and renew the culture but one that comes with an "avowed hostility" to culture itself in the minds of intellectuals, professors, and artists. Kristol suggested that culture and art are merged into a new self-consciousness, and a new sense of mission that was "secular, humanistic, and redemptory." He continued: "All traditional ties with religion were severed. The sacred was now to be found in 'culture' and 'art' where 'creative geniuses' … were in the future to give meaning to our lives and sustenance to our aspirations."

In other words, there is no transcendent order or purpose for human life. It's up to us to create that for ourselves. This is an old story that never ends well. In the following I will deal with some more details of the Sixties revolution, as analyzed in Roger Kimball's *The Long March*. This book helps us understand the profound significance of Kristol's definition.

A DAMAGE REPORT

Kimball writes that in pondering the state of American cultural life he concludes that it has suffered "some ghastly accident that has left it afloat but rudderless, physically intact, its 'moral center' a shamble." He goes on to say that the cause of this "disaster" is like a protracted and spiritually convulsive detonation – "one that trembled with gathering force through North America and Western Europe from the mid-1950s through the early 1970s and tore apart, perhaps irrevocably, the moral and intellectual fabric of our society."

The author explains that his purpose in writing *The Long March* is to explore the effects of the cultural revolution, which he calls "part cultural history, part spiritual damage report." Above all, he stresses that the impact of the Sixties revolution is not only a passing event easily forgotten, but it continues "to reverberate throughout our culture." He writes:

> It lives on in our values and habits, in our tastes, pleasures, and aspirations. It lives on especially in our educational and cultural institutions, and in the degraded pop culture that permeates our lives like a corrosive fog. Looking afresh at the architects of America's cultural revolution, The Long March provides a series of cautionary tales, an annotated guidebook of wrong turns, dead ends, and unacknowledged spiritual hazards.[6]

Although the 1960s revolution in America was accompanied by plenty of violence and destruction, Kimball thinks that the kind of radical upheaval of the French and Russian revolutions is almost unthinkable in America. Here the efforts to transform society have been channeled into cultural and moral life. Thus, the success of the cultural revolution is not in the destruction of buildings and toppled governments but in "shattered values" and in what the author calls the "spiritual deformations" that affect every aspect of life.

I am not assured that the likes of the French and Russian revolutions will not occur in America, for the efforts to radically transform society may well lead to the chaos and hatreds of civil war. It has happened before. Here I am thinking of President Abraham Lincoln's warning issued in 1838:

> At what point, then, is the approach of danger to be expected? I answer, if it ever reaches us, it must spring up amongst us. It cannot come from abroad. If destruction be our lot, we must ourselves be its author and finisher. As a nation of freemen, we must live through all times, or die by suicide.

Perhaps the most destructive feature of the revolution is the movement for sexual "liberation," which often turned into outright debauchery, closely allied to the "mainstreaming of the drug culture

---

[6] Roger Kimball *The Long March: How the Cultural Revolution of the 1960s Changed America* (New York: Encounter Books, 2000), 5.

and its attendant pathologies." Kimball argues that the two are related because "both are expressions of the narcissistic hedonism that was an important ingredient of the counterculture from its development in the 1950s."

The idealization of youth played a major role in the counterculture. This has not only led to the spread of the adolescent values and passions, but to the "eclipse" of adult virtues like circumspection, responsibility, and restraint. Kimball asserts that the most far-reaching and destructive effect has been the "simultaneous glorifications and degradation of popular culture." Even the most vacuous products of that culture are included in the subjects for the college curriculum, as the character of popular culture itself becomes ever more "vulgar, vicious and degrading."

In addition to the general coarsening effect of life, Kimball writes that this triumph of vulgarity has helped to create the twin banes of political correctness and radical multiculturalism. Abandoning the intrinsic standards of achievement has created a "value vacuum" in which "everything is sucked through the sieve of politics and the ideology of victimhood."

Another feature of the counterculture is its ideological commitment to the Radical Left. That's why its proponents believe that the existing society is corrupt and must be destroyed so that a new one can be built on the ruins of the old. Hence the call for the long march through the institutions so that society is reduced to a mass of individuals beholden to the all-powerful state. In other words, the so-called intermediate institutions, which in a free society serve as a bulwark of freedom independent of the state, must be eliminated

.

A MARXIST VOICE

The Marxist philosopher Herbert Marcuse (1898-1979) became a prominent leader of the cultural revolution. His books Eros and Civilization (1955), a book that became a bible of the counterculture, and One-Dimensional Man (1964) became popular in the counter cultural ranks. He wrote that the march through the institutions would be accomplished not by direct confrontation but by "working against the established institutions while working in them." This tactic has been an overwhelming success, especially in the university, the media, and government. Kimball writes that these tactics of insinuation and infiltration rather than confrontation are the primary means by which "the counter cultural dreams of radicals like Marcuse have triumphed."

Is it not ironic that this Marxist philosopher – who represents and advocates a philosophy that everywhere it is applied brings nothing but slavery – pontificates about the abolition of repression in all personal relations including (especially) the man-woman relationship? Kimball writes that Marcuse "blends Marx and Freud to produce an emancipatory vision based on polymorphous, narcissistic sexuality...."

In other words, the old-fashioned notion of faithfulness in marriage and the biblical instruction to help raise the next generation, must be discarded. Here is his reasoning in his own words, reported by Kimball: Marcuse speaks glowingly of "a resurgence of pregenital polymorphous sexuality" that "protests against the repressive order of procreative sexuality." He recommends returning to a state of "primary narcissism," that is,

> the Nirvana principle not as death but as life.... This change in the value and scope of libidinal relations...would lead to a disintegration of the institutions in which the private interpersonal relations have been organized, particularly the monogamic and patriarchal family.[7]

If you had to fit this convoluted argument into one sentence, you could say: "We want freedom from the institution of the family because it is a cage of enslavement."

Kimball summarizes the purpose of this book as follows: "The aim of *The Long March* is to show how many of the ideals of the

---

[7] Ibid., 168.

counterculture have quietly triumphed in the afterlife of the Sixties and what that triumph has meant for America's cultural and intellectual life."

In my view he has been amazingly successful, and for that he deserves our gratitude, as well as many thousands of readers

3 Conspirators of the Sixties Revolution

That the ideology of the Sixties has insinuated itself, disastrously, into the curricula of our schools and colleges; it has significantly altered the texture of sexual relations and family life; it has played havoc with the authority of churches and other repositories of moral wisdom.... It has even, most poignantly, addled our hearts and innermost assumptions about what counts as the good life: it has perverted our dreams as much as it has prevented us from attaining them.[8]

Every major cultural movement of radical change requires an infrastructure of leadership in the opinion-shaping agencies, especially the media, academia, schools, and the arts, which is able to inspire a sizable section of the population.

The Sixties revolution was no exception and was able to draw on a wide range of public figures. The following is a profile of four persons who played a major role in this culture-changing event in American

---

[8] Kimball, 14.

history. I am extensively relying on the information provided by Roger Kimball.

SUSAN SONTAG (1933-2004)

Susan Sontag was born in New York City, but never got to like her country of birth. She was a precocious child and became a prolific author, critic, novelist, playwright, filmmaker, professor, and political activist. She studied at major universities in England, France, and America.

In 1960 she obtained a teaching position in the Department of Religion at Columbia University. Her long list of novels, plays, nonfiction essays, monographs, and films paved her way into celebrity status in the world of letters and academia. Some referred to her as "The Dark Lady of American Letters." The New York Review of Books called her "one of the most influential critics of her generation."

Her philosophy of life and her view of sexuality made her a powerful contributor to the moral perversion of the Sixties Revolution. She was openly bisexual, and was married at age 17 (1950) to Philip Rieff, her teacher at the University of Chicago. Their son David was born in 1952; they divorced in 1958. Subsequently, she consorted with a number of men and women.

Sontag became embroiled in the controversies surrounding America's wars in Vietnam and the Middle East, as well as the Cuban revolution masterminded by the Castro brothers. As did many on the political left, she harbored a strong sense of resentment not only toward her own country, but toward the entire Western civilization. In 1967, she wrote in the *Partisan Review* that America "deserves" to have its wealth "taken away" by the Third World. She then stated that all the benefits and cultural riches of the West "don't redeem what this particular civilization has wrought upon the world. The white race is the cancer of human history."

She visited Cuba in 1968, after which she wrote about the "right way" to love the Cuban revolution. She contrasted what she perceived to be the deadness of the American way of life with the Cuban "new sensibility," that is, a natural "southern spontaneity, gaiety, sensuality and freaking out." She followed up with this canard that "the Cuban revolution is astonishingly free of repression and bureaucratization... No Cuban writer has been or is in jail, or is failing to get his work published." Sontag wrote in a similar vein about her visit to North Vietnam in her essay "Trip to Hanoi." She dutifully repeated the outrageous lies she had been told by her hosts about the good care the American prisoners of war were receiving. She admitted that her report tended to idealize the North Vietnamese, but that was because she experienced that country as one which "deserves to be idealized." Before her trip to Hanoi in 1968, she wrote that the U.S. ("a criminal, sinister country") is brutally and self-righteously slaughtering a small nation.

Barely two weeks after the 9/11 treacherous attack on America, she wrote in The New Yorker of September 24, 2001: "The disconnect between last Tuesday's monstrous dose of reality and the self-righteous drivel and outright deception being peddled by public figures and TV commentators is startling, depressing.... Where is the acknowledgement that this was not a 'cowardly' attack on 'civilization' or 'liberty' or 'humanity' or 'the free world' but an attack on the world's self-proclaimed superpower, undertaken as a consequence of specific American alliances and actions?"

NORMAN MAILER (1923-2007)

Norman Mailer was born in Long Branch, New Jersey. He attended Harvard University at age 16 where he studied aeronautical engineering and began to take an interest in writing. He published his first story at age 18.

After he graduated in 1943, he was drafted into the American army and served in the Philippines and Japan.

In 1948, while studying at the Sorbonne in Paris he published his first book, *The Naked and the Dead*,[9] drawing on his army experience. It became an instant success and was on the *New York Times* best seller list for weeks. It was declared to be one of the best American wartime novels, and the Modern Library called it one of the "one hundred best novels in the English Language." Mailer wrote more than 40 books and many essays which catapulted him into the role of anti-establishment guru. The critic Philip Beidler succinctly summarized Mailer's ambition as follows:

> There is no doubt that Mailer as a literary intellectual wished to assume the mantle of '60s youth-illuminatus, at once existential prophet and pied piper. Accordingly, his career across the decade revealed a relentless, almost obsessive wish to be the voice of '60s adversarial culture in its broadest sense: a voice uniting the radical intelligentsia and dissenting youth in a new project of revolutionary consciousness spilling over from bohemian lofts and campus enclaves into the streets of the nation at large.[10]

In all his extensive writings Mailer displayed a total lack of respect for all traditional norms for social and political relations. He was obsessed with the sexual. He wrote in Advertisements for Myself that "the only revolution which will be meaningful and natural for the twentieth century will be the sexual revolution one senses everywhere." He was married six times and fathered eight children.

His attitude to crime and punishment reverses the roles by making the criminal appear to be the heroic victim of an oppressive establishment, as in his *The Executioner's Song*. Mailer befriended Jack Abbott, a violent convict who sent him long letters about life in prison. He helped Abbott to publish these letters in a book with the title In the Belly of the Beast.

---

[9] Norman Mailer, *The Naked and the Dead* (New York: Rinehart & Company, 1948), 64.

[10] Kimball, *The Long March*

In the introduction Mailer described Abbott as a radical intellectual and potential leader with a vision of a better world through revolution. Mailer helped Abbott get early release from prison. But shortly after his release he went to New York and killed a 22-year-old Cuban-American waiter. When Mailer was asked about the family of the victim, he stated that he was willing to gamble with a portion of society to save this killer's talents.

CHARLES REICH (1928-)

Charles Reich was born in 1928 in New York City. Roger Kimball writes that few embody the spirit of the Sixties better than Charles Reich, one-time Yale law professor turned guru of a higher consciousness. His *Greening of America*, "was both a blueprint for America's cultural revolution and a paean for its supposedly glorious results." Published by Random House, it became an instant best seller as well as a national preoccupation. Yet there were also a few critics, including Stewart Alsop in *Newsweek*, who refused to join the choir. In fact, he described the book as "a bag of scary mush."

However, that did not stop this book from becoming a sensation. Here is a taste of the author's hubris when he predicts in the beginning of his book that there is a revolution coming. He writes:

> It will not be like revolutions of the past. It will originate with the individual and end with culture, and it will change the political structure only as its final act.... It promises a higher reason, a more human community, and a new and liberated individual. Its ultimate creation will be a new and enduring wholeness and beauty – a renewed relationship of man to himself, to other men, to society, to nature, and to the land.[11]

Reich depicts America as a "vast, terrifying anti-community" in thrall to a false consciousness that strips away all creativity and personal uniqueness. To counteract this robotic kind of existence he developed a three-fold typology, which he called Consciousness I, II and III.

---

[11] Charles A. Reich, *The Greening of America* (New York: Banptam), 180.

Consciousness I originated in the nineteenth century when rugged independence, capitalism, character, morality, hard work and self-denial were the dominant motivators. Reich's list of Consciousness I types include farmers, small business owners, AMA-type doctors, gangsters, Republicans, and "just plain folks."

He thinks that this type of consciousness has been overtaken by its successor, Consciousness II, which by now also has passed its "best before" date since it is dominated by the American Corporate State. This began with the New Deal, but that progressive initiative has run its course. According to Reich, its "ethic of control, of technology, of the rational intellect... was the real enemy of liberation."

Kimball writes that Reich's Consciousness III is hard to describe, yet it spread like the measles. Its power to attract must lie in its rejection of all authority, schedules, accepted customs, and deference. As Reich puts it: "Accepted patterns of thought must be broken; what is considered 'rational thought' must be opposed by 'non rational thought' – drug-thought, mysticism, impulses."

Perhaps the core meaning of Reich's thoughts – which explains its instant popularity among the university students and professors – is most clearly centered on his notion of liberation. He states that "the meaning of liberation is that the individual is free to build his own philosophy and values, his own life-style, and his own culture from a new beginning." A more contemptuous and defiant statement about the human condition is hard to imagine.

ELDRIDGE CLEAVER (1935-1998)

Eldridge Cleaver was born in Arkansas and grew up in the Watts section of Los Angeles. Early in life he started getting into trouble with the law for theft and for selling marijuana. In 1954 he was sent to prison for possession of drugs. In 1957 he was arrested again and sentenced to a maximum of fourteen years in prison for rape and attempted murder. While in prison he read revolutionary authors such as Marx,

Lenin, Bakunin, as well as contemporary authors Norman Mailer, Allen Ginsberg, William S. Burroughs. He was released from prison in 1966.

While in prison he began writing a number of philosophical and political essays, which were first published in Ramparts, then in 1968 republished in a book titled, *Soul on Ice*.[12] It became a major source of inspiration in the black power movement, and The *New York Times* Book Review declared it to be "brilliant and revealing." It helped to boost Cleaver into a position of influence in the leadership of the Black Panther Party, becoming its Minister of Information from 1967 to 1971.

Soul on Ice is a collection of Cleaver's thoughts on prison life, race relations, and especially his sexual obsession with white women. It has often been assigned reading in schools and colleges. The critic Maxwell Geismar wrote this in the book's introduction: "Cleaver is simply one of the best cultural critics now writing." Here is a sample of the tenor of his musings:

> I'd like to leap the whole last mile and grow a beard and don whatever threads the local nationalism might require and comrade with Che Guevara, and share his fate, blazing a new pathfinder's trail through the stymied upbeat brain of the New Left....

Cleaver bragged that he became a rapist, first of black girls in the ghetto,

> but then he crossed the tracks and sought out white prey.... Rape was an insurrectionist act. It delighted me that I was defying and trampling upon the white man's law, upon his system of values, and that I was defiling his women.... I felt I was getting revenge.

Though he later renounced his stand on rape, he did not display any regrets for the content of his *Soul on Ice*.

In 1968 Cleaver led a gunfight with Oakland police in which he and two officers were wounded and a young Black Panther member was killed. Cleaver was charged with attempted murder, but managed to escape to Cuba, and later lived in Algeria and France. He returned to

---

[12] Eldridge Cleaver, *Soul on Ice* (Toronto: Delta Publishing, 1968).

America in 1975; his murder charge was dropped, and he was ordered to perform several hundred hours of community service.

Cleaver later became a Christian, a follower of Sun Myung Moon, a Mormon, and a Republican. During his wanderings through these discordant spiritual/political "homes" he found the time to lead what he called the Eldridge Cleaver Crusades, preaching a mixture of Islam and Christianity that he called "Christlam."

Despite Cleaver's decline into a pathetic figure in his later years, the spirit and tenor of Soul on Ice lives on in the minds of the current crop of radicals who long to complete the cultural revolution of the 1960s.

4 Black Power's Slide into Lawlessness

Woe to those who call evil good and good evil, who put darkness for light and light for darkness, who put bitter for sweet and sweet for bitter (Isaiah 5:20).

It is important to understand what the Sixties turmoil was about, for the youth culture that became manifest then is the modern liberal culture of today. Where that culture will take us next may be impossible to say, but it is also impossible even to make an informed guess without understanding the forces let loose by the decade that changed America.[13]

The Black Panther Party, first named the Black Panther Party for Self-Defense, was one of the most controversial and violent organizations that became an important feature of the 1960s counter cultural revolution. It rejected Martin Luther King's call to seek a peaceful way for removing the barriers to full and equal treatment facing all blacks, especially in the American South.

---

[13] Robert H. Bork, *Slouching Towards Gomorrah* (Regan Books, (1996), xiii.

Instead, it adopted a revolutionary program of destroying the existing culture, which it described as grievously oppressive. (Mao Zedong's Red Book became required reading among the BPP membership.) To be sure, there were plenty of reasons for black people to demand an end to the discrimination they endured. But the Panthers were not interested in improving the existing culture.

What they had in mind was the radical overturning of the existing structures and then rebuilding them according to the Marxist blueprint. Never mind that wherever such a revolution has been imposed, the results were always disastrous to the wellbeing and freedom of uncounted millions whose blood still cries out to the heavens.

The Black Panther Party had its beginning in 1966 in Oakland, California, under the leadership of Huey Newton and Bobby Seale, ostensibly to protect the black people against the abuse of police power. It soon became one of the most militant organizations of the 1960s revolution, often involved in violent encounters with the police. In 1967 they marched on the California State Capitol in protest of a ban on weapons. By 1968, their Party had established local branches in most of the major cities in the U.S.

Below is the "Ten Point Program" of the BPP, adopted in October 1966, the year of its founding:

We want freedom. We want power to determine the destiny of our black Community.

We want full employment for our people. (We believe that the federal government is responsible and obligated to give every man employment or a guaranteed income....)

We want an end to the robbery by the white man of our black Community.

We want decent housing, fit for shelter of human beings.

We want education for our people that exposes the true nature of this decadent American society....

We want all black men to be exempt from military service.

We want an immediate end to POLICE BRUTALITY and MURDER of black people.

We want freedom for all black men held in federal, state, county and city prisons and jails.

We want all black people when brought to trial to be tried in court by a jury of their peer group or people from their black communities, as defined by the Constitution of the United States.

We want land, bread, housing, education, clothing, justice and peace. And as our major political objective, a United Nations-supervised plebiscite to be held throughout the black colony in which only black colonial subjects will be allowed to participate for the purpose of determining the will of the black people as to their national destiny.

HUEY PERCY NEWTON (1942-1989)

Newton was born in Monroe, Louisiana in 1942, one of seven children in a family who eventually settled in Oakland, California. His father was a lay preacher; though the family was poor, it was close-knit, and Newton did not suffer hunger or homelessness in his childhood. But he wrote in his autobiography, *Revolutionary Suicide*, that he was humiliated for being black:

> During those long years in Oakland public schools, I did not have one teacher who taught me anything relevant to my own life or experience. Not one instructor ever awoke in me a desire to learn more.... All they did was to rob me of the sense of my own uniqueness and worth, and in the process nearly killed my urge to inquire.

He graduated from high school without being able to read although he was obviously intelligent, and later taught himself to read. In 1974, he obtained a bachelor's degree from the University of California. In

1980 he "earned" a Ph.D. in the history of consciousness on the basis of his doctoral dissertation, *War Against the Panthers*.[14]

At age 14, Newton was arrested for vandalism and gun possession. He burglarized homes and got involved in other petty crimes. He once wrote that he studied law to become a better criminal, but later admitted that he was a fool for having such limited ambitions.

Newton read widely in the literature of the major thinkers of the revolution: Karl Marx, Vladimir Lenin, Frantz Fanon, Malcolm X, Mao Zedong, and Che Guevara. The Panthers adopted Malcolm X's slogan: "Freedom by any means necessary." Malcolm X was assassinated in 1965 at age 39 by three members of the Nation of Islam.

Newton had numerous confrontations with the police that led to charges of assault and murder. He was convicted of attacking someone with a steak knife in 1964. Newton once told a crowd in San Francisco: "Every time you go to execute a white racist Gestapo cop, you are defending yourself." In October 1967, he was found guilty of the murder of Oakland police officer John Frey, and sentenced to prison for two to fifteen years. In 1970, the California Appellate Court overturned the conviction; after two mistrials the case was dropped.

Subsequent charges of murder and assault were laid against Newton. He fled to Cuba in 1974. He returned to the U.S. in 1977, and stood trial for the assault charge, of which he was acquitted. The murder charge against him (of a 17-year old girl) ended in a jury deadlock, after which the prosecution decided not to retry Newton.

On August 22, 1989, Newton was killed by a member of the Black Guerrilla Family, Tyrone Robinson, who accused him of abandoning jailed Panther members and being guilty of some of the killings within the Party. Robinson was convicted of murder and sentenced to 32 years in prison.

---

[14] Huey P. Newton, *War Against the Panthers: A Study of Repression in America* (Santa Cruz: UC Santa Cruz Ph.D. Dissertation, 1980).

BOBBY SEALE

Seale was born in 1936 in Dallas, Texas. In the 1940s his family settled in Oakland, California, where he attended high school. He joined the U.S. Air Force in 1955, but was discharged in 1958 for insubordination.

At the founding of the Black Panther Party in 1966, Seale became its first Chairman while Newton became its Minister of Defense. (These high-sounding designations were intended to underscore their estrangement from the American state.)

Seale was one of the original "Chicago Eight" who were charged with inciting the riot at the 1968 Democratic Convention in Chicago. During the trial the defendants managed to create chaos in the courtroom. Judge Julius Hoffman ordered Seale to refrain from his outbursts. After Seale refused, the judge ordered him bound and gagged and severed him from the case. He was declared to be in contempt of court and sentenced to a four-year prison term. He was released from prison in 1972. In 1973 he ran unsuccessfully for mayor of Oakland.

Having been the co-founder with Huey Newton in 1966, as well as the chairman of the Black Panther Party, Seale played a prominent role in the hectic and violent activities of the Panthers. He helped develop the statements of purpose and spoke and wrote passionately about the right to defend themselves against what he called the fascist American state. He was a popular and eloquent speaker at various events and played a prominent role in the affairs of the Party. But all of that came to a crashing end.

SECOND THOUGHTS OF DAVID HOROWITZ

Horowitz started as a Marxist and at first believed that the Black Panther Party members were idealistic and courageous defenders of the oppressed blacks in America. As he got to know them and discovered that they were in fact a band of criminals, he had second thoughts and decided to tell the truth about them. That realization did not come easily because it meant that he had to discard his Marxist faith and to admit that the Panthers were a threat to the peace and wellbeing of America. It also meant that his own life was at risk.[15]

The evidence of the corruption and violence of the Panthers became clear to everyone who wanted to face the truth. Yet to this day the liberal establishment continues to venerate them as courageous defenders of a long-suffering minority. What follows is a sample of such veneration by Professor Cornel West of Princeton University who called the vision, courage and sacrifice of the BPP's gallant effort to view the people's needs as holy.... He concluded:

Indeed, so holy, democratic, and precious that we now struggle for a new great awakening that shatters the sleep-walking in our time. And the Black Panther Party remains the enabling and ennobling wind in our backs![16]

But reality was not what it seemed on the surface. In fact, the leadership of the Panthers were in the process of punishing and killing their own.

Newton had established himself as the undisputed and feared leader who relished the privilege of power, money and sex. As to the latter, the Panthers had no respect for marriage, and Newton demanded that the women in his entourage would be available for his pleasure. He also became addicted to drugs.

By 1974 the relationship between Newton and Seale began to unravel. At a discussion about a planned film about the Panthers, they had a heated argument and Newton, backed by his bodyguards, beat Seale so severely with a bullwhip that he required major medical treatment. He fled to Cuba and was forgotten by his former allies.

---

[15] In this section I draw on information provided by David Horowitz in his book *Radical Son: A Generational Odyssey* (New York: Free Press, 1997) and his frontpage-mag.com article "Black Murder Inc.," Dec. 13, 1999.

[16] David Hilliard, ed, *The Black Panther Party* (Albuquerque: UNM Press, 2008), x.

MURDER INC.

The internal discipline within the Panthers, sometimes involving murder, was meted out by Newton's personal bodyguards, called the Squad. They were thugs who at the command of Newton would terrify, beat and murder his "enemies." It made for an atmosphere of distrust and fear since no one was able to stand up to Newton.

A number of Panthers who feared Newton's wrath simply fled. Several murders were traceable to Newton's enforcement squad, or to Elaine Brown, who took over from Newton during his stay in Cuba. She was his equal in cruelty and hunger for power. In her book *A Taste of Power* she has the gall to describe in detail her sadistic delight in seeing an exlover beaten by squad members into a bloody pulp.

In December 1974, Betty Van Patter, a secretary in the BPP office, was murdered; a month later her body was found floating in the San Francisco Bay. The murder shook David Horowitz who had cooperated with the Panthers in the operation and funding of a school for poor children. He had begun to have serious doubts about the behavior and intentions of the Panthers. The murder forced him to face the ugly truth about the criminality of the Panthers; he was convinced that they had killed Van Patter.

Horowitz was deeply troubled by the murder because it meant that he had been wrong in everything he once believed about the Panthers' cause against the American "establishment." He also felt somewhat responsible since he had recommended Van Patter for the position with the BPP. He wrote that some on the Left may privately have held reservations about the Panthers:

> But no one on the Left – no one – had disassociated themselves from the Panther cause. No one had publicly said: "These are criminals. These are dangerous people, and to be avoided." There was a reason for this reticence. It would have meant saying, "The police are right, and deserve our support. We have been wrong." Everyone who identified with the Left understood, for the record, that the Panthers were of us and for us. Because they had been made

the symbol of the revolution, they could not be condemned without negative consequences for everything we stood for and had said.[17]

Horowitz describes his discovery of the truth about the Panthers as bringing him to the brink of the abyss, causing him a great deal of emotional turmoil. It also brought him the unmitigated hatred of his former allies who denounced him as a traitor. But that has not stopped him from becoming one of the most courageous and prolific defenders of what is good and true about America and the free West. His many books and the David Horowitz Freedom Center are excellent sources of information and insight that help make sense out of the confusion and turmoil all around us.

---

[17] Horowitz, *Radical Son*, 254.

5 The March Through the Institutions

The universities ...were the scenes of the most violent confrontations and abject betrayal of principle.... What we had witnessed was the spectacle of wholesale capitulation – a liberal capitulation to the grim yet smirking radicalism whose goal was the destruction of an intellectual tradition and, ultimately, a way of life.[18]

This collection of essays is about what has been called the long march through the institutions. The reason this is a significant topic is because institutions are the skeleton, or the framework, that provide the space for a private sphere of society – in distinction from the political realm.

In fact, the private/public distinction is indispensable for a wholesome, free and civilized society. These institutions include the churches, the family, schools/universities, the arts, the media, science, medicine, the economy, politics, and a host of voluntary organizations.

---

[18] Kimball, 99.

Of course, institutions do not come out of thin air. They derive their existence from the minds and hearts of people. This inevitably involves beliefs or worldviews, also called religion. Broadly speaking, there are two ways in which people adopt a particular worldview; it is either a product of the human mind (humanism), or it comes to us from a source outside of ourselves, that is, the Creator God who has revealed himself in the Bible of the Old and New Testaments. All of mankind has in common that we face three questions: Who are we? What are we here for? What is truth? The reality is that we give different answers to these fundamental questions of human existence.

IN THE ACADEMY: WHEN MOB RULE TAKES OVER

These different starting points, however, do not mean that Christians should not concern themselves with those who have a different worldview. On the contrary, Christians are called to love all mankind and to seek the welfare of all people. One way to do that is to be very much aware of the signs of our times. One such epic sign is that among the elite of Western society there is a determined effort to eliminate the institutions that are the backbone of a free society. This is exactly what the march through the institutions is all about.

In this chapter we will consider how this march through the American universities has fundamentally changed the purpose of higher education with the aid of Roger Kimball's, *The Long March*. The same process is happening in Canada, without the starkly racial dimension of the United States. Author/columnist Barbara Kay had the following to say about the Canadian university scene:

> The counterculture of the 1960s drew a bright line between all past understandings and the present understanding of what universities were for.... In a word, the universities, formerly independent custodians of objective knowledge governed by the rubric of free academic inquiry, have become politicized engines of social change.

Intellectual investigation has been subordinated to non-intellectual and even anti-intellectual imperatives.[19]

Along the same lines, Kimball writes that,

perhaps no phenomenon more vividly epitomizes the long march of America's cultural revolution than the student uprisings that swept across college and university campuses from the mid-1960s through the early 1970s.

He adds that the fury and suddenness of these outbreaks amounted to a serious attack on "the intellectual and moral foundations of the entire humanistic enterprise."[20]

On many campuses across the land, students seized buildings, smashed property, and acted like thugs for whom the ordinary rules of civil behavior did not apply. University officials were humiliated and sometimes held hostage, their offices were ransacked, and files were stolen or destroyed. In nearly all situations (with very few exceptions) university administrators and faculty were intimidated and prepared to surrender to the most outrageous demands. A review of events at Cornell University in 1969 and at Yale University in 1970, tell a depressing story.

DYSFUNCTION AT CORNELL

The turmoil at Cornell University began in 1968 when black students charged a visiting professor of economics with racism because he had judged African nations by "Western" criteria. The administration cravenly required an apology, which the professor provided. But the students were not satisfied and took over the office of the economics department while holding the chairman and his secretary "prisoner" for eighteen hours.

The students were not punished; an investigating dean "exonerated" the professor, but nonetheless charged Cornell with

---

[19] Barbara Kay, *Acknowledgments: A Cultural Memoir and Other Essays* (Toronto: Indigo, 2013), 73.

[20] Kimball, 102.

"institutional racism." The authorities clearly signaled that they did not have the conviction to defend the integrity of their institution by punishing the students' criminal behavior. Not surprisingly, this sign of the university administration's cowardice was all the students needed to step up their thuggish behavior.

They escalated a pattern of demands and violence, as well as the occupation of buildings and hostage taking. In February 1969, at a symposium, president Perkins attempted to defend Cornell's investments in South African companies. A black student jumped onto the stage, grabbed Perkins and took his microphone. When a security guard rushed to help Perkins, another black student wielding a two-by-four kept the agent at bay. Meanwhile, blacks in the audience were beating on the bongo drums the university had recently bought for the students, while Perkins was heard to whisper, "You better let go of me."

In April 1969 during parents' weekend one hundred black students took over the Willard Straight Hall before 6 a.m. and gave the occupants ten minutes to leave. Several doors were broken down with crow bars. Parents and college staff were forcibly ejected from the building. While University officials stood by passively, black students armed themselves with knives, rifles and ammunition. Militant members of the Students for a Democratic Society (SDS) stood guard outside, while the students settled down for what became a thirty-five-hour occupation of the building.

A student radio broadcast reported that the protest had taken place because of Cornell's "racist attitudes" and because it "lacked a program relevant to the black students." Some white students broke into the building and scuffled with the occupiers. One black student shouted that "if any more whites come in… you're gonna die here."

CRIME WITHOUT PUNISHMENT

The aftermath of this student uprising displayed even more of the cowardice and lack of conviction among the university's administration and faculty. The perpetrators of the lawless behavior demanded that the disciplinary action against three of the black students involved in the turmoil be dropped. The vice-president for public affairs promised to recommend to the faculty to drop the penalties. An agreement was worked out and the black students vacated the building clutching rifles and ammunition belts, their clenched fists raised in victory.

What Kimball describes as perhaps "the last show of spine by an academic body in the U.S." was that the Cornell faculty voted 726 to 281 not to drop the penalties, also called reprimands. The response of the students was quick; now white and black radicals joined forces and occupied a faculty building. They soon attracted some 2,500 students.

Tom Jones, one of the gun-toting blacks involved in the previous occupation of Straight Hall, said on a local radio station that the faculty had voted for a "showdown." He warned that seven faculty members and administrators would be "dealt with," then intimated that their lives might be at stake. Several professors then moved their families to motels for the night.

The faculty met the next day to reconsider their vote on the three students' penalties. The vast majority of the faculty had changed their minds and now voted by a voice vote of 700 to 300 to dismiss the penalties. They all felt badly about changing their vote. Kimball gets to the heart of what is at stake here: "The handwringing rationalizations of the Cornell faculty for this unconscionable collapse make for nauseating reading."

Tom Jones addressed a crowd of students after the vote and bragged: "That decision was made right here. They didn't make any decision; they were told from this room what to do."

Not all members of the faculty were cowards. James J. John, professor of history, told his wavering colleagues:

if we had a good reason for not dismissing the charges on Monday... we have a stronger reason for not doing so today.... This university, I believe, can survive the expulsion or departure of no matter what number of students and the destruction of buildings far better than it can survive the death of principle.[21]

Professor Allan Bloom who taught at Cornell, resigned in disgust over the cowardice of the administration and most of his colleagues. He said that the threats of the black students, some of whom were carrying guns, and the capitulation of the faculty, amounted to an abandonment of the university's judicial system. In a conversation with a *New York Times* reporter about the violence at Cornell, Bloom said that "the resemblance on all levels to the first stages of a totalitarian takeover are almost unbelievable."[22]

In 1987, Bloom published his famous lament about what he saw as the decomposition of the American universities, significantly entitled: *The Closing of the American Mind: How Higher Education Has Failed Democracy and Impoverished the Souls of Today's Students.*[23]

REVOLT AT YALE

While the mayhem at Cornell had racial overtones, they were even more so at Yale University since it played out against the background of the Black Panthers' radicalism. The occasion was the murder trial of Bobby Seale, chairman of the Black Panther Party, and eight other Panthers. They had been busy fomenting unrest inside and outside of Yale, while arguing that the Panthers would not get a fair trial.

At a Panther fundraising event in one of the Yale buildings, Doug Miranda, area captain of the Black Panthers, claimed that Yale is "one

---

[21] Kimball, 117.

[22] Ibid., 115.

[23] Allan Bloom, *The Closing of the American Mind: How Higher Education Has Failed Democracy and Impoverished the Souls of Today's Students* (New York: Simon & Schuster, 1987).

of the biggest pig organizations" and part of the "conspiracy" against the Panthers. He said,

> Basically, what we are going to do is create conditions in which white folks are either going to have to kill pigs or defend themselves against black folks.... We're going to turn Yale into a police state.... You have to create peace by destroying the people who don't want peace.

At a meeting of the campus radicals in April 1970, some outrageous proposals to help the Panthers were considered, including kidnapping Yale president Kingman Brewster, shutting off New Haven's water supply, starting a student strike, and demanding that the Yale corporation donate half a million dollars to the Panther defense fund. At a later meeting, Doug Miranda suggested that they hold a strike vote and call on Yale to demand that the Panthers be released.

At all 12 of Yale's residential colleges students met to discuss the Panthers' demands and to vote on a student strike. The few that tried to introduce a note of reality were ignored; there was a lot of confusion about what to do. One female undergraduate at Jonathan Edwards College was reported to have said, "Why don't we just vote to strike tonight, and we'll decide tomorrow what we're striking for."

Kimball writes that the two most prominent university spokespersons in this drama were Yale president Kingman Brewster and the university chaplain, the Rev. William Sloane Coffin, Jr. He described Coffin as "one of those self–infatuated radicals who poached on the authority of religion to bolster his sensation of righteousness." Coffin delighted in organizing acts of civil disobedience, and stated that the "white oppressors" of the Panther Party should be treated as the American colonials treated George III. He claimed that the trial was "legally right but morally wrong," and that the Panthers should be set free.

Yale president Kingman Brewster was cut of the same cloth as William Sloan Coffin. Kimball writes that Brewster was a model of "cunning equivocation. With a symmetry that connoisseurs of hypocrisy will admire for decades to come, he showed himself capable of the ultimate pliability." When asked his opinion about Coffin's support of the Panthers, he answered that the university chaplain was "worth three full professors."

Just before the faculty was scheduled to take a strike vote, Brewster declared his neutrality in the matter (of the Panthers' trial). But a few days later at a faculty meeting, while some thousand students and Panthers had gathered outside, he had this to say: "I am skeptical of the ability of black revolutionaries to achieve a fair trial anywhere in the United States."

Eventually, some kind of strike took place. Classes were suspended and the faculty modified academic expectations for the term. A May Day demonstration attracted 15,000 people including the heroes of the countercultural revolution – Tom Hayden, Allen Ginsberg, Jerry Rubin and Abbie Hoffman.

The entire nation was following the events at Yale, which amounted to an attack on the legitimacy of the U.S. justice system. Even more so, it involved very directly the independence and integrity of higher education. Even the *New York Times* understood the seriousness of these events. In an editorial "Murdering Justice" it pointed out: "Those students and faculty members at Yale who are trying to stop a murder trial by calling a strike against the university have plunged the campus into a new depth of irrationality."

Undoubtedly, the turmoil at Cornell and Yale in the 60s and 70s replicated at many other campuses, took direct aim at two indispensable pillars of a free and civilized society. Unless these pernicious attacks on institutions are understood and corrected, America will fail to remain the land of the free and the home of the brave.

6 Radical Ideas

Blowing in the Wind

The only path to the final defeat of imperialism and the building of socialism is revolutionary war. Revolution is the most powerful resource of the people... (The Banner of Che).

Revolution is a fight by the people for power. It is a changing of power in which existing social and economic relations are turned upside down. It is a fight for who run things, in particular, for control by the people of what we communists call the means of production....[24]

The organization that in 1969 grew out of the Students for a Democratic Society (SDS), was out to cause trouble especially for the police and university authorities. They were part of a massive anti-America protest movement against the Vietnam War and the systemic discrimination allegedly suffered by black Americans.

---

[24] *Prairie Fire: Political Statement of the Weather Underground* (SF: San Francisco Communications Co., 1974). Republished *in Sing a Battle Song*, Bernardine Dohrn, Bill Ayers, Jeff Jones (New York: Seven Stories Press, 2006), 240-241.

They succeeded all too well, much to the consternation of their targets, who were often outmaneuvered and out-bullied by the violence and brutality of their attackers.

The Weather Underground went beyond issuing declarations filled with contempt for the American "establishment" and praise for the revolutions in Cuba, China, Vietnam and other communist countries. Their leaders wanted to bring the struggle to the streets of America by organizing riots, confrontations with the police, and bombing buildings such as the Capitol, the Pentagon, police stations and banks. After six years of spreading mayhem and fear, the organization came to a dismal ending marked by internal feuding and betrayal.

But this was not the end of the ideology that fired the WU organization. Their leaders never recanted the ideas that had motivated them. On the contrary, they found a much more effective way to spread their revolutionary ideas by way of infiltrating the institutions they formerly attacked.

THE WEATHER UNDERGROUND: AN EXERCISE IN DEGENERATION

The founding of the Weather Underground took place in 1969 at a meeting of the SDS at the Ann Arbor campus of the University of Michigan. Soon the SDS faded out of the picture, and the WU became the prime instigator of the violent attempts to overthrow the American capitalist "fascist" system. The name is taken from a Bob Dylan song: "You don't need a weatherman to know which way the wind blows." This became the title of the manifesto adopted by the SDS convention in Chicago in June of the same year. It contained the following Statement of Purpose:

> The most important task for us toward making the revolution, and the work our collectives should engage in, is the creation of a mass revolutionary movement, without which a clandestine revolutionary party will be impossible .... Rather it is akin to the

Red Guard in China, based on the full participation and involvement of masses of people in the practice of making revolution; a movement with full willingness to participate in the violent and illegal struggle.[25]

Buoyed by the "successful" riots at the 1968 Democratic National Convention, the WU planned what became known as the "Days of Rage" in Chicago scheduled for October 8-11, 1969. The organizers predicted large crowds to respond to the call for action in the streets, but fewer than 600 showed up on day one. After firing up the crowd with a rousing speech, Bernardine Dohrn led the mob running towards downtown Chicago's commercial center, breaking windows in stores and cars and fighting with the police.

Six people were wounded by police gunfire and dozens were hospitalized; 68 were jailed although most were quickly bailed out. The second and third day was a repeat, although with even smaller numbers. Dohrn was arrested the second night; this only enhanced her status as a revolutionary leader. 75 policemen had been injured. City official Richard Elrod was paralyzed from the neck down. 300 WU members were arrested.

The WU held a "War Council" in December 1969 to review their tactics. John Jacobs gave the concluding speech. He condemned the pacifism of the white middleclass youth in America. He nevertheless predicted the success of a revolution that would draw the youth toward the goal of building a better, which in their view meant a socialist world. But first the existing order must be destroyed. Jacobs explained how that was to be done: "We're against everything that's good and decent in honky America.... We will burn and loot and destroy. We are the incubation of your mother's nightmare."[26]

---

[25] *Wikipedia*, "Weather Underground."

[26] Mark Rudd, *My Life with SDS and the Weathermen Underground* (New York: William Morrow/Harper Collins, 2009), 189.

GOING UNDERGROUND

The deliberations at this council resulted in the decision to go underground and to "engage in guerrilla warfare against the U.S. government" without attempting to organize a mass movement. This was also the time that the leadership of the SDS was taken over by the WU, resulting in the dismantling of the SDS. Mark Rudd, the chief SDS leader of the violence and mayhem at Columbia University in 1968, summarizes this time in his book as the "most notorious" period of this organization:

"We want more group sex, LSD acid tests, orgiastic rock music, violent street actions.... We were by now a classic cult, true believers surrounded by a hostile world that we rejected and that rejected us in return. We had a holy faith, revolution, which could not be shaken, as well as a strategy to get there. The foco theory.[27]

The *foco* theory is Spanish term for Che Guevara's revolutionary method.

We were revolutionaries, about to move to a "higher level" and begin armed struggle against the worst imperialist state in modern world history. We were the latest in a long line of revolutionaries from Mao to Fidel to Che to Ho Chi Minh, and the only white people prepared to engage in guerrilla warfare in the imperial homeland.[28]

It was at this War Council meeting, so-called, where Bernadine Dohrn uttered her contemptuous description of the Charles Manson gang's murder of the pregnant actress Sharon Tate and the LaBiancas. "Dig it," she said. "First they killed those pigs, then they ate dinner in the same room with them. They even shoved a fork into the victim's stomach! Wild!." Rudd explains that the Weathermen do not care one

---

[27] Rudd, 184.
[28] Ibid,, 185.

whit for conventional values. "There were no limits now to our politics of transgression."[29]

On March 6, 1970, members of the WU were busy building a nail bomb to be detonated at an army dance at Fort Dix. They were using a "safe house" in New York's Greenwich Village to construct the bomb. Something went wrong and it exploded, killing two men and one woman, while two others in the house including Kathy Boudin, escaped unharmed.

This is the same Kathy Boudin who was complicit in the Brink's armored car robbery in 1981 in Nanuet, New York, where two policemen and one guard were killed. She pleaded guilty to one count of felony murder and robbery in exchange for one 20-years-to-life sentence. In 2003 she was granted parole. During and after her incarceration she published articles in various publications, including the *Harvard Educational Review*, while also pursuing her doctoral studies at the City University of New York and Columbia University.

Despite her violent history, she was appointed adjunct professor at Columbia University School of Social Work, much to the disgust of those who remember that she was involved in a crime that took the lives of three men who were simply doing their jobs.

A STATE OF WAR

The violent death of the bomb builders in Greenwich Village sent a shockwave through the ranks of the WU. They were rudely confronted with the realization that what they were planning to do would inevitably lead to bloodshed. Now their own blood had been shed and they were forced to reconsider their tactics. Consequently, they took pride in the fact that they only destroyed buildings and property, not human lives. Whatever such claims are worth, the reality is that the WU used plenty of words intended to incite hatred and contempt for "the enemy." One of the resolutions at the December, 1969 War Council was "to engage in guerrilla warfare against the U.S. government."

---

[29] Ibid., 189.

One of the prominent leaders of the WU was Bernadine Dohrn, who on July 31, 1970 made a public "Declaration of a State of War" which included the following announcement:

All over the world, people fighting Amerikan* imperialism look to America's youth to use our strategic position behind enemy lines to join forces in the destruction of the empire. Che taught us that "revolutionaries move like fish in the sea." The alienation and contempt that young people have for this country has created the ocean for this revolution. We fight in many ways. Dope is one of our weapons. The laws against marijuana mean that millions of us are outlaws long before we actually split. Guns and grass are united in the youth underground. For Diana Oughton, Ted Gold and Terry Robbins [killed in the Greenwich Village explosion] and for all the revolutionaries who are still on the move here, there has been no question for a long time now – we will never go back. Within the next 14 days we will attack a symbol or institution of Amerikan injustice.

Most of the leading figures in the Weather Underground, including Bill Ayers and Bernardine Dohrn, spent the 1970s on the run, while their organization slowly disintegrated. It was succeeded by a new organization called Prairie Fire – a name derived from Mao Zedong's statement that "a single spark can start a prairie fire."

In 1974, Bernardine Dohrn, Bill Ayers, Jeff Jones, and Celia Sojourn published Prairie Fire: The Politics of Revolutionary Anti-Imperialism. The authors explain in the Introduction that they are mapping out a political ideology and strategy to create a revolution in the U.S. They write: "We need a revolutionary Communist Party in order to lead the struggle, give coherence and direction to the fight, seize power and build the new society."

What stands out in all the documents and statements of the WU is that they were inspired by the communist revolutionaries in Cuba, Nicaragua, North Vietnam and Russia, especially by the sadistic killer,

Che Guevara. Several American delegations traveled to Havana to pay tribute to the Castro-led revolution. Bernadine Dohrn led one such delegation, which met with Havana officials, who gave them the usual Potemkin village treatment. She was interviewed by Cuba's Tricontinental magazine and met with dignitaries from the revolutionary third world.

Dohrn and her colleagues also met with a delegation of Vietnamese headed by Huynh Va Ba, a member of that government. He told them that they had similar experiences with organizing by recruiting among the middle class and young people prepared to fight. Then Huynh told them that the war was entering its final phase, and he urged them: "You must begin to wage armed struggle as soon as possible to become the vanguard and take leadership of the revolution."

Dohrn assured him that they would try their best to be worthy of that honour. As if to solemnize their unity of mind, the Vietnamese gave the WU people rings forged from the metal salvaged from downed American fighter planes.[30]

"FREE AS A BIRD"

In 1980 Bill Ayers and Dohrn surrendered to the authorities and then found that all the charges against them had been dropped because of an "improper surveillance" technicality. Ayer is reported to have said, "Guilty as sin, free as a bird. America is a great country." He then used his freedom to radicalize America from within its mainstream institutions, especially the education establishment. He earned a master's degree in Childhood Education, and in 1987 he received a doctorate in Curriculum and Instruction from Columbia's University's Teachers College.

Also in 1987, Ayers became a professor, and later a Distinguished Professor of Education at the University of Illinois, a position he held until 2010. Although he is now retired, he holds a number of key

---

[30] Peter Collier and David Horowitz, *Destructive Generation: Second Thoughts about the Sixties* (Orangeville: Summit Books, 1989), 83.

positions in various phases of the educational system. In 2008 he was elected as V.P. of Curriculum Studies at the American Educational Research Association, a position that gives him direct influence over what is taught in American teacher-training colleges and its public schools.

In a speech in December 2012 at New York University, Ayers advocated that the education system be used to indoctrinate young people to transform Amerikan society. He also serves on the board of *In These Times*, a Chicago-based socialist journal. He was a strong supporter of the Occupy Wall Street organization. His influence is international, since he was an admirer of the late Venezuelan Marxist president Hugo Chavez. Ayers is a board member of the Miranda International Center; a Venezuelan government think tank promoting Cuban style education in Venezuelan schools.[31]

Ayers actively spreads his ideas. He is the author of at least ten books most of them dealing with education, and one giving the story of his life, Fugitive Days; Memoirs of an Antiwar Activist, in which he attempts to put a positive spin on hating and betraying his own country.

His wife Bernardine Dohrn is no less radical in attempting to fundamentally transform America. She proved to be a fanatical leader in the fight against Amerika. Just like her erstwhile lover, and later husband Ayers, she left her life of preaching and living the revolution after she surfaced in 1980.

NO REGRETS

Dohrn first worked at a Chicago law firm, and in 1991 she became an adjunct Professor of Law at the Northwestern University School of Law in Chicago where she is also director of the Legal Clinic's Children and Family Justice Center. She is still in a leadership position, but now at a

---

[31] Bill Ayers, DiscoverTheNetwork.org.

position of prestige where she is able to mold the minds of generations of students.

Besides being able to influence the lives of university students, she is also in a position to do that through membership in various Left-wing organizations. She is a popular speaker at various events such as university graduations. Her present position enables her to spread her ideas far more effectively than she ever could before. It's a heady experience to move from being a revolutionary fugitive to becoming an honored member of the intelligentsia.

The Ayers-Dohrn team has attempted to account for this transition and to justify their Weather Underground behavior. Ayers' *Fugitive Days: Memoirs of an Antiwar Activist* is devoted to that purpose. The short version is in his article "Revisiting the Weather Underground." Dohrn did the same in her "When Hope and Mystery Rhyme." Both articles are published in *Sing a Battle Song.*[32]

They admit to having some regrets, but those are only about tactics, not substance. What these writings amount to is no renunciation of their contempt for their own country, the demonization of the "establishment," the rejection of all traditional authority, the debauchery of language and morals, the thrashing of the institution of marriage and family, and their determination to fundamentally change America.

Their worst insult against common sense and their own country is that they are unrepentant admirers of communism as practiced and preached by the likes of the Castro brothers, Che Guevara, Ho Chi Minh, the Vietcong, Lenin, Marx and other thinkers of the radical Left. They have closed their eyes to the reality that these regimes are responsible for killing hundreds of millions and condemning untold millions more to a life of misery and hopelessness.

---

[32] Bernardine Dohrn, Bill Ayersand Jeff Jones; Weather Underground Organization, *Sing a Battle Song: The Revolutionary Poetry, Statements, and Communiques of the Weather Underground 1970-1974* (New York: Seven Stories Press, 2006).

It is ironic and deeply troubling that the radical critics who viciously attacked the universities are now controlling them. Their strategy to move from violence to infiltration has been brilliantly successful. But that "success" has contributed, perhaps fatally, to what Allan Bloom has called The Closing of the American Mind. There are no winners in this story.[33]

---

[33] NB: The "k" in Amerika is not a typo, but an allusion to the KKK.

7 The Endangered Family

If I were the devil I would convince the young that the Bible is a myth... that man created God instead of the other way around.... that marriage is old-fashioned, that swinging is more fun, that what you see on TV is the way to be (Paul Harvey, 1965.)

At the heart of liberty is the right to define one's own concept of existence, of meaning, of the universe, and of the mystery of human life. (U.S. Supreme Court, Planned Parenthood v. Casey, 1992)

"The march through the institutions" is a phrase coined early in the 1960's by student activist Rudi Dutschke. The phrase has been mistakenly attributed to the Italian Marxist Antonio Gramsci (1891-1937), mainly because he spent his life vigorously promoting exactly what the phrase meant.

It signifies what the Communists intend to do with their radical revolution, namely, to capture all the institutions of a culture and thus obtain total control of society.

SOUNDS OF THE COMING REVOLUTION

Such a radical change occurred in a very short order in Russia, China, Cuba, and other Communist countries, as well as in Nazi Germany.

What they all have in common is the elimination of the distinction between civil society and the state. In other words, all institutions, such as the family, church, school, university, the media, entertainment, the arts, and every voluntary organization are destroyed or become incorporated into the totalitarian state. History, even recent history, has provided overwhelming evidence that such revolutionary changes spell nothing but evil and misery.

So far the free West has been spared such evil. The bitter irony is that the same revolution that happened relatively quickly in other countries is occurring slowly and surreptitiously in the West as well. We need to recognize this reality and become alert to what is really happening. What are the forces that are pushing our still-free Western countries in a direction that many will come to regret? What are the signs of our time, and what should we do about them?

Obviously, these are huge issues that are complex and critical to the future of the West. Here I want to focus on two issues: secularization and its impact on the institution of the family.

The first thing to keep in mind is that secularism is a dominant force in Western culture. This means that Christianity plays no effective role in the formation of most people's views of the world and of their place in it. This is how the Humanist Association of Canada summarized its contribution to the spread of secularism: "Promoting the separation of religion from public policy and fostering the development of reason, compassion and critical thinking for all Canadians through secular education and community support."

The American Humanist Association stated in its Manifesto II, published in 1973, the following:

We find insufficient evidence for belief in the existence of a supernatural; it is either meaningless or irrelevant to the question of survival and fulfillment of the human race. As nontheists, we begin with humans not God, nature not deity.... We can discover no divine purpose or providence for the human species.... No deity will save us; we must save ourselves....

A CHILD OF THE ENLIGHTENMENT

The core meaning of secularism, as is evident from the above quotations, is the declaration of human independence from God. This radical idea was succinctly expressed in the slogan of the late 18th century French Revolution: "No God, No Master." Secularization is the application of the belief in human autonomy, and it comes to expression in every detail of life.

Contemporary secularism is a child of the Enlightenment, the 18th century intellectual movement spearheaded by thinkers such as Voltaire and Rousseau. An excellent source on the Enlightenment is Crane Brinton's, *The Shaping of Modern Thought*. He describes the worldview of this movement as "the belief that all human beings can attain here on this earth a state of perfection hitherto in the West thought to be possible only for Christians in a state of grace, and for them only after death."[34] Another excellent source on this topic is Benjamin Wiker, *Worshiping the State*.[35]

The following is a very brief summary of the main themes of the Enlightenment:

It is atheistic. Consequently, there is no authoritative rule or sovereign above us to whom we owe allegiance. Instead, we are the designers and creators of our own "values."

Human reason (rationalism) is the final arbiter and source of what is good and true.

---

[34] *Cane Brinton, The Shaping of Modern Thought* (Upper Saddle River, NJ: Prentice-Hall, 1964), 109.

[35] Benjamin Wiker, *Worshiping the State: How Liberalism Became the State Religion* (Washington DC: Regnery Publishing, 2013).

Human fulfillment can only be achieved by our own efforts in this world through mastery over nature, especially by means of science and technology.

Human nature is essentially good. Evil is caused by the structures of society, notably by the maldistribution of power and wealth, which can be overcome by radical changes in those structures via social engineering. (Think President Barak Obama's "fundamental transformation.")

All social structures are purely historical and eminently malleable.

IDEAS HAVE CONSEQUENCES

The big problem faced by secularism is how to construct a society that is just and peaceful if all moral concepts are relative. If there is no given, abiding and authoritative standard of truth, ultimately all distinctions become problematic. It is then impossible to make judgments about right and wrong, truth and falsehood. We are left with deciding what is convenient, pleasant, or necessary for survival, but we cannot say that something should be done because it is right, or something should be believed because it is true. In fact, to do so is to risk the charge of being judgmental, arrogant and intolerant.

The denial of a transcendent and sovereign lawgiver and standard of truth means that the very existence of a moral order is denied. The issue is not that people engage in wrong (immoral) behavior but that they deny the very existence of a standard or norm by which to distinguish between right and wrong. This has a devastating impact upon the possibility of agreeing to a common set of standards by which society is to be guided. Let's take another look at the radicalism of the secular faith as expressed in the Humanist Manifesto:

We affirm that moral values derive their source from human experience. Ethics is autonomous and situational, needing no theological or ideological sanction. Ethics stems from human need

65

and interest.... Human life has meaning because we create and develop our futures.... We strive for the good life here and now.

Such a radical, alternative faith does not merely touch the margins of life and society but is all-pervasive since it goes to the very basis of our existence in this world. It represents a radical denial of everything the Bible teaches, and its effects are revolutionary. But none of this is new. Secularism's modern expression has its roots in the original Fall, man's rejection of the sovereign God, coupled with the attempt at finding the divine within the human. "You will be like God," Satan said.

No just and peaceful society can exist without some kind of order, some general notion of right and wrong. If the God-ordained order is rejected, a pseudo order will be designed. But such an endeavor becomes entirely arbitrary and unreliable. For if people believe that there is no transcendent authority, why should they worry about the wellbeing of their neighbour, their society? Why should they concern themselves with doing justice or being truthful or faithful? The bitter irony is that this kind of relativism always ends up in totalitarianism.

The secular faith (yes, it is a faith) leads to a strange paradox. Whereas it glorifies individual liberty and questions all traditional moral constraints in the private sphere, even to the extent that traditional norms are held in contempt, we witness the increasing reliance on legislation and the (coercive) power of the state. In the words of Supreme Court of Canada Justice Beverley McLachlin: "Today, it is not to religion or the community that society looks to regulate and remedy its evils – it is to law, primarily the criminal law."[36] In other words, the state is given the task of controlling society. A more dismal prospect is hard to imagine.

WHAT ABOUT THE FAMILY?

The family is a bulwark of a free society, because it is the first and foremost institution in which every life begins, is nurtured into maturity,

---

[36] *Western Report*, July 19, 1993.

and serves as the indispensable means for the continuation of the human race. It obviously belongs in the private sphere of life, but where secularization takes over it will be accompanied by the ongoing expansion of state power at the expense of the other non-state institutions. It is especially the family and marriage that are now besieged from many sides. Michael Novak, a Roman Catholic author, eloquently describes the freedom-defending task of the family, as follows:

> Between the omnipotent State and the naked individual looms the first line of resistance against totalitarianism: the economically and politically independent family, protecting the space within which free and independent individuals may receive the necessary years of nurture.

Many families are in trouble because they are dysfunctional, but dysfunction is aided and abetted by myriad outside forces, especially those who call for a radical revolution. They understand the point made by Novak that the independent family is the first line of resistance against totalitarianism.

William Gairdner is a Canadian author who describes himself as "a parent who speaks out on the political, economic, and social policies that threaten us all." And speak out he did in his 655-page book, *The War Against the Family*, published in 1992. In 1990, he had also argued in defense of the family in, *The Trouble with Canada*.[37]

Still, Gairdner does not call himself a Christian, but in both books, he provides a vigorous defense of a Judeo-Christian notion of freedom over against what he perceives to be a slide into a form of statism that constitutes a direct attack on the family. As Gairdner and many others

---

[37] William D. Gairdner, The War Against the Family: A Parent Speaks Out (Boston: Stoddart Pub., 1993) and *The Trouble with Canada: A Citizen Speaks Out* (Boston: Sstoddart Pub., 1990).

have stressed, we need to be alert to the way the deliberate destruction of the family is being played out.[38]

RADICAL FEMINISM AND PLANNED PARENTHOOD

Radical feminism is fueled by the kind of revolutionary fervor that motivated the 1960s rebels who declared that the West is totally corrupt and needs a radical transformation. As we have seen in previous chapters, these revolutionaries invariably sided with totalitarianism of the Marxism/Leninism type. Many of them often traveled to the Soviet Union, North Vietnam, China and Cuba to learn first-hand how to bring about the Revolution, returning home to become propagandists for the most barbarian regimes. The worst offenders in spreading these lies were and are many university professors whose job it is to tell the truth to their students.

Gairdner's two books provide a wealth of information and a detailed, historical overview of the developments that brought us to the current anti-family patterns of behavior and public policies. He traces that history back to Plato who advocated that families should be incorporated into the state so that all blood ties would be abolished. The Communist Manifesto also lists the abolition of the family as a major item of the Marxist agenda. The late Robert Bork, author of *Slouching towards Gomorrah*, penned a succinct description of the destruction wrought by radical feminism.

Radical feminism is the most destructive and fanatical movement to come down to us from the Sixties. This is a revolutionary, not a reformist, movement, and it is meeting with considerable success. Totalitarian in spirit, it is deeply antagonistic to traditional Western

---

[38]Cf., e.g., George Grant, *The Family Under Siege: What the New Social Engineers Have in Mind for You and Your Children* (Ada, MI: Bethany House Pub., 1994) and Mary Eberstadt, *How the West Really Lost God: A New Theory of Secularization* (West Conshohocken, PA: Templeton Press, 2014).

culture and proposes the complete restructuring of society, morality, and human nature.[39]

One of the most influential organizations in furthering the radical feminist agenda is the Planned Parenthood Federation of America, affiliated with the International Planned Parenthood Federation, usually shortened to Planned Parenthood. Its roots go back to the first birth control clinic in Brooklyn, New York in 1916 started by Margaret Sanger. In 1942, it was renamed Planned Parenthood and has grown into an international organization with affiliates in many countries, including China, where it assisted the government with its one-child per couple policy. The Planned Parenthood Federation of Canada reports that it provides clinical services of "information and counseling on sexual and reproductive health issues" in 68 communities across Canada.

Margaret Sanger (1879-1966) saw it as her life's function to remove the veil of ignorance about sex and reproduction. But in the process, she adopted all the negative ideas about family relations, calling for the total rejection of the traditional ideas about sex and family.

That's why she became the darling of the radical feminists. In the literature, Planned Parenthood stresses its work in reproductive health and education. But in reality, its education is teaching even the very young about free sex, homosexuality and other variations of sexual acts. It is also fanatically pro-abortion in its counseling and education services.

Planned Parenthood is the nation's largest abortion provider, which is one out of every four abortions in the United Sates. In 2009 it performed 332,278 abortions, which is an average of 910 abortions each day. Abby Johnson, the former director of Planned Parenthood's clinic in Bryan, Texas, said that in 2009 her clinic was given an increased

---

[39] Robert Bork, *Slouching towards Gomorrah* (New York: Harper Perennial 2003), 193.

abortion quota to raise revenue, "because that's where the revenue was."[40]

Sex education is a good thing, but it should be done in an age-appropriate manner, while the parents have the right and duty to ensure that it is done without violating their beliefs. The reality is that abortion has become big "business" and a major source of income for Planned Parenthood. But taking the life of a helpless baby (whether partly or completely formed) is evil. And so is sex education to the very young that will give them a wrong start in one of the most intimate, sacred, and mysterious components of life (see Solomon's *Song of Songs*). It is stealing the innocence of little ones, which is a loss that can never be undone.

---

[40] Charmaine Yoest, *National Review Online*, April 26, 2011.

8 Anti-Americanism: A Home-Grown Illness

Events of the last few years, and 9/11 in particular, have made the under-standing of anti-Americanism a far more compelling task than it used to be, although the phenomenon has been with us for a long time. Its first incarnation, European anti-Americanism, has deep roots, and its stereotypes spread over much of the world.[41]

Since the early 1990s, Europe has developed a strain of anti-Americanism that is, according to Robert Fulford, is almost Canadian in its odious condescension and ignorant resistance to fact.[42]

Why do so many Americans hate their own country? Anti-Americanism is a complex and hard to understand phenomenon. It is impossible to grasp without understanding that it is not in the first place against what America

---

[41] Paul Hollander, ed., *Understanding anti-Americanism: Its Origins and Impact at Home and Abroad* (Chicago: Ivan R. Dee, 2004), 3.

[42] *National Post*, March 22, 2003.

does, but what it is. That explains why even the good it does – such as liberating a country (Iraq, Kuwait, Afghanistan) or a continent (Europe), or rushing to help alleviate the impact of natural disasters – makes no difference to the diehard haters of America. Anti-Americanism has a long history, but it has spiked since World War II, especially during the Vietnam War and the subsequent wars in the Arab world.

A WORLDWIDE PHENOMENON

One obvious reason has to do with radical Islamists, led by the late Osama bin Laden, who have declared war on America, which they call "the Great Satan." The result of that war has become very obvious since not a day goes by that we are not reminded of its repercussions affecting America as well as the entire Western world. What should be a surprise to many is that anti-Americanism is not only an international issue, but it has a very large homegrown presence in America itself. This topic has been broached in previous essays. In this essay we will elaborate, beginning with a few quotations from European public figures. I am indebted to Paul Hollander's extensive description of this topic in his *Anti-Americanism: Irrational and Rational*,[43] as well as his more recent, *Understanding Anti-Americanism*, quoted at the beginning of this chapter.

Harold Pinter, the leading British playwright, upon receiving an honorary degree in Turin, Italy in 2002, drew a comparison between his cancer surgery as a,

> personal nightmare and an infinitely more pervasive public nightmare – the nightmare of American hysteria, ignorance, arrogance, stupidity, and belligerence; the most powerful nation the world has ever known effectively waging war against the rest of the

---

[43] Paul Hollander, *Anti Americanism: Irrational and Rational* (Piscataway, New Jersey: Transaction - Publishers, 1995).

world.... The U.S. administration is now a bloodthirsty wild animal. Bombs are its only vocabulary.[44]

Pinter also stated that the atrocity of 9/11 was inevitable retaliation "against constant and systematic manifestations of state terrorism on the part of the United States over many years, in all parts of the world." On another occasion he stated: "The U.S. is really beyond reason now.... There is only one comparison: Nazi Germany."

Carlos Fuentes, a prominent Mexican author, has compared the United States with past totalitarian systems, claiming that the U.S. government, then headed by president George W. Bush, was a more capable dictatorship than that of Hitler or Stalin because it had no external counterforce. Fuentes asserted that "Bush claims to act in the name of the people of the United States.... Such a declaration locates us, once more, before the 'great lie' that Hitler so astutely evoked...."[45]

The German philosopher Martin Heidegger (1889-1976) viewed the United States as the embodiment of injustice and oppression. He gave this definition of Americanism: "The still unfolding and not yet full or completed essence of the emerging monstrousness of modern times." Heidegger believed that Russia and America were similar from a meta-physical point of view because the result in both countries was "the onslaught of what we call the demonic, in the sense of destructive evil." In his view America represented the greater threat since "Bolshevism is only a variant of Americanism."[46]

WHY THE SELF-HATRED AT HOME?

If one listened only to the strident voices of the Left on the American intellectual and political landscape, one would think that America is

---

[44] Hollander, *Understanding Anti-Americanism*, 92.

[45] Ibid., 29.

[46] James Ceaser, "A Genealogy of Anti-Americanism," *The Public Interest,* Summer, 2003.

fast becoming a totalitarian country where all dissent is smothered by the juggernaut of the right-wing establishment. But when the White House was occupied by a man on the political left, the tone and content of the public debate changed. Yet the conflict between the two sides of American politics (statism versus a clear separation between state and civil society) is very much alive, though increasingly confusing and troubling.

Future generations may look back to our time with puzzling amazement that while America was enjoying a period of unprecedented freedom, leisure, and prosperity, a virulent hate-America mentality arose because of an alleged failure to satisfy the demands of a large segment of the population. A great deal of that hatred is animated by the intellectual leadership in the opinion-shaping institutions, especially the universities, the media, and the popular entertainment culture.

Roger Kimball writes in his chapter in *Understanding Anti-Americanism* that "Sartre's explosive anti-Americanism set the tone of elite opinion in Europe and, increasingly, in the United States. Vietnam fanned the smoldering resentment into a raging conflagration." The result was that the Vietnam War became the catalyst for the surge in Anti-Americanism in the United States.

But Kimball is convinced that the war was not the central issue. Rather, it soon became clear that Vietnam, was merely the occasion for disparagement … that went far beyond any specific government policy. Vietnam became the banner under which the entire range of radical sentiment congregated." Jerry Rubin, one of the leaders of the black revolutionaries, bluntly admitted that if the Vietnam War ends, "we'll find another war."[47]

While American politics has changed a great deal, anti-Americanism has not gone away. In fact, it has migrated closer to the center of American politics. (More about that later.) Let's be sure to distinguish

---

[47] Ibid., 240-242,

legitimate criticism of America from hatred of America. Being critical of Anti-Americanism is not about the free flow of conflicting opinions, the open and vigorous debate of different viewpoints, conducted in a respectful and civilized manner. Such is the legacy of an open and free society where all viewpoints can be tested in the public marketplace of ideas and beliefs.

Anti-Americanism is very different. It is an ideology that is based on the belief that something at the center of American life is evil and it threatens the entire world. Paul Hollander uses this term "to denote a particular mindset, an attitude of distaste, aversion, or intense hostility, the roots of which may be found in matters unrelated to the actual qualities or attributes of American society or the foreign policies of the United States."

One of the most prolific and garrulous critics of the United States is the darling of the radical left, Noam Chomsky, professor of linguistics at the Massachusetts Institute of Technology. He is the ever-ready pundit commenting on all things pertaining to the character and role of the United States. He is best known for his interviews, speeches and books in which he details the evil of the American "empire" as the epitome of capitalism and oppression. Shortly after 9/11 he denounced the U.S. as "a leading terrorist state." After the start of the war against Iraq, Chomsky wrote in the *New York Times* that, "The most powerful state in history has proclaimed it intends to control the world by force."

During the Vietnam War, Chomsky joined the stream of travelers to Vietnam with other revolutionaries such as Jane Fonda and Susan Sontag, to cheer on the Communists in the hope that the American military would lose the war. He assumed no responsibility for the many thousands of Vietnamese who were killed, imprisoned and died trying to escape the victorious Communist regime or for the murder of 2 million Cambodians after the American military left in 1973. He first denied that such a genocide happened, but when the reality could no longer be denied, he insisted that whatever happened in Cambodia was the fault of America.

Although Chomsky is an extremist and some are inclined to dismiss him as a self-promoting crank, his influence is still widespread since he has been able to pass on his despicable views to many generations of students. He eagerly serves in the "blame America first" army, that reaches even into the churches. For example, Tom Driver, of the Union Theological Seminary in New York, quoted Jesus' words, "Those who take the sword will die by the sword" as a way to understand the horrific crime of 9/11. He added: "The violence that America has long exported has now come back upon us in a covert operation of masterly, although diabolical, planning."[48] The list of those who admire Chomsky as a hero is long. In the privileged world of the American academia anti-American ideology is firmly entrenched. Chomsky is no exception.[49]

A REVOLUTIONARY MINDSET

Countless articles, essays, and books are devoted to anti-Americanism, a topic loaded with controversy, animosity and contradiction. Yet another chapter, in yet another book, will hardly do it full justice, but we can make a start in understanding the ideological underpinnings that give anti-Americanism its staying power.

It is instructive to view anti-Americanism as an outcropping of what is endemic to our modern, secular age – that is, an ideology of rejection and estrangement. This involves an overriding sense that there is something fundamentally wrong with the United States (and by extension the entire West) that cannot be corrected by piecemeal reforms, but requires a total uprooting of existing conditions and structures, if necessary, by force; in other words, what is needed is a Revolution.

---

[48] "Straight Answers to Moral Confusion in National Crisis," November 8, 2003.

[49] Cf., David Horowitz, *The Professors: The 101 Most Dangerous Academics in America* (Washington DC: Regnery Publishing, 2007).

The big question is who does the analysis, and who will lead the way? The intellectuals are eager to take on that task. Norman Birnbaum wrote in 1988 that he had full confidence in their ability to provide the leadership in the needed revolution. He explained:

The intellectuals] bear the responsibility for deciding anew how the world really is, or how it ought to be.... Installed, with all due modesty, in the vanguard of an aroused citizenry, we may set forth once again to redeem a not quite fallen world.... We secular thinkers will find ourselves in the midst of those who take their social conscience ... their self-definition from ecclesiastical tradition.[50]

At its core, anti-Americanism is driven by the attempt to eliminate the past as that has been influenced by the Judeo-Christian faith, and to replace it with a thoroughly secular understanding of the good life. That worldview was succinctly defined in the 1973 Humanist Manifesto, in which its authors stated that there is no supernatural, no divine purpose, and no deity to save us, but that we must save ourselves. The same principle is summarized in Marx's Communist Manifesto. History is rife with painful evidence that such ideas of self-redemption inevitably end up in cruel tyrannies. (The same goes for life under sharia law.) The problem with the current revolutionaries who want to tear down what exists in America is that they are in denial about reality in countries ruled by dictators inspired by the Marxist or humanist manifestos. Many are the "pilgrims" of the West who have traveled to the worst kind of gulags, and yet who returned with glowing reports. They sealed the fate of millions condemned to a life of misery and fear. That's how it is possible that the Castro brothers and the late Che Guevara are still heroes of the radical left. Lenin used to call them "useful idiots."[51]

---

[50] Norman Birnbaum cited in Hollander, *Understanding Anti-Americanism...*, 13.

[51]Cf., Paul Hollander, *Political Pilgrims: Travels of Western Intellectuals to the Soviet Union, China, and Cuba* (Oxford: Oxford University Press, 1981).

America has provided a home for millions of newcomers who experience their new country as a place of freedom and opportunity. Thousands if not millions are refugees of countries where the revolutionary ideas were put into practice. These are the people who speak from bitter experience about living in a tyrannical and lawless culture where fear and terror keep the population in bondage. Many of them have written about their lives in slavery, and we should pay attention.

AN INFLUENCE FOR GOOD

I can imagine that some readers might say to me: "Do you mean to say that the Americans are the embodiment of goodness and that anyone who dares to criticize them is evil?" I do not mean any such thing.

The United States is suffering from the same spiritual malaise that afflicts us all. It is burdened by all the forces of secularism with its rampant hedonism and materialism, evident in the breakdown of marriage and the family, abortion on demand, crime, drug addiction, corruption, political correctness, sleazy politics and ditto entertainment. The list is lengthy.

However, the United States is not one uniform entity of evil and corruption, as depicted by its homegrown and foreign radical critics. Despite all the wrongs so clearly and often falsely trumpeted by so many, one will find wholesome families and communities, schools and churches, a love of freedom, the conviction that some things are worth fighting for, and a spirit of generosity that comes to expression in helping the needy near and far.

To call the United States a terrorist state, a threat to the world and responsible for the impoverishment of the Third World is furthering the spread of malicious lies. These lies are also repeated endlessly in the Arab/Muslim world, and add immensely to the difficulties the United States is facing. Some are so blinded by their hatred that they want the United States to fail in its attempt to help establish freedom in other parts of the world.

This is the time to stand with the United States against the lies and distortions hurled against it, even if there are legitimate reservations and misgivings about the details. The world situation is precarious. There are evil forces out to destroy and kill. To defend against them requires more than endless conferences and United Nations' resolutions. Sometimes what are needed are military force and the kind of determined leadership that is becoming all too scarce.

America is undergoing a serious crisis of identity and belief. As the leading nation of the democratic West, we are all affected by America's current turmoil and division, especially in Canada because we are close neighbors.

Many prominent Christian leaders in America have reminded us that America's upheavals and threats from within and without are first of all of a spiritual nature.

What America now needs is utterly beyond our human capacity. But it is not beyond the power of God to renew and heal. May God continue to bless America.

9 Multiculturalism:
Road to Nowhere

Depending on stereotype, ensuring that ethnic groups will preserve their distinctiveness in a gentle and insidious form of apartheid, multiculturalism has done little more than lead an already divided country down the path to further social divisiveness.[52]

Among the many irrational ideas about racial and ethnic groups that have polarized societies over the centuries and around the world, few have been more irrational and counterproductive than the current dogma of multiculturalism.[53]

Canada is supposed to be the shining example of harmoniously merging a wide variety of ethnic, racial and religious communities into a peaceful and unified nation. We pride

---

[52] Neil Bissoondath, *Selling Illusions: The Cult of Multiculturalism in Canada* (Toronto: Penguin Canada, 1994, 2002), 82-83.

[53] Thomas Sowell, *National Review Online*, March 15, 2013.

ourselves on being so much superior to the American melting pot by fashioning a much more vibrant and colorful mosaic.

John Ibbitson of the *Globe and Mail*, gushes about the Aga Khan Foundation's interest in establishing a global center for pluralism in Ottawa. He writes:

> [G]overnments around the world increasingly look to Canada as the world's most successful pluralist state. We have found a way, despite many strains, of accommodating the founding French and English cultures, and have welcomed succeeding waves of European, Asian, Hispanic and African immigrants. Unlike the rest of the world, the more polyglot Canada gets, the more politically and culturally stable it becomes.[54]

But reality is not quite that simple. To be sure, Canada has always been a country of immigrants. Most of us trace our roots back to other parts of the world. For some of us that requires a couple of centuries of backtracking. For many of us, the tracks from our countries of birth are still fresh.

After World War II a flood of immigrants began arriving in Canada. (My family was part of that flow.) The question was how to accommodate this large number of people who increasingly came from non-Western countries. At the same time English-French tensions called for a fresh approach. Toward answering the question, a Royal Commission on Bilingualism and Biculturalism was appointed in 1963, which published a voluminous report in 1969.

A NEW DEFINITION

While its main focus was on the special status of Quebec within Canada, this Royal Commission went much further by proclaiming Canada to be a nation of not just two but one of many cultures. It did not take long before the concept of cultural pluralism or

---

[54] *Globe and Mail*, February 6, 2004.

multiculturalism was elevated to the defining characteristic of Canada. And that's how a process was put into motion that has left many people scratching their heads – or should have.

Not surprisingly, this outcome did not please the Quebecois, since they would prefer to keep the limelight on just the two founding cultures. But then Prime Minister Pierre Elliott Trudeau became an enthusiastic booster of the newly discovered insight. (Could it be that this wily enemy of Quebec nationalism knew that multiculturalism would help dilute the special status of Quebec in Canada?)

On October 8, 1971, the Prime Minister announced in the House of Commons that the Liberal government had accepted all the recommendations contained in Volume IV of the Royal Commission on Bilingualism and Biculturalism. He explained:

> A policy of multiculturalism within a bilingual framework commends itself to the government as the most suitable means of assuring the cultural freedom of Canadians. Such a policy should help break down discriminatory attitudes and cultural jealousies. National unity if it is to mean anything in the deeply personal sense, must be founded on confidence in one's own individual identity....
> A vigorous policy of multiculturalism will help create this initial confidence. It can form the base of a society which is based on fair play for all.

On the same day, the government adopted a statement of policy, "Appendix to Hansard," that amounted to an unqualified endorsement of the Prime Minister's comments. It noted that cultural diversity is to be treasured in contrast to what it called "assimilation programs forcing our citizens to forsake and forget the cultures they have brought to us."

The government further assured that Canadian identity will not be undermined by multiculturalism. It declared that

> cultural pluralism is the very essence of Canadian identity.... To say we have two official languages is not to say that we have two official cultures, and no particular culture is more 'official' than the other. A policy of multiculturalism must be a policy for all Canadians.

In 1973 the Ministry of Multiculturalism was established. In 1982 the Charter of Rights and Freedoms was amended to say that it must be interpreted to enhance "the multicultural heritage of Canadians."

In 1988 the Canadian Multiculturalism Act became law, proclaiming that the policy of the government of Canada is to

> recognize and promote the understanding that multiculturalism reflects the cultural and racial diversity of Canadian society... [and that] multiculturalism is a fundamental characteristic of the Canadian heritage and identity and that it provides an invaluable resource in the shaping of Canada's future.[55]

Much has changed since the 1960s. The old Canada with its strong Anglo-Saxon and broadly Judeo-Christian stamp has made way for a much more diverse population. How have the newfangled, "pluralist" policies worked out in practice? What has been gained – or lost? How do we truly evaluate the outcome of policies that are over four decades old?

We should all be able to agree that Canada's welcoming and open policies to its new arrivals is admirable. The generosity and goodwill that exists among neighbors of different races, nationalities and religions is something to be treasured and safeguarded, which is the responsibility of every one of us. If this is what multiculturalism is all about, we should all be wholehearted supporters.

A NEW DOGMA

But much more is implied in the kind of multiculturalism that has been declared to be the defining characteristic of Canada. As applied in Canada, this policy assumes the status of a sacred dogma that brooks no disagreement. Therein lies the problem.

One may dislike my use of dogma, because calling something dogmatic has unfavorable connotations. But the language of the

---

[55] CMA 3(1) a, b.

policies and legislation is loaded with words which suggest that issues of fundamental meaning and substance are at stake here. Though the term culture can mean different things, the language used throughout indicates that culture does not only refer to the arts, different customs, cuisine, social conventions, and other outward expressions. In fact, it refers to something much more fundamental, that is, a whole way of life and a way of being a nation. The absolutist-sounding language leaves little room for a different conclusion.

Multiculturalism is said to assure our cultural freedom, enhance our confidence in our own identity, help break down discriminatory attitudes, and so contribute "to a richer life for us all," and so on. This is the language of the true believers.

FOUR OBJECTIONS

There are at least four weighty problems with the assumptions and implications of multiculturalism as applied in Canada.

One. It is driven by a typically modern, or even post-modern, belief that all cultures are of equal value. Therefore, no single culture is better than any other. For example, we cannot say that the largely "Judeo-Christian" Western democracies are superior to other cultures. To make such a claim is seen as cultural imperialism that is responsible for the injustice and oppression of the past.

The ideology undergirding this cultural equivalence, or relativism, makes it impossible to speak of better or worse, right or wrong. The practical effect is that we are living in a moral wasteland where no abiding standard of truth and goodness may be applied.

Two. This means that we now tiptoe around all kinds of political and ethical pressure points and no longer call a spade a spade. We change definitions or, as the late American Senator Daniel Patrick Moynihan has famously said, we have "defined deviancy downward."

For example, instead of using traditional concepts of justice, we now declare equality to be the uppermost principle. If people of certain national or racial backgrounds display particular tendencies to turn to a life of crime or family breakdown, we are forbidden to say anything about such facts. Those who break that taboo are quickly denounced as bigots and racists. That's what happens when you declare all cultures to be the same. It dispenses with the ability to make moral judgments. The main intended result is of course that it enables us to escape responsibility – or so we think.

The outcome is a culture of hypocrisy, doubletalk and cowardice. That's why there is so little honest discussion about immigration and refugee policies in this country. The irony is that it is now considered a sign of sophistication and broadmindedness to deny all universal absolutes, whereas at the same time we are busy inventing our own brand of absolutes. We then declare ourselves to be progressive. Multiculturalism is one of such new absolutes.

Three. A further bitter irony is that multiculturalism as government policy has undermined the very integrity and substance of Canadian culture. Instead of insisting that newcomers become acquainted with Canadian history and institutions, we tell them that there is nothing distinctive or excellent about Canada.

Then secretary of state for multiculturalism, Sheila Finestone, stated on a CTV panel discussion on January 31, 1995, "In my view there isn't any one Canadian identity. Canada has no national culture." She received a lot of flak from the public. But she was only restating what Prime Minister Trudeau had said in 1971: "[T]here is no official culture, nor does any ethnic group take precedence over any other."

Four. As a few brave critics have explained, multiculturalism has not led to more harmony and understanding but to the further fragmenting of this divided country. Let's take a closer look at what a few commentators have said about this topic.

THE EMPEROR WITHOUT CLOTHES

Neil Bissoondath, Trinidad-born, of East Indian descent, Canadian playwright and novelist, will have none of the self-congratulation about Canada's success in building a multiculturalist nation. His *Selling*

Illusions is a blunt yet thoughtful reminder that, as he puts it, the emperor of multiculturalism has no clothes.

Bissoondath encountered not just criticism but vilification. He found that his East Indian and immigrant background gave him no immunity against the charge of being a bigot and racist. To question multiculturalism is to question what he calls "a holy cow." But he is unrepentant and has plunged into the thick of the controversy that many do not want to touch.

His skill as a novelist is evident in the sensitive way he describes his own roots and the challenges faced by those who leave their homeland to start a new life for themselves in a strange country. Bissoondath has little time for those who insist on retaining their loyalty to the country left behind rather than making Canada their true home.

He has little good to say about the celebration of ethnic diversity that amounts to no more than sentimental celebration of ethnic stereotypes. He argues that multiculturalism that wants to hang on to the ancestral homeland, with its insistence that "There is more important than Here," serves to encourage the ghettoizing of the different ethnic communities.

This divided loyalty has led some born in this country to return to take up arms on the side of the Croatians during the war in Kosovo. More recently many more Islam believers have joined the jihad in places where open warfare has broken out.

The other side of that coin is that old feuds in the homeland of immigrants have been introduced into Canada – sometimes with deadly results. The advocates of multiculturalism do not honestly face up to the fact that many ethnic communities and races harbor deadly animosities within themselves. They refuse to face up to that ugly truth because it would expose a fatal flaw in their grand design of nation building.

ETHICAL CHAOS

Bissoondath argues that the elevation of diversity to public policy is empty without setting out some limits. But where to draw those limits when some immigrant communities (at least their spokespeople) argue that female circumcision is part of their culture? Or what about the demand to adjust criminal law enforcement in the case of wife or child abuse in certain communities; or the demand for exclusive black schools; or polygamy, and sharia law for Muslims? The author writes that we do not know how to answer these questions

> because we have so blithely accepted the mentality of division, we find ourselves lost in a confusion of values. Multiculturalism has made us fearful of defining acceptable boundaries.... And so we find ourselves in danger of accepting, in its name, a slide into ethical chaos."[56]

Ironically, multiculturalism has been exploited to feed the sense of alienation in many ethnic communities – inevitably coupled to, what else, the notion of victimhood. We now must be careful to avoid giving any offence to minorities, especially visible ones. This kind of anti-discrimination fetish has flourished especially in the academy and among the literati. Entire books and plays that do not meet the new standards of race and gender sensitivity have been declared to be unacceptable.

A vicious fight has been going on against writers who, like Bissoondath, want simply to write honest stories. The new racist and sexist vigilantes now insist that only blacks can write about blacks, women about women, Africans about Africans, aboriginals about aboriginals. And so on. Here is a case in point, one of many that could be cited.

A number of years ago, University of Toronto professor Jeanne Cannizzo was driven from her position after she curated an exhibition called "Into the Heart of Africa" at the Royal Ontario Museum. Some black groups denounced her as a racist and picketed the ROM, plastered confetti on her house, disturbed her classroom lectures, and

---

[56] Bissoondath, *Selling Illusions*, 139.

threatened her with physical harm. She withdrew from teaching and left the country.[57]

Where were the university leaders, her colleagues, the "human rights" champions, and for that matter the police, standing up for academic freedom, even the basic freedom from criminal attacks?

Bissoondath responded to an essay by Susan Crean who attempted to justify professor Cannizzo's attackers. He wrote that the Crean article "in the end, reveals the confusion often found in white left-liberal circles: not the exercise of intellect but the abdication of it, not exploration of ideas but conversation in a confessional."

The vaunted tolerance has made way for hateful intolerance, and Bissoondath has had his share of the slings and arrows for his breach of the new orthodoxy. But he is unbowed. He says: "Any attempt to padlock the mind is a question of fundamental liberty. Any limitation of subject matter or point of view ... represents for us all a severe restriction on the free play of the imagination."

You need not agree with everything in this book to find this a refreshing change from the doublespeak that appears to be endemic to the subject of multiculturalism. The bitter irony, which Bissoondath points out, is that the much-hyped multiculturalism in Canada does not deliver what it promises.

The road toward a more healthy and vigorous nationhood begins with an acknowledgment of the truth about multiculturalism. That road is difficult and treacherous. But *Selling Illusions* is full of suggestions to make a start at least with the first steps on that road.

MOSAIC MADNESS

Sociologist and professor at the University of Lethbridge, Reginald Bibby, has joined the discussion about Canada's dilemma in attempting to be all things to all people. His study of life in Canada

---

[57] Ibid., 152.

published in 1990 bears the revealing title, *Mosaic Madness: The Poverty and Potential of Life in Canada.*[58]

In his opinion, multiculturalism is a form of relativism that puts a common basis for nation building out of reach. He writes that we want to be so open-minded (pluralistic) that we are not very loyal to anything except to a rather "tenuous willingness to coexist."

The problem, says Bibby, is that in this country pluralism means that if someone dares to advocate a position on the basis of an ethical, moral, or religious principle – for example, on premarital sex, marriage structure, homosexuality or abortion – such a person is typically considered narrow-minded, if not a threat to the public well-being.

Bibby thinks that religion, which is concerned with what is true, should help us find a way of living together within one nation. But relativism means that truth may mean different things to different people. And this is exactly the tar pit of modernity that lands us into what Bibby calls a "visionless existence."

He describes religion in Canada as not very aggressive nor is it expected to be very demanding. Most Canadians have no strong convictions about religion, which at best has only a marginal place in their lives.

Bibby's study of religion and its impact on society in Canada has caused him to believe that religion in Canada lacks authority and has therefore lost the ability to make a contribution to the creation of social cohesion. He concludes: "Sadly, religion, rather than decrying the excesses of individualism and relativism, has tended to embrace them. It therefore has lost both its message and its vocal cords."

---

[58] Reginald Bibby, *Mosaic Madness: The Poverty and Potential of Life in Canada* (Toronto: Stoddart, 1990).

CONCLUSION

Selling Illusions is intense, bold, detailed with some helpful suggestions. Bissoondath takes on the advocates of multiculturalism right on their home turf – and has the scars to prove it.

Mosaic Madness does not go much beyond some well-meaning admonitions to keep on striving to do better. Bibby concludes that there is still much hope that "madness can yet give way to sanity."

I am not so sure. One thing is certain: Christians who want to take their confession seriously and want to take part in the public discussion about the very foundation of our nation need to do their homework. The two books mentioned here, though quite different in tone, provide compelling proof of the urgency of that assignment.

10 The Media's

Romance with Obama

The traditional media is playing a very, very dangerous game with its readers, with the constitution, and with its own fate. The sheer bias in the print and television coverage of this election campaign is not just bewildering, but appalling.[59]

Many Americans must still be scratching their heads, wondering how it was that Barack Obama, an unknown academic turned community organizer and then Senator from Illinois, managed to capture the first prize of American politics and become President of the most powerful nation in the world.

Undoubtedly, Obama's victory had to do with his eloquence, political savvy, energy and boundless ambition. But while these characteristics would have brought him far, they wouldn't in themselves have been sufficient to defeat his competitors in the Democratic Party and carry him to victory in the 2008 election.

---

[59] Michael S. Malone, cited in ASL, 21.

The one, decisive factor in Obama's rise to the presidency was the role of the mainstream media in American politics. Bernard Goldberg spent 28 years as a correspondent with CBS News, and has been an outspoken critic of systemic bias in the mainstream media. According to Goldberg, the media has changed from being an impartial observer to an unapologetic advocate of mostly left-wing causes. Goldberg suggests that this transformation is a threat to the integrity of the media, and an impediment to public confidence and the health of a free society. His 2001 book[60] won Goldberg no plaudits from his colleagues, many of whom considered him a traitor, but it became a *New York Times* #1 best seller.

OBAMA IS CROWNED KING

In 2009, Goldberg published *A Slobbering Love Affair*.[61] The title says everything you need to know about the theme of this book. Goldberg refers to a number of studies that expose a lack of fairness in the media and suggests an obvious double standard in reporting about Democrats versus Republicans. But his main argument is that the media helped Obama by mostly writing glowing stories about his performance and his crowd-inspiring speeches.

Veteran reporters such as Chris Matthews of MSNBC's program "Hardball", were reduced to making the most embarrassing and juvenile claims about their hero Obama. Many will remember Matthews' comment about the thrill going up his leg when listening to Obama. And the editor of *Newsweek*, Evan Thomas, raised flattery to a new level when he praised Obama's June 2009 Cairo speech as follows: "I mean in a way Obama's standing above the country, above – above the world, he's sort of God."

---

[60] Bernard Goldberg, *Bias: A CBS Insider Exposes How the Media Distort the News* (Washington DC: Regnery Publ., 2001).

[61] Bernard Goldberg, *A Slobbering Love Affair: The True (and Pathetic) Story of the Torrid Romance between Barack Obama and the Main-stream Media* (Washington DC: Regnery Publ., 2009).

MSNBC Keith Olbermann said this about Obama's famous Invesco Field speech: "For forty-two minutes not a sour note, and spellbinding throughout in a way usually reserved for the creation of fiction." Olbermann intended to praise Obama, but in an odd sort of way, he spoke the truth when he referred to the "creation of fiction."

Putting a glow on Obama's every utterance was bad enough, but the most important way in which the media became an apologist for Obama was to shield him from damaging information. This happened when some critics who had not fallen for the Obama adoration syndrome took a hard look at his previous relations with some shady characters from the hard Left, people including Bill Ayres (an unrepentant 1960s terrorist), Bernardine Dohrn, Jeremiah Wright (the racist, American-hating preacher at the church Obama attended for 20 years) and the Association of Community Organizations for Reform Now (a left-leaning network of advocacy groups whose government funding was revoked in 2009 after allegations of corruption and fraud). The complete list of Obama's radical affiliations is much longer – see Pamela Geller's, *The Post-American Presidency*.[62]

DAMAGE CONTROL

If anyone were to mention these connections, Obama and his staff would shrug them off by saying that relations with these people and organizations were only incidental and of no consequence. This looked like it might change, however, when the story about the real Jeremiah Wright broke in February 2007, not in the mainstream press but in *Rolling Stone*. This coincided with the distribution of Wright's most outlandish and racially-charged sermons.

Rather than condemn Obama's affiliation with Wright, the media, led by the *New York Times*, swung into action to minimize the damage.

---

[62] Pamela Geller and Robert B. Spencer, *The Post-American Presidency: The Obama Administration's War on America* (New York: Threshold Editions, 2010)

The spin masters were so effective that they managed to turn the tables on anyone who wanted to pursue this story by smearing them as hatemongers and racists.

The other significant way the media protected Obama was not to ask hard questions during his numerous interviews on all the major news outlets. Goldberg listed ten questions that were never put to Obama. Here are three of them:

Is it fair to say that if Jeremiah Wright's sermons had not been made public you would still be worshipping at his church?

What did your wife really mean when she said, referring to your candidacy, that it was the first time she was proud to be an American?

Regardless of your age at the time of Bill Ayers' bombings, why would you have anything – anything – to do with a man like Ayers, who not only planted bombs at the Pentagon and the Capitol, but who said his only regret was that he did not do more to stop the war in Vietnam?

Goldberg does a masterful job of shining the light of truth on the duplicity of the mainstream media that abetted Obama in covering up information about his past associations with left-wing radicals. Obama made it very clear that he wanted to bring about a fundamental change in America. If you want to know what he had in mind, read Goldberg's book. Then also take the time to study what the radicals mentioned here and a raft of like-minded revolutionaries are advocating.

Goldberg writes with a quiet passion because he is convinced that the new advocacy role of the media is not only its undoing, but also a threat to society at large. Worst of all, the media is doing immense harm to the freedom that is indispensable for a healthy and thriving democracy. The simple reason for this is that freedom and truth are indelibly interconnected. Or to use biblical language, "…the truth will set you free" (John 8:32). In my opinion, this book should be required reading at the high school level and beyond. Thank you, Mr. Goldberg.

11 How the Media Distorts the News

Liberal minds flocked to the USSR in an unending procession, from the great ones like [George Bernard] Shaw and Gide and Barbusse and Julian Huxley and Harold Laski and Sidney and Beatrice Webb, down to the poor little teachers, crazed clergymen and millionaires, driveling dons, all utterly convinced that, under the aegis of the great Stalin, a new dawn is breaking in the world, so that the human race may at last be united in liberty, equality and fraternity for evermore....

These liberal minds are prepared to believe anything, however preposterous, to overlook anything, however villainous, to approve anything, however obscurantist and brutally authoritarian, in order to be able to preserve intact the confident expectation that one of the most thoroughgoing, ruthless and bloody tyrannies ever to exist on earth can be relied on to champion human freedom, the brotherhood of man, and all the other good Liberal causes to which they had dedicated their lives....[63]

---

[63] Malcolm Muggeridge, *Confessions of a Twentieth Century Pilgrim* (New York: Harper Collins, 1988), 87.

One of the biggest challenges we face is how to make sense of the avalanche of information about world and national affairs. Who is able and willing to distinguish and tell the truth about what is really going on? The army of reporters and commentators all claim to be objective and fact-based. The problem is that much of what the mainstream media produces is determined by the ideological biases not dissimilar to what Malcolm Muggeridge (1903 –1990) encountered when he served as the correspondent for the Manchester Guardian in Moscow in 1932-1933.

TRAVELLING TO THE PROMISED LAND

His story is an account of his and his wife Kitty's initial enthusiasm for the communist revolution in Russia that promised to build a new society where capitalism and injustice are eliminated. Muggeridge writes that they wanted to live there for the rest of their lives so that their son will

> grow up in a sane world with a future instead of in our crazy run-down one with only a past.... Where we were going, we assured ourselves and one another, there was hope and exhilaration. It was the wave of the future – a phrase even then current.[64]

Of all the fellow travelers, the Muggeridges came with superb credentials. They had the blessing of Sidney and Beatrice Webb, who was Kitty's aunt. The Webbs were ardent admirers of communist Russia who published sycophantic books about the Russian Revolution, including The Truth About Soviet Russia and Soviet Communism: A New Civilization? (The question mark was dropped from later editions.)

Travelling on the Soviet ship Kooperatsia to Russia, Muggeridge thought back to the time he sailed for India on his way to "tired

---

[64] Macolm Muggeridge, *The Green Stick: Chronicles of Wasted Time* (New York: William Morrow/Harper Collins, 1973), 227.

imperial glory," but this time they are headed for "the veritable future of mankind." He describes the other passengers as follows:

These fellow-passengers provided my first experience of the progressive elite from all over the world who attached themselves to the Soviet regime, resolved to believe anything they were told by its spokesmen. For the most part, they were academics and writers... all upholders of progressive causes and members of progressive organizations, constituting a sort of Brechtian ribald chorus in the drama of the twentieth century.... The fall guys of history...who throw themselves under the wheels of the great Juggernaut. I was to speculate endlessly about them, rail against their credulities and imbecilities, ridicule their absurdities and denounce their servility before the nakedness of Soviet power. The more so because I knew inwardly that I was one of them; in my heart, too, the same death wish.[65]

Muggeridge found it easy to be a correspondent for the Manchester Guardian as long as he stayed within the rules enforced by the state censors. Those rules required that they never write anything that would reflect unfavorably on the regime. In other words, the only source of news was the Soviet press, which was preoccupied with reporting the many "successes" in all the major sectors of the economy.

DISILLUSIONMENT

Being of a critical if not cynical mindset, Muggeridge was no fool and soon discovered the truth about Russia. Unlike many other communists, he turned against his erstwhile belief and then became a convinced and eloquent opponent of the Soviet Union. When he sent his last dispatch to the Guardian in which he wrote the truth about the murderous Stalinist regime, he realized that his career as a correspondent in Moscow would be over. The Green Stick is a

---

[65] Ibid., 235-6.

fascinating explanation of the author's change from admirer to bitter critic of communist ideology and practice.

The change of mind was not long in coming because Muggeridge saw closeup the lies used to prop up a system that squeezed every ounce of honesty and freedom out of life. He and his fellow journalists in fact were enablers of the lies they were fed by the state-controlled media. He summarized: "In the beginning was the Lie, and the Lie was made news and dwelt among us, graceless and false."[66]

Muggeridge toyed with the idea of telling the head of the Press Department of the Soviet Foreign Office, Oumansky, that he was not really a foreign correspondent but a comrade who had come to the USSR to help build Socialism. But by this time his desire for citizenship in the "Kingdom of Heaven on Earth" had begun ebbing away. Instead, he began to wrestle with basic questions about the validity of the Soviet regime often while walking in Red Square or passing through Lenin's tomb, ironically, at the center from which the monstrous Soviet ideology emanated.

He was fascinated by the massive Kremlin buildings, an extravagant fortress then housing not an anointed king or emperor, not an elected president, or a chosen Pope, but the Dictatorship of the Proletariat. This represents a new abstraction that transcends Louis XIV's claim to be the embodiment of the state and the people. That's what the ruler in the Kremlin claimed for himself. Muggeridge writes:

All the toiling masses everywhere, their will, their purpose, their very being, embodied in this one man, who spoke and acted, and even lived, on their behalf. And everyone else… must be abolished. Then at last history would be over, paradise would have come to earth, and the Dictatorship of the Proletariat, in the person of the man in the Kremlin, would reign forevermore.

Walter Duranty (1884-1957) was the *New York Times'* correspondent in Moscow. Muggeridge described him as "a little sharp-witted energetic" and controversial person. Muggeridge writes that there was

---

[66] Ibid., 240.

something "vigorous, vivacious, preposterous, about his unscrupulousness which made his persistent lying somehow absorbing." No one else followed every shift and change in the Party Line as he did. Oumansky constantly held him up to the rest of the foreign correspondents as an example that they should imitate. Muggeridge once called Duranty "the greatest liar I have met in journalism."

Duranty served as the Moscow Bureau Chief of the *New York Times* from 1922 -1936; thereafter he was on retainer until 1941. He excelled in concocting glowing stories about the communist revolution in Russia where, as he reported, the collectivization of agriculture was going well, with no famine conditions anywhere.

He also thought that the harsh treatment of those accused of undermining the Russian state and spying for the enemy was deserved, and that the judicial procedures were fair. Duranty's acquiescent attitude about the monstrous lies and most ridiculous charges against the accused earned him a privileged position so that he had no difficulty in getting a visa, or a house, or other favors.

Muggeridge thinks that in some strange way, Duranty's favorable depiction of the Soviet regime was a response to some need of his nature, not that he believed in the Revolution or in its beneficial outcome for Russia, or for mankind. No, he admired Stalin and the regime for its strength and ruthlessness. "I put my money on Stalin," was one of his favorite sayings. In their last conversation, Duranty admitted that the agricultural situation was a disaster and there was a severe famine, although he told his readers the very opposite. For that he was awarded the Pulitzer Prize.

A MAN-MADE CATASTROPHE

During his years as a reporter for the *New York Times* in Moscow, Duranty came to be seen as the great Russian expert in America whose views influenced President Roosevelt in his policies towards Russia.

(Might this explain how Eastern and mid-European countries ended up under the Stalinist boot after World War II?)

Muggeridge writes that Duranty's reports were nonsensically untrue, yet the Times accepted them because it wanted to be deceived and Duranty provided the necessary cover for that deception. This kind of treasonous denial of the murder of millions and the destruction of civilized life has been repeated in many other countries, such as in Cuba, in Vietnam, and in Latin America.

Rumors of famine in the Ukraine, though a forbidden topic, were reaching the expatriates in Moscow. Muggeridge decided to see for himself, and he travelled by train through the Ukranian countryside. He had to be careful not to attract the attention of the authorities, which is the reason that he travelled without any prearranged stops. He did manage to stop at various villages where he saw not just a famine, but a deliberately planned and executed calamity that he can never forget.

It was not just a famine due to any natural catastrophe like drought or floods. This particular famine was brought about by the forced collectivization of agriculture, "an assault on the countryside by party aparatchiks...supported by strongarm squads from the military and the police." In March 1933, Muggeridge sent three articles to the Guardian in which he told the truth about this man-made famine in one of the most fertile parts of Russia. There was not only a famine but "a state of war, a military occupation." He tried to describe all the horrors he saw.

> (T)he abandoned villages, the absence of livestock, neglected fields; everywhere famished, frightened people and intimations of coercion, soldiers about the place, and hard-faced men in long overcoats. One particularly remarkable scene I stumbled on by chance at a railway station in the grey early morning; peasants with their hands tied behind them being loaded into cattle trucks at gunpoint...; all so silent and mysterious and horrible in the half-light, like some macabre ballet.[67]

---

[67] Ibid., 286-7.

No other foreign journalist had visited the famine areas in the USSR except under official auspices and supervision, so Muggeridge's account stood by itself, and he was accused of being a liar in the Guardian correspondence columns and elsewhere. Meanwhile Duranty's voice in the *New York Times* trumpeted a very different story of granaries overflowing with grain, apple-cheeked dairymaids and plump contended cows, not to mention George Bernard Shaw and all the other distinguished visitors who testified that there was not, and could not be, a food shortage in the USSR.

Muggeridge once attended a Sunday church service in Kiev that made a deep impression on him. The church was crowded, but he managed to squeeze into a spot where he had a good view of the worshippers. He writes:

Never before or since have I participated in such worship; the sense conveyed of turning to God in great affliction was overpowering. Though I could not, of course, follow the service, I knew little bits of it; for instance, where the congregation say there is no help for them save from God. What intense feeling they put into these words! In their minds, I knew, as in mine, was a picture of those desolate abandoned villages, of the hunger and the hopelessness, of the cattle trucks being loaded with humans in the dawn light.

Where were they to turn for help? Not to the Kremlin, and the Dictatorship of the Proletariat, certainly; nor to the forces of progress and democracy and enlightenment in the West.... Every possible human agency found wanting. So, only God remained, and to God they turned with a passion, a dedication, a humility, impossible to convey. They took me with them; I felt closer to God then than I ever had before, or am likely to again.[68]

After leaving Russia in April 1933, Muggeridge wrote that his mind "was endlessly preoccupied with thoughts of the Soviet regime. I felt

---

[68] Ibid., .288.

furious about the whole experience, as though I had been personally cheated..."

A PROFOUND MYSTERY

The Russian Revolution of 1917 was born in times of great upheavals. It began seven decades of a murderous regime led by men with hearts of steel, such as Lenin, Trotsky and Stalin, who cared not for God or men.

They exploited the existing confusion and rudderlessness to fight their way to the top by brute force and indescribable cruelty.

Many of the Western elite in charge of the academy and the media were and are in denial about the true character of communism. Malcolm Muggeridge, gifted with the power of words, told the awful truth, and for that he was blacklisted and treated with contempt.

In contrast, Walter Duranty denied that the communists were ruling with an iron fist that destroyed the lives of millions of terrified people. Stalin honored him for assisting in establishing diplomatic relations between the U.S. and the Soviet Union. He was widely perceived as an expert on the Russian Revolution and was awarded the Pulitzer Prize in 1932.

All of this came crashing down when the truth of the Stalinist regime could no longer be hidden. The *New York Times* fired Duranty, and there were growing public demands to strip him of his Pulitzer. In 2003, the Times appointed one of its editorial board members, Karl Meyer, to write a signed editorial in which he called Duranty's articles "some of the worst reporting to appear in this newspaper."

Subsequently, the Times issued a statement about this shameful episode in which it put all the blame on Duranty and on the Pulitzer board's refusal to withdraw the award since it found "no clear and convincing evidence of deliberate deception" in his reporting.

It is hard to find the right words to describe the role of the *New York Times* for allowing its pages to be used as a propaganda tool for one of the most evil and cruel dictatorships in the history of mankind. In one sense, Duranty is a small bit player in the Revolution inspired by Karl

Marx, whose ideas fired the imaginations of millions of followers – and victims. Instead of the promised land of peace and brotherhood, we get what the Soviet Union, China and North Korea created, saturated with the blood and tears of millions.

Their blood still cries out, but the Times has never owned up to its responsibility in furthering the cause of such evil. Instead, it blamed its underlings, and subsequent events show that it has learned nothing. It continues to promote the cause of the Revolution now renamed as progressivism.

Many on the Left still revere as a hero the late Cuban mass murderer Che Guevara. And the Times correspondents' reports at a crucial phase in the Castro-led revolution may well have been the decisive turning point that has condemned the Cuban people to a life of slavery and squalor.

I find it a profound mystery that the liberal progressives, so well described in all their banality and foolhardiness by Malcolm Muggeridge, have embraced the worst tyrants of our time. Do they not know that the Revolution they so admire will devour them too? (Think Leon Trotsky, and the 1938 Moscow Show Trials.)

Their willful blindness may have something to do with G.K. Chesterton's famous saying: "When men no longer believe in God, they do not believe in nothing, but they will believe in anything."

12 How the Media Sold Out to Cuba

In all essentials, the battle for Cuba was a public relations campaign, fought in New York and Washington. Castro's principal advocate was Herbert Matthews of the New York Times, who presented him as the T. E. Lawrence of the Caribbean...so the Times sponsored Castro. This swung round the State Department.[69]

The cult of Ernesto Che Guevara is an episode in the moral callousness of our time. Che was a totalitarian. He achieved nothing but disaster. Many of the early leaders of the Cuban Revolution favored a democratic or democratic-socialist direction for the new Cuba. But Che was a mainstay of the hardline pro-Soviet faction, and his faction won.[70] One of the most shameful betrayals of modern times occurred when Fidel Castro led the revolution in Cuba against the then president Fulgencio Batista and replaced his dictatorship with a far worse, Stalinist one. The Castro revolution outdid the Russian communists in per capita execution, torture and

---

[69] Paul Johnson, *Modern Times* (1983), 621.

[70] Paul Berman, "The Cult of Che," www.Slate.com, September 24, 2004.

imprisonment. The bitter reality is that the Cuban island with its beautiful beaches, pleasant weather and its relatively advanced economy was transformed into a gulag where the blood of millions of innocent victims still cries out.

The irony is that the Castro revolution succeeded not because of the bravery and cunning of the Castroites, despite the myth they managed to propagate so successfully. Castro succeeded because he was a master propagandist in presenting himself as an honest man who wanted nothing but to build a free and tolerant country. He swore that he was not a communist, but a democratic reformer. But soon the mask came off and he began to smother all freedom with unspeakable cruelty. Cuba became a gulag like the one in the Soviet Union, if not worse.

A BITTER IRONY

The bitter irony is that Castro's hide was saved by the Western, mostly American media and intellectual elite, who slavishly served as propagandists for him. Even after more than half a century of the Cuban disaster, they refuse to face the ugly reality. Nor have they shown any remorse for delivering the Cuban people into the hands of ruthless murderers who wrecked their economy, tore their families apart, and destroyed their culture. Castro built a police state where you can be jailed, tortured and killed for not showing sufficient admiration for the Great Leader and his sadistic sidekick Ernesto Che Guevara, who was killed in 1967 when he was attempting (unsuccessfully) to export the Cuban-type revolution into Bolivia.

Those who want to look behind the myths and lies about Castro's Cuba have a wealth of information at their fingertips, including the stories from Cubans who speak from personal experience. Armando Valladares spent twenty-two years in Castro's prisons, where he suffered unspeakable insults and torture at the hands of sadistic guards. He describes this ordeal in his prison memoirs, Against All

Hope (1986), providing an inside look at Cuba's descent into a place where mass murderers had free rein.

Humberto Fontova escaped from Cuba with his family in 1961 when he was seven years old. He is the author of three books, *Exposing the Real Che Guevara: and the Useful Idiots Who Idolize Him*[71] and *Fidel: Hollywood's Favorite Tyrant*.[72] His most recent book, *The Longest Romance*,[73] explains in detail how the American media created and sustained the myth that the Castro revolution built what *Newsweek* described as "one of the best countries in the world to live."

On April 21, 1959, Castro attempted to put Americans at ease about his true agenda:

I am not a communist for three reasons: communism is a dictatorship and for my entire life I have been against dictatorships. Furthermore, communism means hatred and class struggle, and I am completely against such a philosophy. And finally, because communism opposes God and the Church. I say this to set your minds and spirits at rest.[74]

Fontova reports that well before Castro made this statement, he had already been hosting Soviet secret service agents and made the preparations for the Stalinization of Cuba. In the meantime, the mainstream media, including the influential *New York Times* were solidly committed to the falsehood that Castro was a democrat and a hero who deserved to be welcomed as a liberator of a long-suffering people.

---

[71] Humberto Fontova, *Exposing the Real Che Guevara: and the Useful Idiots Who Idolize Him* (New York: Sentinel, 2008).

[72] Humberto Fontova, *Fidel: Hollywood's Favorite Tyrant* (Washing DC: Regnery Publishing, 2005).

[73] Humberto Fontova, *The Longest Romance: The Mainstream Media and Fidel Castro* (New York: Encounter Books, 2013).

[74] Fontova, *The Longest Romance*, ix.

THE MYTH-MAKER

Castro had assured Cuban mothers that he would solve all Cuba's problems without spilling any blood. When entering Havana on January 8, 1959, welcomed as a hero by a jubilant crowd, he had singled out all Cuban mothers to tell them: "Let me assure you that because of me you will never have to cry."

Just one day after he told that lie, more than a hundred men and boys were machine-gunned down without trial and bulldozed into a mass grave, while many wives and mothers wept uncontrollably on a nearby road. On that same day The Observer (U.K.) wrote the following: "Mr. Castro's bearded, youthful figure has become a symbol of Latin America's rejection of brutality and lying. Every sign is that he will reject personal rule and violence."

Prior to his arrival in Havana, Castro had written a letter to fellow revolutionary Melba Hernandez in which he explained his strategy:

We cannot for a second abandon propaganda. Propaganda is vital – propaganda is the heart of our struggle. For now we use a lot of sleight of hand and smiles with everybody. There will be plenty of time later to crush all the cockroaches together.[75]

Che Guevara, who was in charge of crushing the "cockroaches," was of the same mind as his boss. He stated that on his watch "judicial evidence" will be done away with as an "archaic bourgeois detail. We execute from revolutionary conviction.... I don't need proof to execute a man – I only need proof that it's necessary to execute him." Fidel, who abolished habeas corpus, fully agreed because he said that legal proof is impossible to obtain against war criminals. "So we sentence them based on moral conviction."

Shortly after Armando Valladares was taken prisoner, he was interrogated and accused of being an enemy of the revolution because he had attended a school run by priests. Valladares defended himself

---

[75] Ibid., viii.

by saying that Fidel Castro had attended a similar school. The interrogator responded:

> Yes, but Fidel is a revolutionary. You, on the other hand, are a counter revolutionary, tied to priests and capitalists, and so we are going to sentence you to jail." Valladares then said that there is no evidence against him. The Castro minion then admitted: "It's true, we have no proof, or rather no concrete proof against you. But we do have the conviction that you are a potential enemy of the Revolution. For us that's enough."[76]

While addressing the U.N. General Assembly in December 1964, Guevara told his audience that execution in Cuba will continue as long as necessary. Obviously, as Fontova suggests, the necessity he had in mind was to eliminate those who stand in the way of the Stalinization of Cuba.

The Black Book of Communism, composed by French scholars and published by Harvard University Press, reports that by the early 1970s the Cuban firing-squad executions had reached fourteen thousand – which on a percentage basis would be the equivalent of over three million executions in the U.S. And yet, despite all the evidence provided by millions of Cubans whose families have direct experience of the most cruel and heartbreaking suffering imposed by the Castro regime, there is no shortage of propagandists for this regime in the West. So it is that the New Yorker writer Jon Lee Anderson in his 814-page biography of Che Guevara claims that "I have yet to find a single credible source pointing to a case where Che executed an innocent" (Exposing the Real Che Guevara, (2008, p. xxiii).

THE SCOOP THAT SAVED CASTRO

The *New York Times*' correspondent Herbert Matthews was the first of many American journalists to interview Fidel Castro in February 1957 while Castro was still hiding out in the Sierra Maestra mountains of Eastern Cuba. Soon a stream of journalists and other fellow travelers

---

[76] *AAH, 9.*

were following in his footsteps, so the revolution in Cuba under the elusive Castro became front page news in all the major American media outlets.

Jonathan Alter, writing in the *New York Times* nearly half a century later catches the momentous significance of the events reported by Matthews as follows: "The front-page scoop...was a sensation at the time and transformed Castro's image from a hotheaded Don Quixote into the youthful face of the future of Cuba."[77]

The New York Times of February 24, 1957 carried Matthews' first of three articles that contradicted the government announcement of Castro's death. "Cuban Rebel is Visited in Hideout: Castro is Still Alive and Still Fighting in Mountains," is how the Times announced one of its most famous breaking news stories. Indeed, it was the beginning of a movement that would establish a communist base and an extension of Soviet power a mere 90 miles from the U.S. coast.

Matthews was not shy in boasting about outsmarting Batista's army and meeting with Castro for a three-hour interview that became the substance of a series in praise of his host in the jungle hideout. Following are a few excerpts of Matthews' evaluation of Castro as published in the *New York Times* of February 1957.

> The personality of the man is overpowering. It was easy to see that his men adored him and also to see why he has caught the imagination of the youth of Cuba all over the island. Here was an educated, dedicated fanatic, a man of ideals, of courage and of remarkable qualities of leadership... He [Castro] has strong ideas of liberty, democracy, social justice, the need to rescue the constitution, to hold elections....

The program is vague and couched in generalities, but it amounts to a new deal for Cuba, radical, democratic and therefore anti-Communist.

---

[77] Matthews, *New York Times*, April 23, 2006.

Matthews quoted Castro: "You can be sure we hold no animosity towards the United States.... Above all we are fighting for a democratic Cuba and an end to dictatorship.".

Ever since Matthews landed the scoop of his life in 1957, he excelled in serving as the propagandist for the Castro dictatorship begun in earnest after Castro's triumphant entry into Havana. A slew of admirers of the Castro revolution, including such media celebrities as Barbara Walters, Andrea Mitchell and Diane Sawyer, began to trek to Cuba where they were always accompanied by guides trained in the art of deception.

The guides had an easy job, since most of the "political pilgrims" were motivated by anti-Americanism and left-wing ideology. They were not interested to follow up on stories about the horrors inflicted on those who refused to bow to the new tyrants.

The Castro worshippers came to see what their hosts wanted them to see, and they did nothing to help the many who, like Armando Valladares, were condemned to long prison sentences, torture and death. They turned a blind eye to the plight of untold Cubans who were worked to death or executed without any recourse to a fair trial. Guevara summed up how the naïve admirers of Castro played a major, if not the decisive, role in the "success" of the Castro revolution: "Foreign reporters – preferably American – were much more valuable to us than any military victory. Much more valuable than recruits for our guerrilla force were American media recruits to export our propaganda."

BARBARIANS AT WORK

It is hard to describe or read the horrendous suffering imposed on defenceless victims, but it is worth knowing, remembering, and honoring the names of brave men and women whose lives were turned into a nightmare or cut short by the new barbarians in Havana. Against All Hope contains the names, pictures and a brief note of forty-nine victims of the Castro regime. This is just a small percentage of the hundreds of thousands who suffered and perished. According to the Cuba Archive

Project, the Castro regime with firing squads, prison tortures, forced-labor camps and drownings at sea, has caused the deaths of an estimated 100,000 Cubans.

Castro's lackeys showed no respect for women prisoners. Their "crime" was that they were related to "enemies of the revolution." In the section, "Castro's Chambers for Women," Fontova writes that communist prison guards while transferring the women dragged them around like "dead animals." The prisoners were incapable of walking because of the constant beatings and being confined to cells littered with excrement and other body fluids. The cells were barely big enough to stand in and were entirely sealed except for tiny airholes. The women were confined underground in total darkness, like tombs, except that their occupants were still alive, if only by ultra-human perseverance.

Ana Lazaro Rodriguez recalled that one of her cellmates, "Chirri, was just a kid, barely 18. Tiny, blonde and beautiful, she should have been going to high school dances. Instead, because her father had been involved in a plot against Castro, she was squatting in a dark filthy cell...."

Rodriguez writes that some girls were even younger than 18, having been raised in a Havana Catholic orphanage. She and her cellmates could hear the shrieks of pain and horror of a 13-year-old girl coming from a nearby torture chamber. The women prisoners were pounding on things, nearly going mad with anguish, and screaming in protest.

Ana shouted at one of the guards, "She is a little girl. How can you let this happen?" The guard said nothing and walked away. Next they threw the girl in with "Sappho," a notorious lesbian with a multi-scarred face who was in jail for murder. Ana writes, "It was another half-hour before the little girl's screams finally ended."[78]

---

[78] Fontova, 209.

The priest, Javier Arzuaga, had the duty of comforting many of Che Guevara's murder victims and their families. During one of his rounds he was surprised to find a 16-year-old boy named Ariel Lima among the condemned "war criminals" who were slated to be executed by Guevara's firing squad. The boy was dazed and terrified. The priest attempted to plead the boy's case. Guevara snapped: "So what's the big deal? What's so special about the boy?" He dismissed the priest's pleading, but said that the Appeals Tribunal would reconsider, which it did, by confirming the death sentence to be administered that same night. As they left the hearing, Ariel's mother ran up to Guevara and threw herself on the ground begging him to save her son. "Woman," he sneered at her, pointing at the priest, "go see that guy... padre Javier Arzuaga is a master at consoling people." Then looking at the priest he said: "She's all yours, padre."

That night Ariel was still in a totally dazed condition as they tied him to the execution stake. Then came the order to fire. "And the volley shattered Ariel's quivering little body." Fontavo writes that Guevara was probably watching from his window, installed so that he could watch his "darling firing squads at work."

Part II: The Stubborn Truth of Islam

13 The Breeding Ground of Jihad

Allah is our objective. The Prophet is our leader. Qur'an is our law. Jihad is our way. Dying in the way of Allah is our hope (Muslim Brotherhood motto).

[T]he issue of terrorist financing in the United States is a fundamental example of the shared infrastructure levered by Hamas, Islamic Jihad and al Qaeda, all of which enjoy a significant degree of cooperation and coordination within our borders. The common link here is the extremist Muslim Brotherhood – all these organizations are descendants of the membership and ideology of the Muslim Brotherhood.[79]

One of the challenges facing all students of Islam is to sort out the many different shades of Islam that have emerged since its founding under the charismatic leadership of the Prophet Muhammad in the year 622 in Medina, in what is now Saudi Arabia.

That history includes rapid territorial expansion in the first one hundred years, severe internal conflicts, the formation of two major

---

[79] Richard A. Clarke, before the Senate Banking Committee, Oct. 22, 2003.

branches with numerous subdivisions, a series of setbacks, and decline in the past 400 years.

After World War II Islam experienced a revival of militancy as it attempted to face the overwhelming forces of modernity. This revival was powerfully aided by the demise of the Western colonial overlords and the simultaneous flow of hundreds of billions of dollars to the Islamic oil-producing countries. The renewed militancy is directed especially at the Western democracies, the U.S.A, (also known as the "Great Satan"), and the Jewish state established in 1948 (the "Little Satan").

The volume of literature produced by Muslim as well as non-Muslim authors, now expanded and speeded up via the Internet, is massive and wide-ranging. What adds to the challenge is that these sources represent a wide range of viewpoints, often diametrically opposed. What really complicates matters is that the language and concepts of Islam are very different from those steeped in the Western notion of freedom, truth, justice and logic.

There are compelling reasons why we should try very hard to understand that difference. This essay will attempt to do that by taking a careful look at one of the major organizations that has been spearheading militant, jihadist Islam: the Muslim Brotherhood.

This Brotherhood has gained a lot of experience in waging jihad during its 86 years of turbulent existence. It has also learned a lot of lessons in operating in the "shadow" of the openness and freedom within the Western democracies.

AN INCUBATOR OF JIHAD

In 1928, the Egyptian schoolteacher, Hassan al-Banna (1906-1949), founded the Muslim Brotherhood dedicated to the spread of Islamic orthodoxy. Al-Banna was an admirer of Adolf Hitler and had *Mein Kampf* translated and widely distributed in the Arabic world. One of his disciples, Haj Amin al Hussein, the mufti of Jerusalem, was also a Muslim Nazi who recruited Muslims for Hitler's armies and planned to build gas chambers in the Middle East. That plan came to nothing after the German army was defeated at El Alamein.

The Muslim Brotherhood began when six men paid al-Banna a surprise visit and demanded that he become their leader. This is part of the pledge they made, expressing a deeply held conviction that has marked the Brotherhood during its entire history:

We despise this life, which is one of dishonor and enslavement. Arabs and Muslims no longer have a place here in this country, nor do they enjoy any dignity. And they do nothing about their state of bondage as wage earners working for foreigners.

As for us, we have nothing to offer but our blood, which circulates in our veins with boiling rage. We have nothing but our souls, which sparkle with faith and dignity....

We do not know how to serve the fatherland, the faith and the Muslim Ummah. Thou hast the answer....

Thou shalt be responsible for us and our actions, responsible for an entire community of devoted [fighters] which takes an oath in front of Allah to live only according to religion and to die for him....[80]

What these men had in mind with their passionate statement of belief and commitment was to devote their lives to a cause that was bigger than themselves. They were dedicating themselves to stand against the laxness and defeatism among Muslim believers; and externally, against the colonial regimes, especially Britain and France. The Brotherhood's founding took place only four years after the abolition of the rule by Islamic clergy (caliphate) in Turkey under the leadership of Kemal Ataturk. (Osama bin Laden has described that event as a grievous insult that he listed as a motive for his declaration of war on the West.)

---

[80] Amir Taheri, *Holy Terror: Inside the World of Islamic Terrorism* (Chevy Chase, MD: Adler & Adler, 1987) 45.

Al-Banna lamented the end of the caliphate as a separation of "the state from religion in a country [Turkey] which was until recently the site of the Commander of the Faithful." He saw this as part of a "Western invasion, which was armed and equipped with all [the] destructive influences of money, wealth, prestige, ostentation, power, and means of Propaganda." He summarized the Brotherhood's worldwide ambition as follows:

> "...it is a duty incumbent on every Muslim to struggle towards the aim of making every people Muslim and the whole world Islamic, so that the banner of Islam can flutter over the earth and the call of the Muezzin can resound in all the corners of the world: God is greatest [Allahu akbar]!"[81]

Consequently, the Muslim Brotherhood set out to reverse the trend of secularization and made the spread of sharia law the purpose of its existence. At first Al-Banna chose the route of peaceful opposition by debate and persuasion. But after absorbing the teachings and examples of other Muslim leaders who preached a message of violence and murder, in 1938 he declared that Islamic rule in Egypt must be established "by force if necessary." He also began forming an "alternative administration" that would in time take over the government and wage war "against 'the heathen, the apostate, the deviant,' who would, when judged too dangerous, be put to death in the name of Allah."[82]

In the 1940s the Brotherhood began a campaign of terror and assassinations that became a model for Muslim organization in other countries. Many came from the surrounding countries to learn the deadly art of murder and mayhem. Mass arrests followed and Al-Banna was executed in January 1949, though his writings are still in circulation and continue to inspire those who long for the worldwide caliphate.

---

[81] Cited in Robert Spencer, *Onward Muslim Soldiers: How Jihad Still Threatens America and the West*, Washington DC: Regnery Publishing, 2003), 218.

[82] Taheri, 51.

The following decades saw more violence and death, which led to the Brotherhood's being banned in Egypt for a number of years, but its offspring is now active in many other countries as well.

Tariq Ramadan, grandson of Al-Banna, now living in the U.S., is one of the most effective defenders of the Brotherhood.[83]

THE FATHER OF MILITANT ISLAM

The second influential leader of the Brotherhood was Sayyid Qutb (1906-1966) who has been called "the father of modern [Islamic] fundamentalism." He studied in the U.S. from 1948 until 1950, where he acquired a strong aversion to what he perceived to be the moral degeneration of that country. After his return to Egypt, he joined the Muslim Brotherhood and he served in the Ministry of Education from which he was dismissed in 1952. (He is considered to be the main inspiration for the ideas of Osama bin Laden, who was a student of Sayyid's brother Muhammad Qutb, professor of Islamic studies.)

Although imprisoned from 1954-1964 and executed by the Egyptian government in 1966, he developed a huge following as a result of his involvement in the activities of the Muslim Brotherhood in opposition to the government in power. Even more important is the legacy of his voluminous writings. They include a 30-volume commentary on the Qur'an (In the Shade of the Qur'an – of which a 15-volume English translation is in progress) and his Signposts on the Way, also called Milestones. The latter is a passionate argument for the elimination of all man-made laws to be replaced by the worldwide rule of Islamic law.

In chapter 4 of Milestones, "Jihad: the Cause of God," Qutb describes the various stages of Islamic progress. He elaborates on the notion of freedom in the Qur'an as stipulated in Sura 2: 256: "There is no compulsion in religion." But in trying to balance the idea of freedom

---

[83]Cf., Caroline Fourest, *Brother Tariq: The Doublespeak of Tariq Ramadan* (New York: Encounter Books, 2007).

with the absolute claims of divine authority of the Qur'an, he seems to assume that if the followers of Allah provide the right environment of universal Islamic rule, everyone will voluntarily submit.

However, until such perfect conditions materialize, presumably by persuasion and discussion, the enemies of Islam must be dealt with. Qutb leaves no doubt about the approach to be used. After quoting Sura 2: 256, he writes that Jihad in Islam on the other hand,

tries to annihilate all those political and material powers which stand between people and Islam, which force one people to bow before another people and prevent them from accepting the sovereignty of God. These two principles [human freedom v. divine sovereignty] have no relation to one another nor is there room to mix them.... The Islamic Jihad has no relationship to modern warfare, either in its causes or in the way it is conducted. The causes of Islamic Jihad should be sought in the very nature of Islam and its role in the world, in its high principles, which have been given to it by God and for the implementation of which God appointed the Prophet – peace be on him – as Messenger and declared to be the last of all prophets and messengers.

Qutb continues in this vein, explaining that Islam amounts to a universal declaration of the freedom of all mankind (not just Arabs and Muslims) from servitude to other men and to his own desires. In contrast, any other system in which humans are seen as the final authorities deifies humans and thereby become usurpers of the authority of God.

He writes that because Islam teaches the freedom of man from all authority except that of God, it is faced in every period with obstacles and opposition of many kinds, it must first of all deal with the obstacles of political power. Thus, Islam strives from the beginning to abolish all those systems and governments based on man-made rules, which, according to Qutb, are by definition a form of slavery.

Qutb deals in detail with the different methods and timing of Jihad. He insists that in an "Islamic system there is room for all kinds of people to follow their own beliefs, while obeying the laws of the country which are themselves based on the Divine authority." You can be sure that the defenders of radical Islam will readily quote the first part of the last sentence, but the real meaning lies in the last part.

THE BIBLE VERSUS THE QUR'AN

Again and again, Qutb returns to his overarching concept of the absolute authority of God and how that is the source of human freedom. There is an odd surface similarity here with what the Bible teaches about this topic, but there is a world of difference between the two religions.

The Bible also teaches that God is the sovereign authority and sustainer of all that exists. Secondly, it teaches that true human freedom is found in surrendering our lives to His service. But the difference between the biblical and the Islamic understanding of freedom is like that between day and night, or light and darkness.

This is a topic that needs far more commentary, but let me give a brief summary of the difference between the teachings of the Qur'an and the Bible about the central issue of human freedom. The main difference lies in what the Qur'an and the Bible teach about divine love and compassion.

The love of God is revealed first of all in that Christ came to save the world and reconciled sinful human beings to a holy God, by giving his life as a ransom for our sins. Consequently, salvation and true human freedom is a gift of God's grace, which is open to all people. Now we are called to love God above all and our neighbour as ourselves. Jesus teaches that we are even to love our enemies and to pray for them.

In the Qur'an, as interpreted by Qutb and like-minded teachers, God is depicted as a hard, unpredictable taskmaster, who can only be pacified by having our good deeds outnumber our bad ones. Qutb explains that the main struggle in life is to establish Islamic rule worldwide. Those who refuse are considered unworthy, unclean, infidels, destined for hell. Depending on circumstances, they are declared to be second-class citizens (dhimmis), to be persecuted, or killed in the name of Allah.

There is also a fundamental difference between the Islamic and the Christian notion of a just and free society. The Bible teaches principles and guidelines for all human relations and social structures, summarized in the call to love God and our neighbors. There have evolved within Christianity over the centuries certain insights with respect to the different roles and authorities of the various social structures. This has led to the recognition that the boundary between the public and private spheres must be respected. "Give to Caesar what is Caesar's and to God what is God's." Behind this recognition lies the fundamental freedom of conscience and belief.

The contrast with Islam could not be more acute. It teaches that sharia (Islamic law), based on the Qur'an and the Hadith, contains all of the instructions for the proper conduct of politics and all others areas of life. There is no separation between the mosque and the state, but the supreme authority for every aspect of life belongs to experts in Islamic law. This is the establishment of a theocracy in which there is no freedom of religion – and therefore no freedom at all. In fact, where sharia law dominates there is a death penalty on renouncing the Islamic faith.

THE TWO FACES OF JIHAD

There is more than one way to impose sharia law on a nation. One is well known because it is violent and often spectacular, such as the hijacking of planes and the destruction of 9/11, as well as the daily violent attacks by jihadists in the Middle East, Africa and Asia. The other way to spread Islam is quite different because it hides its goal by stealth and subterfuge. It comes with a smiley face and preaches peace and goodwill. The Muslim Brotherhood is a major player in this process. This is an excerpt of a 2004 Dutch Secret Service report about the Muslim Brotherhood's tactics in the Netherlands:

Radical branches of the Muslim Brotherhood employ covert Dawa [proselytizing] strategies. Rather than confronting the state power with direct violence, this strategy seeks to gradually undermine it by infiltrating and eventually taking over the civil service, the judicature, schools, local administrations, et cetera. Apart from clandestine infiltration, covert Dawa may also be aimed at inciting Muslim minorities to civil disobedience, promoting parallel power structures or even inciting Muslim masses to a revolt."[84]

Nonie Darwish, courageous defender of Christianity and the free West, has summarized this two-fold, confusing characteristic of Islam as follows:

The lesson America needs to learn and get united under is that we, the West, right now are under assault by the good old Islamic doctrine of Terror and Lure; two sides of the polar opposite and deceptive face of Islam. If the West continues to believe that Islam is a religion of peace, then unfortunately for the West they will suffer irrevocable consequences.[85]

We do well to listen to her advice, especially now that we have abundant resources available to help us in our efforts to separate truth from the Lie.

---

[84] Cited in Erick Stakelbeck, *The Brotherhood: America's Next Great Enemy* (Washington DC: Regnery Publishing, 2013), 43.

[85] "The Islamic Tactic of Terror and Lure, FPM, June 30, 2014.

14 In the Shadow of the Qur'an

In an open and free society, those who underestimate the evil of such men [as Khalid Sheik Mohammed, al Qaeda chief] become unwitting partners in crimes imagined and then perpetrated against the unwary and innocent citizens of that society.[86]

J ihadists who preach and practice violence in the cause of Islam, have perfected the art of playing the bad cop/good cop routine. And they are mightily assisted by the naiveté and division within the West, including the U.S., which finds itself on the frontlines of the Western defenses.

The confusion about the true nature of militant Islam was amply demonstrated in a story reported in a *Washington Post* (Sept. 11, 2004) article by John Mintz and Douglas Farah, "In Search of Friends Among the Foes." In May 2000 when Ishaq Farhan, a Jordanian leading opposition politician affiliated with the Muslim Brotherhood,

---

[86] Salim Mansur, *Western Standard*, April 23, 2007.

disembarked in New York, he was extensively interrogated by federal agents, refused entry to the U.S. and ordered to return to Jordan.

But then U.S. Embassy officials in Jordan swung into action and effectively undid the security officials' work. A State Department representative personally delivered an immediate visa to Farhan as well as the United States' "deep regret for the difficulties Dr. Farhan experienced."

CONFLICTING SIGNALS

Sending conflicting signals by two different agencies of the same American administration is emblematic of a similar kind of confusion in the media about the nature of the enemy that has declared war on the free West. On the one side of this controversy are those who take seriously the threats against the free West by the Muslim Brotherhood and a slew of like-minded terrorist organizations.

On the other side are those who look for the "root cause" of the Muslim hatred toward us within the West itself. Furthermore, they believe that the Muslim Brotherhood has broken with its violent past and is now prepared to embrace democracy and pluralism. The authors of *"In Search of Friends Among the Foes"* summarize this dilemma well:

FBI agents and financial investigators probe the group for terrorist ties and legal violations, while diplomats simultaneously discuss strategies for co-opting at least its moderate wings. In both sectors of the U.S. government, the Brotherhood often remains a mystery.

How do we separate the moderates from the terrorists? This debate of late has come to focus on the Muslim Brotherhood, described by Mintz and Farah as,

a sprawling and secretive society with followers in more than 70 countries. It is dedicated to creating an Islamic civilization that harks back to the caliphates of the 7th and 8th centuries, one that would segregate women from public life and scorn nonbelievers.

However, the Brotherhood (Ikhwan in Arabic) has also claimed that it has renounced violence in favor of democratic politics and pluralism. (You can find those claims on its website: www.ikhwanweb.info.) Should we believe them? Let's first consider a very informative *Washington Post* article by Mintz and Farah.

They write that the Brotherhood has instigated Islamic revolution in Egypt, Algeria, Syria and Sudan. In the Palestinian territories it has given birth to Hamas, which has sent suicide bombers into Israel and is committed to the destruction of the Jewish state. The Brotherhood has not renounced that position toward Israel. (In fact, the Brotherhood's Supreme General Muhammad Mahdi Akef called for attacks in Palestine, Iraq, and Afghanistan in his weekly sermon.)

The authors show that the Brotherhood has ties to many Islamist extremists worldwide, involving training, financing and indoctrination through an extensive network of Islamist organizations. In the 1950s, the Brotherhood found refuge in Saudi Arabia, and there founded the largest Saudi charities, such as the Muslim World League in 1963 and the World Assembly of Muslim Youth in 1973.

GLOBAL MISSIONARIES

Mintz and Farah explain:

Funded by petro dollars, they became global missionaries spreading the Saudis' austere and rigid Wahhabi school of Islam, whose adherents at times describe all non-Wahhabis as infidels." In 1990 the Brotherhood fell out of favor and was denounced by Saudi prince Nayef as "the source of all problems in the Islamic world.

The authors name names and provide an overview of the multi-faceted activities of the Muslim Brotherhood worldwide and also in the U.S. Ali Ahmed, Washington-based activist closely associated with the Brotherhood, is quoted as saying that among their main goals were "carving out havens for Muslims, propagating Islam in America and backing Israel's destruction."

A U.S. official familiar with the federal investigation of former Brotherhood members stated that they had developed "a disciplined strategy, specific goals to act on their plan to convert Americans, starting with U.S. military personnel, prison inmates and black people." The emphasis here is on patience in pursuing their goals.

In a 1995 speech to an Islamic conference in Ohio, Youssef Qaradawi, a top Brotherhood official and Qatari imam, predicted that victory will come through dawah – Islamic renewal and outreach. He assured his audience: "Conquest through dawah that is what we hope for.... We will conquer Europe, we will conquer America, not through the sword, but through dawah." (In his television program on Al-Jazeera in June 2004, Qaradawi said: "The democracy I call for is the democracy of Muslim society. It has fixed principles it does not violate, and red lines it cannot violate, and some principles that are not up for discussion.")

Mintz and Farah provide the sort of information that would make many of us conclude that the Muslim Brotherhood is a two-faced jihadist organization that in no way can be considered a possible ally in our struggle against radical Islam.

MODERATES OR OPPORTUNISTS?

The impression given by Robert Leiken and Steve Brooke writing in *Foreign Affairs* magazine is quite different.[87] The tenor of their article is to discredit the critics of the Brotherhood and to assure us that the U.S. is making a serious mistake in not regarding this organization as an ally.

They write that the Brotherhood won the battle with its jihadist members and now is completely committed to "the path of toleration" and has found "democracy compatible with its notion of slow Islamization." Leiken and Brooke allow for the possibility that the Brotherhood's commitment to democracy is no more than a tactical and transitory step – an opportunistic move to what Bernard Lewis has

---

[87] *Foreign Affairs*, "The Moderate Muslim Brotherhood," March-April 2007.

described as "one man, one vote, one time." But they hasten to assure us that the Brotherhood is not like that.

They tell us that on the basis of their extensive discussions during the past year with dozens of Brotherhood leaders and activists from Egypt, France, Jordan, Spain, Syria, Tunisia, and the United Kingdom they have concluded that the Brotherhood has rejected "global jihad while embracing elections and other features of democracy." But the evidence they produce is mostly anecdotal and often based on the views of unnamed representatives and allies of the Brotherhood.

They write that the Brotherhood's anticipated way to power is not revolutionary but based on the strategy of "winning hearts through gradual and peaceful Islamization." They believe a "senior member" who assured them that it would be unjust for the Brotherhood to come to power without majority support.

Another spokesman told them that if the Brotherhood would obtain political power and then "should rule unwisely," it would deserve to be defeated. Mintz and Farah conclude this paragraph by saying that in their many conversations with the Brotherhood allies in the Middle East – no specific countries or names mentioned – they "heard many expressions of confidence that it would honour democratic processes."

The article wanders through the Brotherhood's various alleged mutations from jihadist to a trustworthy member of the respectable and peace-loving democratic family. They work hard at putting the best possible face on the Brotherhood policies, though it has never wavered from its position that Israel is illegitimate and the major stumbling block to peace in the Middle East.

Leiken and Brooke report that the Brotherhood is willing to recognize Israel's right to exist but only on the condition that Hamas must first agree to such recognition. The problem is that Hamas has steadfastly stuck to its determination to destroy Israel. In other words, the Brotherhood agrees with those who want to eliminate Israel, while hiding behind the skirts of Hamas, one of its own offspring and a fanatic terrorist organization that is a prime instigator of violence, murder and chaos in the Middle East.

The authors' declaration that the Brotherhood has renounced terrorism is accompanied by a caveat that in fact nullifies that declaration. They admit that it authorizes jihad in countries and territories "occupied" by a foreign power. Consequently, the Brotherhood considers the struggles in Iraq (read the murder of coalition forces and thousands of Iraqis) and against Israel as "defensive jihad" against invaders, a concept Leiken and Brooke describe as "the Muslim functional equivalent to the Christian doctrine of 'just war.'"

This is a short sampling of the arguments with which these authors seek to inform the public about the Brotherhood's internal politics and their policies in a number of host countries. The upshot of their advice to U.S. policy makers is that it makes strong strategic sense, on a case-by-case approach, to begin a conversation with the Muslim Brotherhood.

GLOSSING OVER INCONVENIENT FACTS

The main problem with their advice is that they gloss over many clear indications that the Brotherhood's statements of their commitment to democracy and tolerance is no more than a tactical move to persuade a poorly informed public. In any case, it is clear that those who clamor for the Islamization of a society, which means the application of sharia law, are really calling for the one-party-state, in this case the one-religion state. Such a state is fundamentally opposed to a free and open society. The late Brotherhood's Supreme Guide Mustafa Mashour put that in blunt language: "Democracy contradicts and wages war on Islam. Whoever calls for democracy means they are raising banners contradicting God's plan and fighting Islam."

Leiken and Brooke do not bother to explain the meaning of Al-R "red lines it cannot violate." Instead, their article creates confusion about the difference between fake moderate and real moderate Muslims.

That confusion has the result that real moderate Muslims are intimidated and ignored, and we are deprived of their much-needed expertise and support. Let me conclude by giving voice to one of such Muslims who refuses to be intimidated, Zuhdi Jasser, a former U.S. Navy Lieutenant Commander, a physician, and founder of the American Islamic Forum for Democracy:

> As a devout anti-Islamist American Muslim, I have been struggling to explain to all those who will listen the central incompatibility of the Islamist doctrine with America's pluralist ideology. The literal Islamization of society, consciousness, and government, as advocated by the Muslim Brotherhood is an anathema to America as it is to a pluralistic and liberated Islam. Leiken and Brooke, in effect, whitewash an international organization whose mission is at odds with our own Constitutional system of governance.

15 Islamization of America by Stealth Jihad

The Ikhwan [Muslim Brotherhood] must understand that all their work in America is a kind of grand Jihad in eliminating and destroying the Western civilization from within and 'sabotaging' its miserable house by their hands and the hands of the believers so that it is eliminated and God's religion is made victorious over all religions. Without this level of understanding, we are not up to this challenge and have not prepared ourselves for jihad yet.[88]

What remains, then, is to conquer Rome. This means Islam will come back to Europe for a third time, after it was expelled from it twice. We will conquer Europe. We will conquer America. Not through the sword but through our Dawa [proselytizing].[89]

---

[88] Mohammad Akram Adlouni, "An Explanatory Memorandum on the General Strategic Goal for the Group in North America" (1991). Cited in Erick Stakelbeck, *The Brotherhood*, 46.

[89] Yusuf al-Qaradawi, "Muslim Brotherhood's Spiritual Guide."

The immigration of millions of Muslims into the West is in the process of fundamentally changing the recipient countries. Why is that so different from previous immigration flows, and why is it that political correctness makes it very risky to start a public discussion about this topic?

Muslim immigrants to the West are from a very different background and culture than that of their host countries. Whereas most previous immigrants want to assimilate into their newly adopted home country, many Muslims, though not all, refuse to do so. Instead, they want to remain aloof and to replicate the traditional living arrangements of their home countries. It is not uncommon for them to settle in a section of major Western cities where they form their own enclaves under the rule of Islamic law (sharia). In some instances, they declare their territory to be "no-go zones," that is, non-Muslims are not welcome. Ditto for the police and other local authorities. Why would they do that?

A KIND OF GRAND JIHAD

The answer lies in their Islamic faith. The Qur'an and the Hadith teach that a faithful Muslim is called to help spread the rule of Allah over the entire world, as spelled out in the opening paragraph taken from an important Muslim Brotherhood document. Muslims also are taught that the world is divided into two parts, a world at peace that is ruled by Islamic law (dar-al-lslam), and the rest of the world that is at war (dar-al-Harb).

This is why the influx of Muslim immigrants to the West is seen by the Muslim leadership as a golden opportunity to expand the influence of Islam by infiltrating the major Western institutions, notably the schools, universities, the media, and politics.

One reason that the Muslim faith is a puzzle to most Westerners is that their religion is not distinguished from any other sector or institution of society. In other words, the mosque and state are conflated. It means that Islamic law (sharia) is the final authority in every detail of life including politics. This is why the Muslim

Brotherhood's flag includes two crossed swords, and why the leadership of radical Islam takes seriously this command of Muhammad: "I have been sent with a sword in my hand to command people to worship Allah and associate no partners with him. I command you to belittle and subjugate those who disobey me, for whoever imitates a people is one of them."[90]

Mohammad assumed the dual role of warlord and religious leader. Combining political/military power and religious authority makes for a system that is all powerful. This is what makes Islam different from all other religions; it functions more like a political ideology. This merging of mosque and state inevitably results in a totalitarian dictatorship which leaves no space for any freedom.

The Islamic immigration into the West comes at a time when the West is spiritually and morally in severe decline, so that it does not have the conviction and confidence to counteract a fanatical, supremacist religion such as Islam. In fact, the Western leadership does not understand and therefore is feeble in its reaction to Islam. Regrettably, the West has adopted an attitude of craven inferiority in its dealings with Islam.

The combination of inner defeatism in the West (Mark Steyn called it "civilizational exhaustion") and its failure to grasp the imperialistic intentions of Islam is a ready-made soil for the Muslim Brotherhood to pursue its goal of establishing the worldwide caliphate. Al-Qaradawi and a host of like-minded Islamic leaders know that to succeed they must destroy America as a powerful presence on the world stage. They mean what they say in the 1991 document, namely, that all their work in America is a grand jihad of destruction by boring from within and thus making Islam "victorious over all religions."

---

[90] Cited in mark-durie.com blog, August 12, 2014.

The Muslim leadership in Europe and North America has been amazingly successful in using the freedom and openness of its host countries to freely practice their religion. But their most effective means of outreach and spreading the faith is by means of numerous specialized organizations dealing with all the major issues of a modern society. The Explanatory Memorandum referred to above lists 29 Islamic organizations busy with furthering the spread of Islam in all the vital American institutions and organizations by stealth and obfuscation. Subsequently, a number of other organizations were added, including the Muslim Public Affairs Council and the ubiquitous Council on American-Islamic Relations (CAIR). Erick Stakelbeck summarizes:

> The Brothers' stealth strategy includes gaining and exercising influence in the media, government and educational circles; building mosques across a wide geographical area and establishing self-segregating Islamic enclaves; forging alliances with the political Left; and engaging in mass media blitz to reshape the national conversation (and public policy) when it comes to Islam, Israel, and the broader Middle East. This methodical strategy of infiltration, co-optation, and deception had already been articulated in The Project [the Exploratory Memorandum] and adopted by the international Muslim Brotherhood leadership in the early 1980s.[91]

OBAMA: FUNDAMENTALLY TRANSFORMING AMERICA

Since America is still the most powerful nation in the world, it is a prime target for the Muslim Brotherhood's strategic goal to destroy the Western civilization from within. That's the very reason America is called the "Great Satan."

The Brotherhood has a number of things in its favor, in addition to the flow of Muslim immigration into America where they are free to practice their religion, build their mosques and organize a large array

---

[91] Stakelbeck, 46.

of organizations to infiltrate the major institutions of influence, especially the media, the academy, and the agencies of government.

The most successful campaign to portray Islam as a positive and much misunderstood religion is occurring in the lecture halls of all of the major American (and other Western) universities. Many millions of dollars have flowed from Saudi Arabia's wealthy donors to finance Islamic studies departments at American universities. Here as elsewhere, he who pays the piper calls the tune. This is how the universities have become the preeminent champions of an Islam-friendly worldview. There are many professors who are eager to assist in this process. As well, the Muslim Students Association, founded in 1963, is a major voice at the universities in the promotion of Islamic supremacy and the destruction of the state of Israel.

Typical is John Esposito, who is considered America's foremost authority on Islam; he is the author of more than 20 books on Islam's concept of politics and human rights. He served as the president of the Middle East Studies Association and now teaches at Georgetown University where he serves as professor of religion and international affairs, and professor of Islamic Studies. He also heads the Prince Alaweed Bin Talal Center for Muslim-Christian Understanding.

In addition, Esposito is a Muslim affairs consultant to the Department of State, as well as to corporations and universities worldwide. He believes that the Muslim world is advancing toward an "Islamic democracy that might create an effective system of popular participation" and that the U.S., should not "in principle object to implementation of Islamic law or involvement of Islamic activists in government."[92]

The upshot of these developments in the universities has led to what in the words of historian Bernard Lewis amounts to an

---

[92] Horowitz, *The Professors*, 148-151. Cf. also Stephen Schwartz, "John L. Esposito: Apologist for Wahhabi Islam," *American Thinker*, September 18, 2011.

"ideological strait-jacket" that has locked the Middle East Studies departments in universities all over the country into

> a degree of thought control and limitations of freedom of expression without parallel in the Western world since the 18th century... [which] makes any kind of scholarly discussion of Islam, to say the least, dangerous. Islam and Islamic values now have a level of immunity from comment and criticism in the Western world that Christianity has lost and Judaism has never had.[93]

THE WHITE HOUSE AIDS THE ENEMY

The second reason why the influence of Islam in America is growing is that it meshes very well with President Barack Obama's notion of fundamentally transforming America. Without doubt, the most surprising, indeed shocking reality is that the spread of militant Islam in the U.S. was aided and abetted by none other than President Obama. No one could have foreseen such an outcome, because it makes no sense and can only be attributed to the truly chaotic state of American politics. The reasons for this disconcerting state of affairs are complex and confusing, but it can be understood by those who take the trouble to do some investigating.

A good place to start is the June 4, 2009 speech of President Obama at Islam's oldest and most revered Al-Azhar University in Cairo where he distanced himself from President Bush's policies. In fact, the speech became an apology for America's role in the world while crediting Islam with carrying the "light of learning through so many centuries, paving the way for Europe's Renaissance and Enlightenment." Obama claimed that with him a new day had arrived in America's relations with the Muslim world. Here is a key excerpt from that speech:

> I've come here in Cairo to seek a new beginning between the United States and Muslims around the world, one based on mutual interest and mutual respect, and one based upon the truth that America and

---

[93] Robert Spencer, *Stealth Jihad: How Radical Islam is Subverting America without Guns or Bombs* (Washington DC: Regnery Publishing, 2008), 237.

Islam are not exclusive and need not be in competition. Instead, they overlap and show common principles – principles of justice and progress; toleration and the dignity of all human beings.... And I consider it part of my responsibility as President of the United States to fight against negative stereotypes of Islam wherever they appear.

The mind boggles in trying to grasp the meaning of these words. This must certainly be one the oddest speeches ever given by a president of the United States. The marvel is that it evoked little reaction in the mainstream press, despite the fact that it provides the key to Obama's understanding of one of the most serious threats to America and the entire Western world. Let me try to summarize what I think is the meaning of this historic speech to the Muslim world. Here are five considerations that deserve our attention:

ONE. Note that his comments are nothing short of grandiose in temper and scale. Obama announced that he proposes to tackle the world-impacting challenge of the relationship between Western civilization and Islam, something that after 1400 years has not been accomplished.

TWO. Obama's "new beginning" is a way to ignore and downgrade all previous attempts to deal with the American-Islam relationship. (Remember that Obama was against America's military action in Afghanistan and Iraq.) He signals that he will be the anti-Bush in his dealings with the Muslim world.

THREE. Obama's language is inclusive and pretentious. He refers to the U.S.'s dealing with the "Muslims around the world," and fighting against "negative stereotypes of Islam wherever they appear." For one thing, there is no way he can do so; for another, it is not his duty as president of the U.S. to fight against negative stereotyping of Islam. In fact, it is his duty to fight against the widely believed and assiduously propagated stereotype in the Muslim world, namely, that America is a dictatorial empire that deserves to be called "the Great

Satan." Instead of using this opportunity to defend America against such a vicious falsehood, Obama appointed himself as the defender of the enemies of his own country.

FOUR. In elaborating on his notion of seeking a new beginning of American-Muslim relations, Obama said that mutual interest and respect are needed as well as the recognition that America and Islam are not exclusive and need not be in competition. Then he stated that the two "overlap and show common principles – principles of justice and progress, toleration and the dignity of all human beings."

On this score, Obama ignores the bitter reality that exclusion, hatred, injustice, and violence is built into the teachings of the Qur'an and the other sacred writings of Islam. This is the reason that radical Muslims are butchering the "wrong kind" of Muslims, that Christians and Jews are called infidels who are destined for hell, that right now the Middle East and Africa is in great turmoil, that thousands are killed and millions are threatened, that many of them are forced to flee for their lives, that Israel is again threatened with extinction, and that Christianity is being driven out of the Middle East and some African countries. The terrorists who killed nearly 3000 people on 9/11 were motivated by the hatred that their imams had taught them from their scriptures. So was the Fort Hood killer of his fellow soldiers, and the Boston bombers who ended what was a pleasant social event in bloodshed and shrieks of anguish and pain. And so were the other thousands of suicide bombers who have killed and maimed their victims – all of this in the name of Allah.

Does Obama not bother to read the Qur'an and the other Islamic scriptures? Does he not know that every Friday in thousands of mosques in the Islamic world and in some Western countries as well, the faithful are confirmed in their hatred toward the West? Has he never heard those hysterical crowds in Iran and other Muslim countries screaming, "Death to America!" "Death to Israel!"?

Obama must have known these irrefutable facts. They are there for all to see, unless one does not want to see them. This is called being in denial, which is a very serious malady for a leader of the once great America.

FIVE. There is one more of Obama's polices that deserves our attention since it directly affects the threat of radical Islam against America and the entire Western world. In response to complaints by Muslim spokes-people, Obama ordered a review of all training manuals for law enforcement and national security agencies with a view to purge all references that are offensive to Muslims.

Dwight C. Holton, speaking for Attorney General Eric Holder had this to say:

> I want to be perfectly clear about this: training materials that portray Islam as a religion of violence or with a tendency towards violence are wrong, they are offensive, and they are contrary to everything that this president, this attorney general and Department of Justice stands for. They will not be tolerated.

And thus it was decreed that all efforts to keep the country safe from future attacks by the jihadists must not assume that there is any connection between Islam and terror. In other words, counter terrorism agents are ordered to turn a blind eye to what drives a person to become a terrorist. One would think that such information would be a key factor in the investigation and the prevention of terrorist attacks, but not in Obama's Wonderland.

CONCLUSION

The result: the Justice Department canceled the scheduled training sessions at national security agencies by scholars who are critical of Islam teachings, such as Robert Spencer and Steven Emerson. U.S. Army Reserve Major Stephen Coughlin, an expert on Islamic law at the Pentagon, was fired because he told the truth about Islam-inspired hatred and violence. The murder of 13 military persons by the fanatic Muslim Nidal Hasan at Fort Hood was renamed as a case of "work place violence." What is perhaps most incredulous is that the new anti-terrorist (or workplace violence) training manuals were written with the advice (and consent?) of Muslims.

If Obama would have been true to his oath of office, he could have used this speech to tell the truth about America and its role as a defender of Western civilization. He could have spoken up for the persecuted Christians and Jews and the other non-Muslims in Islam-ruled countries. He could also have defended his own country against the lies that now poison the relationship between it and the Muslim world. That would have been a difficult task, and might not have been accepted very well. But it would have been well worth the effort.

As it was, Obama told his audience what they wanted to hear, and in doing so, as David Warren writes, this speech did "not merely miss an opportunity to speak the truth plainly. It sabotaged every effort to speak the truth plainly, to the darkest tyrannical forces in the Islamic world. It sold out America, it sold out the West, and it sold out the Muslims.

16 Persecution Today:

Why This Story Must be Told

Remember those in prison as if you were their fellow prisoners, and those who are mistreated as if you yourselves were suffering (Hebrews 13: 3).

We are witnesses to murder, and our governments are accomplices. The relentless destruction of the last remnants of the Middle East's Judeo-Christian civilization is well under way. And we are silent. [94]

Many living in the free West take for granted their precious freedoms, such as freedom of speech, belief, association, and movement. But if we begin to reflect on this topic, we soon realize how privileged we are. Just looking back to the last century when millions suffered and died in two world wars should cause us to pause and reflect with gratitude on living in a civilized and free society.

---

[94] Ralph Peters, "Middle East Genocide," *New York Post*, June 1, 2013.

Especially Christians should spare a thought and prayer for the millions of fellow Christians who are – again – suffering severe persecution simply because they are Christians. They are not the only ones suffering hardship and oppression. But this essay will concentrate on the suffering of Christians living in sharia/Islamic-ruled countries.

The Arab Spring, which many hoped would usher in a new phase of openness and freedom in the Arab/Muslim world, did no such thing. Instead, it has enabled a hardline branch of Islam, the Muslim Brotherhood and its offspring, to gain power in Egypt, the most, at least potentially, influential country in that part of the world. Surrounding countries with a majority Muslim population are also experiencing a move toward strict sharia governance.

Turkey is now headed by a government that is determined to change from a secular to an Islamic country. Both Egypt and Turkey are facing strong opposition from its citizens who are rioting in the streets of the main cities. The outcome of these struggles is hard to predict, but so far it appears that the hard liners have the upper hand. The plight of Christians caught in the crossfire in Syria, where a reported 93,000 people have died, is extremely precarious.

THE NEW EXODUS

In the midst of all these upheavals, there is one consistent trend: an increase in the persecution of Christians. The radicalization and upheavals in many sharia-ruled countries is forcing Christians to flee. Where can they go? Many have ended up in refugee camps in Jordan, Turkey, and in Syria prior to the outbreak of civil war. Some have been able to emigrate to the West, but many do not have the means or opportunity to make the journey.

A 2010 report of the Vatican synod on the Middle East exodus stated that Christians numbered about 20% of the population a century ago, but that has now dropped to five percent. Ironically, the Christians in Iraq, the country liberated from the despotic rule of Saddam Hussein in 2003, has seen a large outflow of Christians, particularly after the massacre at Our Lady of Deliverance Church in Baghdad on October

31, 2010, that killed 58 church members, including two priests, and severely wounded many more.

Raymond Ibrahim, author of *Crucified Again*,[95] writes: "Today, Christians are all-but-extinct species in Iraq – more than half have fled – and what few churches remain are still under attack."

Michael Terheyden writes that after the attack in October 2010, terrorists' groups have attacked Christians in their homes. Church leaders were reluctant to hold Christmas services, and about 80% of Christians were afraid to attend church. About ten churches were closed and Sunday school was canceled.[96]

The same story applies to the Christians in Egypt, who have fled in unprecedented numbers. The Egyptian Union of Human Rights Organizations states that 100,000 Christians have emigrated since March 2011. "The Coptic Christians are one of the earliest Christian communities in the world, and they are the largest minority in the Middle East today" (about 10% out of a population of 80 million).

Terheyden reports that Islamist groups have stepped up their campaign of threatening, beating and murdering Christians in Egypt:

Their churches, businesses and homes have been ransacked and burned to the ground. As it turns out, the so-called Arab Spring has allowed Islamist groups like the Muslim Brotherhood and the Salafis to grab power. Some Copts fear this is an ominous turn of events. They worry that life in Egypt will grow much worse in the next few years.

---

[95] Raymond Ibrahim, *Crucified Again: Exposing Islam's New War on Christians* (Washington DC: Regnery Publishing, 2013).

[96] *Catholic Online*, July 30, 2012.

WHY DO THEY HATE?

Attacks on Christians and their churches and homes are happening all over the Muslim world. The perpetrators were encouraged in their violence by the grand mufti of Saudi Arabia, Sheik Abdul Aziz bin Abdullah, who declared on March 12, 2012 that it is "necessary to destroy all the churches of the region."

Thanks to the Internet and to a number of valiant authors, including Raymond Ibrahim, whose new book *Crucified Again*, and his regular monthly reports on the Muslim persecution of Christians, are goldmines of information and insight. In his book he traces the source of Muslim hatred of Christians to the Qur'an and the Hadith (words and deeds attributed to Muhammad). Following is a condensed summary of the information:

The Qur'an contains a number of anti-Christian verses, including Qur'an 5:73, 'Infidels are they who say Allah is one of three,' a reference to the Christian Trinity; and Qur'an 5:17, 'Infidels are they who say Allah is the Christ, [Jesus] son of Mary' (see also Qur'an 4: 171). To be referred to as an infidel (that is, a 'kafir') is to be categorized as an enemy of Islam, who must be either eliminated or subjugated.[97]

Some Koranic verses speak well of Christians but there are many more that condemn Christians. That contradiction is resolved by the doctrine of "abrogation," that is, the later (hostile) verses cancel out the earlier (tolerant) ones, which date back to the time Muhammad but had no political power. The Qur'an's final word on the fate of Christians and Jews is found in Qur'an 9:29:

Fight those among the People of the Book who do not believe in Allah nor the Last Day, nor forbid what Allah and His Messenger have forbidden, nor embrace the religion of truth, until they pay the yizya with willing submission and feel themselves subdued.

The idea of fighting non-Muslims until they pay tribute is embedded in Islam. Muhammad made this claim about himself:

---

[97] Cf., *Qur'an* 9:5 and 9:29. Ibrahim, 18-30.

I have been commanded to wage war against mankind until they testify that there is no God but Allah and that Muhammad is the Messenger of Allah; and that they establish prostration-prayer, and pay the alms-tax [that is, until they become Muslims]. If they do so, their blood and property are protected.[98]

There are hundreds of similar Islamic texts enjoining Muslims to fight non-Muslims until the latter either convert or pay tribute and live in submission.

It is on the basis of such exhortations that Islamic scholars hold that their religion is destined to wage a continuous war against the non-Muslim world. This is how the Muslim scholar Ibn Khaldun explained this feature of Islam, as quoted by Raymond Ibrahim: "In the Muslim community, the holy war [jihad] is a religious duty, because of the universalism of the Muslim mission and the obligation to convert everybody to Islam either by persuasion or by force." Other religions do not have such universalistic duty. "But Islam is under obligation to gain power over other nations." No one can be excused for not knowing that this branch of Islam means what it says about its goal of world domination.

THE CONDITIONS OF OMAR

This historic document also called the Pact of Omar dates back to the reign of the second caliph Omar bin al-Khattab (634-644). It had its origin in an "agreement" between the caliph and the conquered Christians. Muslim scholars disagree about the exact dating and subsequent redaction, but they agree that it is authentic and relevant for today.

The eighth-century Muslim jurist Abu Yusuf declared that the Conditions must "'stand till the day of resurrection' because they are in agreement with the Qur'an and the Hadith literature."

---

[98] Ibn al-Hajjaj Muslim, Sabib Muslim, C9BIN31.

In the 14th century Ibn Qayyim wrote what became accepted as the authoritative document, Rulings Concerning Dhimmis. (Dhimmis are defeated and subjugated non-Muslims.) He praised the conditions for their faithfulness to the essence of Islamic teachings. Here follows a small selection of the Conditions as reproduced in the Ibn Qayyim version, quoted in Crucified Again. The conquered Christians appear to be speaking:

When you came to our countries, we asked you for safety for ourselves and the people of our community, upon which we imposed the following conditions on ourselves for you:

Not to build a church in our city – nor a monastery, convent, or monk's cell in the surrounding areas – and not to repair those that fall in ruins or are in Muslim quarters;

Not to prevent Muslims from lodging in our churches, by day or night, and to keep their doors wide open for [Muslim] passersby and travelers;

Not to harbor in them [churches, monasteries] or our homes a spy, nor conceal any deceits from Muslims;

Not to clang our cymbals except lightly and from the innermost recesses of our churches;

Not to display a cross on them [churches], nor raise our voices during prayer or readings in our churches anywhere near Muslims;

Not to produce a cross or [Christian] book in the markets of Muslims;

Not to congregate in the open for Easter and Palm Sunday, nor lift our voices [in lamentation] for our dead nor show our firelights with them near the market places of the Muslims;

Not to display any signs of polytheism, nor make our religion appealing, nor call or proselytize anyone to it;

To honor the Muslims, show them the way, and rise up from our seats if they wish to sit down;

To host every traveling Muslim for three days and feed him adequately; We guarantee this to you upon ourselves, our descendants, our spouses, and our neighbors, and if we change or contradict these conditions imposed upon ourselves in order to receive safety, we forfeit our dhimma [covenant], and we become liable to the same treatment you inflict upon the people who resist and cause sedition.

Ibrahim points out that these abject humiliations imposed on Christians in the past, are now again inflicted on the Christians in the Muslim world. He quotes part of a recent Friday mosque sermon by the Saudi Sheikh Marzouk Salem al-Ghamdi as follows:

If the infidels live among the Muslims, in accordance with the conditions set out by the Prophet – there is nothing wrong with it provided they pay Jizya to the Islamic treasury. Other conditions are ... that they do not renovate a church or a monastery, do not rebuild ones that were destroyed, that they feed for three days any Muslim who passes by their homes... that they rise when a Muslim wishes to sit, that they do not imitate Muslims in dress and speech, nor ride horses, nor own swords, nor arm themselves with any kind of weapon....[99]

THE SYRIAN DISASTER

The case of Syria is especially tragic with Christians fleeing for their lives because of the civil war, and then running headlong into Islamist rapists and killers.

Their churches are attacked, often with loss of lives. In October 2012 a car bomb exploded near the only Syriac Orthodox Church in the town of Deir Ezzor; five people were killed. There were three attacks on Aleppo churches in four weeks. The number of people killed in the November 2012 attack on the Syriac Orthodox Church in Aleppo was estimated to be between 20 and 80.

In the same month the historic Arabic Evangelical Church of Aleppo was mined and blown up. The pastor Ibrahim Nasir expressed

---

[99] Ibrahim, 30.

bitterness and sadness of all Syrian citizens that makes Christians "inconsolable.... Today is the day when we cry out to Christ to say: my God, forgive them, for they do not know what they are doing."[100]

On June 1, 2013, Mark Durie, Anglican vicar in Melbourne, and author of The Third Choice, posted (markdurie.com blog) a report of Martin Janssen (translated from the Dutch) about the heartbreaking stories of Syrian Christians who had escaped to Jordan. Janssen had participated in a prayer walk for two Syrian clergy, Greek Orthodox Archbishop Paul Yazigi and Syriac Orthodox Archbishop Yohanna Ibrahim, who had been abducted by Syrian rebels. Afterwards he met with a number of Syrian refugees who told him about the hardship and losses they had experienced having been forced to flee their homes and villages when the rebel forces moved in.

The rebels announced that from now on the villagers would be under an Islamic emirate, and were subject to sharia law. The Christian residents were offered four choices:

1. Renounce the idolatry of Christianity and convert to Islam;
2. Pay a heavy tribute (jizya) to the Muslims for the privilege of keeping their heads and their faith);
3. Be killed;
4. Flee for their lives, leaving their belongings behind.

The Janssen report continues:

Some Christians were killed, some fled, some tried to pay the jizya and found it too heavy a burden to bear after the rebels kept increasing the amount they had to pay, and some were unable to flee or pay, so they converted to Islam to save themselves....

The scenario reported by Syrian refugees is a re-enactment of the historic fate of Christians across the Middle East. Even when the Syrian refugees manage to escape to surrounding countries such as Lebanon, Jordan and Turkey, they find no peace. They are not made to feel welcome but experience growing hostility.

---

[100] Ibid., 69.

The Syrian Christians who met with Janssen came from Idlib, Aleppo and villages in the countryside between these two cities. Their testimony was the same. Many of these villages had a large Christian presence until a few years ago, but now Christians no longer live there. One of the group, Jamil, an elderly man, told the following story about his village near Idlib where 30 Christian families had always lived peacefully alongside some 200 Sunni families. That changed dramatically in the summer of 2012.

One Friday trucks appeared in the village with heavily armed and bearded strangers who did not know anyone in the village. They began to drive through the village with a loudspeaker broadcasting the message that their village was now part of an Islamic emirate and Muslim women were henceforth to dress in accordance with the provisions of the Islamic sharia. Christians were given four choices. (See above).

Eventually Jamil fled the village; he lost his land and farm. Some families who could not escape or pay the Jizya converted to Islam. To his knowledge there were no Christians killed in his village, but he heard about a neighboring village where three Christian families survived, who were then murdered in the middle of the night.

Miryam, an Armenian middle-aged woman from Aleppo, told about the looting and plundering by armed militias, stealing wheat, bread and fuel, and entire inventories of schools, businesses and factories. If owners protested they were executed. She said that it is possible to adapt to the most difficult conditions. But it is impossible to live with constant fear that even the simplest daily activities such as taking your children to school, attending church, and trying to sleep when you know that there are people in your neighborhood who consider it their religious duty to kill as many Christians as possible.

Miryam and others in the group saw no future in staying in a country where their lives have been turned upside down. But where can they go? Listening to such stories and trying to imagine what unspeakable trauma these Christians experience is heartbreaking.

What can we do? What should we do?

1. Pray for the persecuted.
2. Be well informed about the Qur'an and Hadith-inspired hatred towards Christians and other infidels in the Arab/Muslim world.
3. Do everything possible to inform others in your families, churches, schools, and communities about the devastation caused in all cultures where sharia law is supreme.
4. Reach out to the persecuted, through international agencies, especially churches.
5. Be ready to welcome a flood of refugees whose lives have been made impossible in the Muslim world.

17 Expelling Christianity from the Muslim World[101]

Instead of falling for overblown tales of Western Islamophobia, let's take a real stand against Christophobia infecting the Muslim world. Tolerance for everyone – except the intolerant.[102]

It is unclear what either Western governments or Western churches think they are achieving by turning a blind eye to the persecution of Christians in the Muslim world.[103]

The so-called Arab Spring has not turned out well for the millions of Christians still living in the Middle East and other Muslim-ruled countries. This has become painfully evident in

---

[101] Orig., *Christian Renewal*, May 2012.

[102] *Ayaan Hirsi Ali, The Daily Beast,* Feb. 6, 2012.

[103] Caroline B. Glick, *Jewish World Review*, Oct. 12, 2011.

Afghanistan and Iraq. These two countries were freed from the dictatorship under the Taliban and Saddam Hussein. Instead of now enjoying the hoped-for freedom to live, work and worship according to their deepest beliefs, Christians in these countries are again suffering under severe persecution.

The recently published annual report of the U.S. Commission on International Religious Freedom names the following 16 countries as the "most systematic freedom violators in the world": Burma, China, Egypt, Eritrea, Iran, Iraq, Nigeria, North Korea, Pakistan, Saudi Arabia, (North) Sudan, Tajikistan, Turkey, Turkmenistan, Uzbekistan, and Vietnam.

Nina Shea, a tireless public defender of persecuted Christians and other non-Muslims, believes that Afghanistan also belongs in the ranks of the world's worst religious persecutors. For instance, the Afghan government has ordered the razing of that country's last remaining church after its lease was cancelled. The Afghan constitution fails to protect the freedom of religion or belief. Instead, it contains a clause that all laws must be in accordance with Islamic law (sharia).

Expatriate Afghanis, on behalf of persecuted Christians in Afghanistan, sent an open letter to the free world in June 2010 in which they pleaded for help because the government of that country is engaged in what they describe as a "campaign to brutalize and eliminate its Christian citizens." The letter reports that Christians have been subjected to frequent searches of homes and businesses, and to arrests and torture, in order to extract the names of Afghan Christian converts and the locations of secret Christian churches. The writers plead with the Body of Christ around the world for help in broadcasting the desperate plight of the Christians in that country.

WORSENING PERSECUTION

Iraq's Christian population was once one and a half million. It is now reduced to fewer than 150,000 – although *The Voice of the Martyrs* puts that number at about 334,000.

Tragically, the post-Saddam government has tolerated, perhaps even supported, the numerous attacks on Christians and their businesses, houses and churches. Writing in the December 2011 of the American Thinker, Michael Curtis said that in the last five years, 18 priests and two bishops have been kidnapped. The archbishop of Mosul was killed in 2008. Since 2004 over 70 churches, 42 of them in Baghdad, have been attacked. In October 2010, 58 Christians were killed and others seriously wounded while attending the Syrian Catholic Cathedral in Baghdad.

Churches have been bombed in Egypt, Nigeria, Pakistan, Indonesia, and the Philippines. In Pakistan a Christian woman by the name of Asia Bibi, is facing the death penalty for having "insulted" Islam.

In Iran, Youcef Nadarkhani has similarly been condemned for the "crime" of becoming a Christian. In desperation to escape these horrific attacks, some Christians have converted to Islam. Curtis writes that in countries such as Syria and Egypt others have supported secular political groups in the vain hope of being protected. Above all, Christians have fled from these countries so that the Arab world, which is now home to very few Jews, is also becoming devoid of Christians. Hence this cruel slogan that makes the rounds in the Arab world: "First the Saturday people, then the Sunday people."

What drives the current intensified persecution of Christians in the Arab/Islamic world? The main reason is the radicalization of the Muslim world, accompanied as always, by hatred for the kafirs – the unbelievers. Perhaps the most important cause is a revival of the belief that Muslims have the duty to spread the rule of Allah, as embodied in sharia law, over the entire world.

Christians living in the free West have great difficulty understanding the agonizing dilemmas facing the hard-pressed Christians in the increasingly hostile Muslim countries. Many have been forced out of their homes and communities where they have lived for countless generations. Where can they go? The irony they experience is that the revolutions that have eliminated the Mubaraks and the Qaddafis may well be replaced by more fanatical tyrants who will make their lives even more burdensome and tenuous.

Habib C. Malik, professor at the Lebanese American University, writes that Christians are genuinely alarmed about the prospect that the collapse of the regimes in Egypt and elsewhere will lead to their replacement by militant, hardline Islamists. He writes that the elephant in the room of the Arab spring is the mistreatment of minority communities, Christians and others, across the Arab world. Malik is convinced that if the Muslim moderates allow these minorities to be victimized with impunity, they will hasten the exodus of Arab Christians and they will lose "their historic chance to induce a lasting positive transformation of dismal Arab realities. Moderation would then be on its way toward its doom" (The Daily Beast, Oct.16,2011).

Professor Malik has a fresh approach to a topic that has been endlessly debated and mostly misreported and misunderstood. He pictures the presence of Christians within a Muslim nation as a healing catalyst. And he is right, although given the current state of Islamic ideology and practice, the prospects do not look promising. Although we should never give up hope, we also need to face realty, especially when it is ugly.

There is no end of horror stories about the persecution of Christians in Islam-ruled countries. One serious problem is that the plight of these Christians is generally ignored in the West. The mainstream media often turn a blind eye or report that the persecution of Christians is really a matter of sectarian strife in which both sides are equally responsible.

NIGERIA TARGETED

Coptic Christian Raymond Ibrahim writes a monthly report published at frontpagemagazine.com about the stepped-up persecution of Christian churches in many, mostly Muslim, countries.

On April 27, 2012, he reported that the terrorist group Boko Haram declared "war" on Christians and is aiming to "annihilate the entire

Christian community living in the northern part of the country" (Nigeria). One Boko Haram spokesman is quoted as saying: "We will create so much effort to end the Christian presence in our push to have a proper Islamic state that the Christians won't be able to stay."

Along with constant church bombings, this organization's new strategy is to convince Christians of the power of Islam by kidnapping their women.

On January 6, 2012, Ibrahim reported that weeks before the Christmas Day church bombings, another jihadi attack by local Muslims left five churches destroyed and several Christians killed. Local Muslims went around town pointing out church buildings and shops owned by Christians to Boko Haram members, who then bombed these churches and shops.

Faith J.H. McDonnell in her article, "Christian Slaughter in Nigeria"[104] reports that Boko Haram is determined to impose sharia law in Nigeria; this group has killed more than 900 Christians in the last two years.

On Sunday, April 29, 2012, Boko Haram attacked Catholic and Protestant worship services at Bayero University in Kano, killing 22 worshippers and wounding many more. Later on the same day, Boko Haram attacked a service at the Church of Christ in Nigeria parish in Jere, killing five people. Halfway during the service, the terrorists shouted "Allah Akbar" and headed straight for the altar where they killed the pastor, Reverend Albert Naga.

Boko Haram members have also focused on newspaper offices and television viewing centers as bombing targets, for example, in Jos, Plateau State. President Goodluck Jonathan has asked the U.S. government for help in dealing with Boko Haram and other terrorists. Despite more evidence that this organization is a terrorist organization with links to Osama bin Laden and to al Shabaab, a Somali terrorist

---

[104] McDonnell, Frontpagemagazine.com, May 4, 2012.

group aligned to al Qaeda, the Obama administration has refused to designate it as such.

U.S. Congressman Peter King, Chairman of the House Homeland Security Committee, recently urged the Secretary of State Hillary Clinton to designate Boko Haram as a terrorist organization. He has warned that this organization is a tremendous threat not only to the Christians and other citizens of Nigeria, but "its tactics, targeting, and fundraising operations appear to be increasingly international in scope, including within the U.S. Homeland."

It seems obvious that the Obama administration's refusal to face the reality of imperialistic Islam can be traced to what Andrew McCarthy has called "willful blindness." If not corrected, this illusion will allow the jihadists, whether by stealth or violence, to expand their ideal Islamic state from which all freedom and justice will be expunged. Wake up America.

THE GRAND MUFTI'S FATWA

The real world is one where according to several Arab news sources, on March 12, 2012, the Grand Mufti of Saudi Arabia, Sheik Abdul Aziz bin Abdullah, declared that it is "necessary to destroy all the churches of the region." His pronouncement was in response to a question from a Kuwaiti delegation about the place of Christian churches in Islamic countries.

The Grand Mufti explained that not to destroy the churches would be to approve them, which would be contrary to the Prophet Muhammad, who is recorded as saying (in the Hadith): "Two religions shall not coexist in the Arabian Peninsula." In other words, the Grand Mufti of Saudi Arabia – who occupies a place of supreme authority in the Muslim world – has declared that the persecutors of Christians are right in what they are doing. Such a fatwa will further fan the flames of hatred and violence toward Christians, not just in the Arabian Peninsula, but also in the rest of the world. These developments have momentous implications for the entire world. Are they perhaps foreshadowing what is to come in the free West?

If this is so, why do the mainstream media turn a blind eye to these issues? Further, why is it that even the Christian churches do not speak up in defense of our long-suffering fellow believers in the Muslim world?

18 Why Radical Islam and the American Left Are Allies

Americans have only begun to understand that, if radical Islam is one phase of our enemy, the other is the radical Left. For 200 years the radical Left has believed in a religion promising a heaven on earth whose end justifies any means. That is why progressives like Lenin and Stalin and Pol Pot killed so many innocent people.[105]

We have in Washington a poisonous government that spreads its venom to the body politic in all corners of the globe. We now resume... our quests... like David going forth to meet Goliath, like Beowolf the dragon slayer.... And modern heroes, dare I mention? Who [Chi Minh] and Mao and Lenin, Fidel and Nelson Mandela and John Brown, Che Guevara who reminds us, "At the

---

[105] David Horowitz, *The Black Book of the American Left, Volume III, The Great Betrayal* (New York: Encounter Books., 2013), 94.

risk of seeming ridiculous, let me say that the true revolutionary is guided by a great feeling of love."[106]

One of the great conundrums of the contemporary world is that the radically secular, mostly atheistic, political Left, and the radically religious, supremacist branch of Islam have a common goal. How is such a commonality possible since their deepest reason for existence is fundamentally opposite? One believes in the reality, even supremacy, of the spiritual, the afterlife, and a system of very detailed Allah-given laws to which all Muslims must adhere. On the other hand, the political Left believes that there is no God, no afterlife, and no transcendent order by which we distinguish between truth and falsehood, good and evil.

In an attempt to understand this apparent contradiction, I will concentrate on the American scene since it is the most influential player in the violent drama of current world events. Let me first summarize, then elaborate on what I suggest makes for an alliance between these unlikely partners.

Firstly, they are united in their hatred of the West, especially America. That is the reason for their similarity in demonizing western civilization and especially America.

Secondly, they are united in the belief that life on earth is insignificant and has no intrinsic worth; both are driven by a death wish. Jihadists express this in their motto, "You love life, but we love death." The radical Left's notion is expressed in Marx's saying, "Everything that exists deserves to perish."

Thirdly, both have as their goal totalitarian, that is, political power, which is also the reason why this alliance will not last.

---

[106] Lynn Stewart cited in David Horowitz, *Unholy Alliance, Radical Islam and the American Left* (Washington DC: Regnery Press, 2004), 163.

AMERICA IN THE DOCK

I am indebted to David Horowitz for a large volume of material produced in defense of America and Western civilization. He grew up in a Communist family and at first followed in the footsteps of his parents by becoming a leader in the 1960s revolution. His Marxist faith was severely shaken in 1974 when colleague Betty Van Patter, a mother of three children, was brutally murdered by members of the Black Panthers party, a ruthless gang of fanatic believers in the socialist revolution. Profound soul-searching followed and led to a complete break with his former comrades. In scores of essays, books, interviews, and through his online news magazine, FrontPageMag.com, Horowitz exposes the treachery and hatred that animate the radical Left in America. He sees his life's mission as

> fighting Marxism in all its forms, not as a conservative ideologue but as a seeker after truth and the meaning of life…. My mission is a personal mission - to undo what I did as a leftist, to witness to the truth that I learned and to try to save even if it's only one or two individuals. That's what I do.[107]

Bill Ayers, together with his wife Bernadine Dohrn, were and are beholden to the ideology of anti-Americanism. Both played a major role in the Weather Underground and its campaign of bombings and rioting during the late 1960s and early 1970s. Ayers told a *New York Times* reporter at the launching of his book Fugitive Days in 2001 that he has no regrets about setting off bombs at the Pentagon and the Capitol because they represent the abuse of American power and are therefore monuments to U.S. domination over the planet. Ayers was radicalized by the Vietnam War, which he saw as a global struggle against U.S. imperialism, a war he wanted America to lose. He said that, "My country stood on the wrong side of an exploding world

---

[107] The complete and riveting story of Horowitz's mission is in his *Radical Son*.

revolution... I thought of myself as a revolutionary, committed to overturning the whole system of empire."[108]

For Ayers, being part of the revolution even during his time in hiding (underground) gave him a sense of invigoration that was different from anything he had known before. He writes,

> There was a sense... of being born again. But, yes, it's true, I was born again, born underground, awakened to new ways of seeing and hearing, the new openings of human possibility.... The underground gave me a whole new world, and I gave myself to it wholly and without reservation.[109]

David Horowitz's *Unholy Alliance,*[110] is a detailed description of the Left's radicalization and its hatred toward America, especially fueled by its opposition to the Vietnam and subsequent wars. This movement received its inspiration from Marxist ideology in its search for a perfect world. Its guiding principle is that the existing world, especially America, is rotten to the core and must be overthrown.

This revolutionary idea at one time made the American Communists look to the Soviet Union as the land of promise. That promise collapsed, but the same motive continues to inspire the true believers. They did not change their loyalty to the Marxist ideology, but to hide their real intentions they begin to call themselves "progressives" or "liberals." The universities played a critical role in making their intentions more palatable to generations of students.

A number of prominent university professors led the way in mapping out a radical stance against their own country. Professor Eric Foner, like Horowitz, grew up in a family of Communists, but he never

---

[108] Cited in Dinesh D'Souza, *America: Imagine a World Without Her* (Washington DC: Regnery Publishing, 2014), 58.

[109] Bill Ayers, *Fugitive Days: Memoirs of an Antiwar Activist* (Boston: Beacon Press, 2009), 242.

[110] David Horowitz, *Unholy Alliance, Radical Islam and the American Left* (Washington DC: Regnery Press, 2004).

left the fold. His history of the United States[111] has been described as an attempt to rehabilitate American Communism. The same can be said about another influential book by another "fellow traveler," the late historian Howard Zinn which presents American history as a story of theft, greed and treachery.[112] There are many others, including Herbert Aptheker, Noam Chomsky, Ward Churchill, Nicholas De Genova, Todd Gitlin, Norman Mailer, Michael Moore and Jeremiah Wright, who serve as propagandists for the hate-America ideology.

The shocking events of 9/11 and their aftermath was the "defining moment" that set off a movement of opposition to the policies of the George W. Bush administration. Again, the tenured university professors led the way. Shortly after the start of the war in Iraq, a group of professors at Columbia University held a "teach-in" where they denounced the American-led military action. Anthropology professor Nicholas De Genova called for "a million Mogadishus." a reference to the 1993 humiliation of American soldiers in Somalia. He said that US patriotism is a form of imperial warfare and white supremacy, and that the "only true heroes are those who find ways to help defeat the US military." He also said that a peaceful world would be one in which "the U.S. would have no place." [113]

David Horowitz has an apt description of the role now played by the universities: "As a result of the Left's colonization of the academic social sciences, this anti-American culture is now part of the educational curriculum of America's emerging elites, and as much as an element of the cultural main stream as any other historical tradition. Indeed, it is a dominant element."[114]

---

[111] Eric Fon, *The Story of American* Freedom (New York: W.W. Norton & Company, 1999).

[112] Howard Zinn, *A People's History of the United States: 1492-2001* (New York: Harper, 2003).

[113] Ibid., 34.

[114] Ibid., 105.

A FAITH WITHOUT A FUTURE

Tracing the highlights of the life and career of the late Eric Hobsbawn (1917 to 2012) will help to understand how the Left has become a prominent influence in the shaping of western culture. Horowitz refers to this lifelong communist and teacher/author as "an icon of the contemporary intellectual Left." Though Hobsbawn remained true to his faith in the Soviet Union, one of the most oppressive empires in history, he was a much-respected history professor in the universities of Europe and America. His book, The Age of Extremes, has been published in 37 languages.[115]

Hobsbawn's faith was shaken by the shocking revelations about Stalinist dictatorship by the very top of the ruling Soviet leadership, the then Premier of the USSR Nikita Khrushchev. Then came the eloquent voice of Alexander Solzhenitsyn exposing the horrors of living and dying in the Soviet Union's death camps. No one had caught the attention of the free world as Solzhenitsyn did with his Gulag Archipelago revelations. He exposed the awful truth about this evil empire, which murdered millions of its people while those who survived were condemned to a life of hopelessness and misery.

Hobsbawn recalls in his autobiography of 2002 that the demise of the Stalinist dictatorship caused him sadness and "nostalgia" rather than outrage and guilt. He wrote, "To this day I notice myself treating the memory and tradition of the USSR with indulgence and tenderness." If he had used those words to describe the German Nazis, he would have been disowned by his academic colleagues. But Hobsbawn never broke with his commitment to the Communist cause because, as he explained, his life

> would lose its nature and its significance without the political project to which he committed himself as a school boy, even though that project has demonstrably failed, and as I know now, was

---

[115] Ibid., 60.

bound to fail. The dream of the October [Russian] revolution is still there somewhere inside me.[116]

It's worthwhile to reflect on the enormity of the implications of Hobsbawn's admission that the "project" he devoted his life to turned out to be an empty shell, a mere utopia. What is worse, as a professor who spent a long career with an international reputation, he likely persuaded hundreds of thousands of students and through them millions of people to believe in an ideology that caused the death and brutalization of untold millions.

What stands out in Hobsbawn's disillusionment about the failure of the Soviet experiment is that he had no regrets about his influence in and responsibility for the spread of the Marxist ideology with devastating consequences for entire generations and nations. He expressed no remorse for the suffering endured by all who had the misfortune to live under a communist regime. Rather, he is sorry that his hope for a successful revolution was dashed on the shores of reality, which is the fault not of himself and his utopian fellow believers, but of the enemy – which first of all is America.

When the Soviet disaster came to an inglorious end in 1991, Hobsbawn wrote an article entitled "After the Fall." In the article, he lamented that the Soviet Union's disappearance meant that the Soviet empire (the lesser evil) was no longer able to check the "predatory designs" of the greater evil – the Western democracies. He sided with Rosa Luxembourg who argued that faced with the choice of socialism (Communism really) or barbarism in 1917, the world may yet come to regret its decision against socialism. In other words, America, which has been a haven for the refugees of many woebegone countries, who enjoy its freedom and its raised living standard, is here called barbaric. (Despite the fact that western nations are now in serious spiritual, moral, and political decline, there is no justification in calling them barbaric in comparison with what the Communist revolutions have wrought.)

---

[116] Cited in Ibid., 61.

The revolutionary academics are able to proclaim from the safety of their privileged positions the idea that Marxism is the way to break down the old order and construct in its place the Communist ideal of a society where equality and justice will rule. We now know that the reality of this ideology is very opposite to its promise. Wherever Communism has been applied, untold millions have been and are condemned to lives of slavery and deprivation. Nevertheless, the instigators and preachers of the Revolution refuse to accept any responsibility for the soul-and life-destroying disasters that result in the application of their revolutionary theories. They are like an arsonist who starts a fire and then stands by to watch the building go up in flames. He then blames (who else) America, of course.

UNITED IN HATE

What is behind the unlikely alliance of the secular political Left in the fanatic religious believers in Islam? The short story is that both want to destroy western civilization and build upon its ruins a better, if not perfect, world of peace and harmony. Until now, they have been busy with the work of destruction. The reconstruction will have to wait, because the two allies are totally opposed on that score. Therefore, all efforts for now are focused on tearing down.

At first sight what David Horowitz calls an "Unholy Alliance" seems impossible because the motives of the two parties are fundamentally different. Yet we have seen this phenomenon before. In the 1950s, Arab nationalists cooperated with the Communist bloc and adopted the Marxist view of the world in line with the anti-American and anti-Western ideology.

Ayatollah Ruhollah Khomeini, the mastermind of the 1979 revolution in Iran, adopted the Marxist concept of the world divided into oppressors and oppressed. By introducing the theme of revolution of the oppressed, Khomeini could attract the support of the political Left. The radical Islamists believe that by conquering nations and instituting sharia, they can establish the caliphate and thus redeem the world for Allah. The political Left believes that by using state power and violent means to eliminate private property, it can bring the new millennium into being.

The radical Left believes with Marx that religion is merely a means of seeking relief from the suffering caused by the capitalist system of private property rights. Hence, removing private property will also remove the need for religion. David Horowitz formulates this Marxist thought process as follows:

> The revolution that removes the cause of this suffering will also remove the religious belief it inspires. Thus, the liberation of mankind from private property – the defeat of America and Western capitalism – will liberate Islamic fanatics from the need to be Islamic and fanatic.

Hamas, founded in 1987 and offshoot of the Muslim Brotherhood, has as its main objective the destruction of Israel. On September 11, 2001, the day the Twin Towers fell in New York City, Hamas issued an "Open letter to America" explaining that the attack on America was in retaliation for America's misdeeds. The reasons listed in this letter offer a clue about the alliance of the anti-American Left and the radical Islamists. The letter states:

> You will face the mirror of your history for a long time to come. Thus, you will be able to see exactly how much you have oppressed, how corrupt you are, how you have sinned – how many entities you have destroyed, how many kingdoms you have demolished! America, oh sword of oppression, arrogance and sin.... Do you remember all the blacks who lived under your wing? Your white sons bound their necks with the fetters of slavery, after hunting them in the jungles and on the coasts of Africa.... Have you asked yourself about your actions against your "original" inhabitants, the Indians, the Apaches?
>
> Why do you pour this continuing oppression on the head of Baghdad as you do on the head of Jerusalem, on the head of Jenin? Every time Dick Cheney and his girlfriend Condoleezza Rice

admonish us, [and] gloat at our misfortune, they incite to more [violence against us]!! We stand in line and beg Allah to give you to drink from the cup of humiliation – and behold, heaven has answered.

David Horowitz writes that the Western radicals are in total agreement with this indictment since their list of American crimes is the same. These radicals had endorsed the enemies of America when they embraced the Palestinian movement in the 1960s, backed by the Soviet bloc, when Arafat created modern terrorism. Assisted by the Castro dictatorship, which the American Left also admires, Arafat organized these terrorist training camps for airline hijackers and hostage-takers.

Thus, the attack of 9/11 occurred with hijacked airliners whose targets were Wall Street and the Pentagon, the very symbols of the American nation. This was the point of convergence where the radical Muslims and the American Left found each other in the fire and smoke of the crashing towers that killed nearly 3000 innocent and defenseless people.[117]

---

[117]Cf., Ibid., 144–5.

19 The Insider Movement Examined

[O]ne of the greatest problems in today's society is not radical Islam, but the type of nominal Christianity in which Christians are woefully unprepared to defend their faith (Dr. Joshua Lingel).

The missionary outreach to the Muslim world has been characterized by controversy and disagreement within the Christian Church. This subject has taken a new turn with the rise of the so-called Insider Movement.

Discussion of this topic has taken place mostly within the church hierarchy and among those who are directly engaged in presenting the Gospel to Muslims. Since the issues at stake concern the very character and meaning of the Church as the Body of Christ, every church member should take a vital interest in the state of this debate. This essay is an attempt in that direction, which can only be done in a very cursory way.

The Insider Movement arose out of an effort to be sensitive to the cultural, political, and social environment of Muslims who are approached with the Christian Gospel. Such an effort is laudable but, as history has shown, it has tendency to water down the Gospel. In this case it has led some to insist that there are many similarities (common ground) in the teachings of the Qur'an and the Bible.

One of the major advocates of the Insider Movement is John Travis who has developed a scheme describing six different types of followers of Christ. One of them (C5) holds that Muslims can become followers of Christ while remaining in their Muslim community – hence the term Insider. They may continue to attend the mosque, participate in the fast, and recite the Shahadah (Allah is the one God, and Muhammad is his prophet). They are sometimes called Messianic Muslims.

THE DEBATE HEATS UP

Recently various events have been scheduled to debate and challenge the underlying assumptions of the Insider Movement. Taking part in this debate are a number of missionaries and authors deeply involved in the work of bringing the biblical message to the Muslim world.

Professor Joshua Lingel, Director of i2 (Islamic Institute), Biola University, hosted an "Insider Movement Conference: A Critical Assessment" on October 13, 2009. In his invitation letter he wrote that he is concerned with the "Islamization" of Christian missions which he calls " Chrislam – neither Christianity nor Islam."

Professor Lingel knows U.S. pastors who are teaching their congregations to preach an Islamicized "Jesus," and they are inviting "Islamo-Christian missiologists" to teach them how to preach from the Qur'an. In doing so they falsify both the Bible and the Qur'an. Lingel takes issue with those who teach that Muhammad is a true prophet and that there is biblical ground for reciting the Shahadah.

The August 2009 issue of the St. Francis Magazine, a journal dedicated to the study of "Religion and mission to the Arab world," devoted ten articles to a discussion of the Insider Movement. The editor, the Rev. John Stringer, introduced this subject as follows:

The Insider Movement, also called C5 or Messianic Islam, has been a pervasive, outspoken presence in the world of missions for the last three decades. Missiological journals, Christian magazines and newspapers have been awash in anecdotes from the field extolling this purportedly, new, biblical, approach to ministry. At times, it has seemed almost unthinkable to offer criticism of this broad movement. That is why this entire issue is dedicated to a detailed examination of the Insider Movement, its theology, methodology and tactics.

The authors include seasoned missionaries and scholars, most of whom provide a thoughtful and critical analysis of this movement. Jay Smith has worked for nearly 30 years reaching out to Muslims in more than 20 countries. Living in London during the past 17 years, he has engaged in what he calls "a highly public confrontational and polemical ministry with the more radical elements within Western Islam." He gives an evaluation of a Common Ground Conference held in Atlanta in January 2009, which had as its purpose the promotion of the Insider method of evangelism to Islam.

Smith assesses 17 core beliefs or paradigms as they were articulated at this conference. He concludes that these touch on what lies at the heart of biblical religion and of the Islamic religion as formulated in its sacred scriptures. If the Bible is true, the Qur'an is not; they cannot both be true, or partly true. After all, those differences are not at the margin, but at the heart of what we are as Christians and as Muslims.

The first tenet of the Insider's beliefs Smith evaluates is the definition of such a person as "One who embraces Jesus, yet remains as light in the oikos (household) so that as many as possible might be saved."

He points to a number of problems this creates, as follows: "New believers in Christ are the most vulnerable to the seduction of Islam, to the spiritual forces within Islam, and especially to the strong control Muslim families have over them, emotionally, socially, and physically. With little contact or discipling from more mature Christians... the new believer can easily fall back into his old faith, and/or allegiances."

Roger L. Dixon, in his contribution published in the St. Francis Magazine, points out that the Insider Movement is attempting to reconcile the Bible with Islamic teachings. This would mean that Muslim believers will be both "Christian" in their core beliefs and "Muslim" in their basic tenets. But trying to reconcile these two opposing worldviews defies all logic. He issues a warning that should not fall on deaf ears: "One of the worst mistakes a Christian evangelist can make is to justify a non-biblical world view. I urge every missiologist to examine these C5 claims in great depth before buying into this immature conception of reality with its grandiose claims of success. The delusion of this approach has led some western missionaries to pray the Shahadah (Muslim confession of faith) and become official members of the religion of Islam. What a tragedy and what an accountability must be given by some."

ASKING THE RIGHT QUESTION

The Rev. Bassam Madany was born in Syria and for 35 years preached the Gospel to the Arab world via the Christian Reformed Church's Back to God Hour radio broadcasts. Retired since 1994, he is still active in the same ministry, while also serving as a rich source of insight for the English-speaking world. His books *Bible and Islam* (1979, 2003) and *An Introduction to Islam*, co-authored with his late wife Shirley (2006), are suffused with biblical wisdom.

Madany joined the debate about the Christian mission to the Muslim world in an article "The New Christians of North Africa & the Insider Movement," available on the website of the Middle East Resources.[118] The following is a summary of that article.

Madany begins with one important question. How do the new converts from Islam to Christianity view their conversion? He writes that those views, which have lately been reported on "reformist" Arabic

---

[118] www.unashamedofthegospel.org/the_new_christians.cfm.

websites as well as in the European media, indicate that the new converts are bold and forthright in their witness and enthusiasm about their new-found faith.

At a conference devoted to "The Defense of Minorities and Women," held in March 2007 in Zurich, a lecturer reported that a considerable number of North African Muslims have embraced the Christian faith. The weekly journal, *Jeune Afrique*, devoted three reports about such conversions in Tunisia, Morocco and Algeria.

The same lecturer mentioned that a key factor that led Muslims to convert to Christianity was "the violence of the fundamentalist Islamist movements." A Christian evangelist working in Algeria stated that these terrible events shocked people to discover that Islam was capable of unleashing all that terror and those horrific massacres, which took place over many years in the 1990s. No one was spared. Many people asked: Where is Allah? Some Algerians committed suicide, others went mad, some became atheists, and still others turned to Christianity.

Another factor that led Muslims to become Christians was the biblical message that God is a God of love. They were overwhelmed by the reality that God loves them and that the Messiah died on the cross and rose again to reconcile sinners with their heavenly Father. This message was especially significant for women who in Islam are seen as the embodiment of evil and therefore must be punished for the simplest act.

NO REGRETS

Madany translated a news item posted on an Arabic-language website, about the conversion of an Algerian policeman and his daughter. Despite being accused of having committed a capital offense, he testified about his newly-won sense of freedom and peace after embracing the Christian faith. His daughter explained that her reason for becoming a Christian,

> was due to her feeling that Islam treated women as maids and concubines, only to be sexually exploited by men. Muslim men regard women only from a physical point of view. Now, having

embraced Christianity, she began to feel dignified as a human being. Her decision is final, and she does not regret it at all.[119]

Madany comments that these courageous new Christians who are not afraid to openly profess their faith in a hostile environment are a powerful testimony against those who say that they need not call themselves Christians nor stop their former Islamic practices. He thinks that this novel Insider methodology, seen as a way to solve the problem of the small number of Muslim converts, amounts to a radical discontinuity with the work of the great missionaries of the past.

As an Eastern Christian who spent most of his life bringing the Good News of Jesus Christ to the followers of Islam, Madany urges his readers to pay careful attention to the biblical directives on missions. Despite the Jewish and Gentile outright rejection of the gospel of the cross, Paul did not hesitate to proclaim it. "For the word of the cross is foolishness to those who are perishing, but for us who are being saved, it is the power of God."

Madany writes that he cannot hide his joy when he hears about the rebirth of the Christian Church in North Africa, and he praises God for the boldness of these new Christians who are not ashamed of the Cross of their Savior.

In considering the case of the Insider Movement in light of the biblical message, we do well to pay careful attention to the testimony of this seasoned, Arabic-speaking missionary to the Muslim world.

---

[119] *Aafaq* [Horizons], April 24, 2009,

20 Why We Must Stand with Israel[120]

Israel is the only country in the Middle East that is democratic yet it is widely accused of being a dictatorial state. On January 28, 2014, The National Post editor had this to say: On the other hand, it is important to remember that Israel is the only country in the world that, for decades, has been systematically singled out for unfair criticism by the world community – especially at the United Nations. Given this deafening chorus of bigotry and denunciation, Israel's few supporters must be full-throated if they hope to provide an effective counterbalance.[121]

We remind ourselves of this history in order to appreciate God's purpose in mentioning the Jews ahead of the idolaters in the ranking of those who are hostile to Islam..... This wicked and most vile nature could only be defeated in past history by Islam and its followers when they truly follow Islamic principles. Our modern world will not be saved from this wicked nature except

---

[120] Orig., *Christian Renewal*, "What Happens to Truth in an Age of Delusion? (Series: Part 10), March 2014.

[121] Editorial, "Anti-Israel Bias on Parade," *National Post*, January 28, 2014.

by Islam, and only when its people implement Islam completely in their lives.[122]

Canadian Prime Minister Stephen Harper used a trip to Israel during the week of January 19, 2014 to reassure his host that Canada is steadfast in its support of Israel's right to exist and to defend itself. In his address to the Israeli parliament, the Knesset, he was direct in summarizing Israel's precarious position and his view of the relationship between the two countries. He said: Are we Repeating the 1930s?

In the 65 years that modern Israel has been a nation, Israelis have endured attacks and slander beyond counting and have never known a day of true peace. And… we Canadians understand that Israelis live with this impossible calculus: If you act to defend yourselves, you will suffer widespread condemnation over and over again. But should you fail to act, you alone will suffer the consequences of your inaction and that consequence will be final. It will be your destruction.

The truth that Canada understands is that many of the hostile forces Israel faces are faced by all western nations. Israel faces them for many of the same reasons we face them. You just happen to be a lot closer to them…. One must look beyond Israel's borders to find the causes of the relentless oppression, poverty and violence in much of the region.

I believe the story of Israel is a great example to the world. It is a story, essentially, of a people whose response to suffering has been to move beyond resentment and build an extraordinary society, a vibrant democracy, a freedom-loving country with an independent and rights-affirming judiciary….

---

[122] Sayyid Qutb, cited in Andrew G. Boston, *The Legacy of Islamic Antisemitism* (Amherst, NY: Prometheus Books, 2008), 38.

You have taken the collective memory of death and persecution to build an optimistic, forward-looking society.... Israel represents values which our Government takes as articles of faith and principles to drive our own national life. And therefore, through fire and water, Canada will stand with you.[123]

THE FUTILITY OF ALL PEACE EFFORTS

Why have all the efforts to reach a lasting peace agreement between Israel and Palestine failed, and why are the current frantic efforts by the U.S. Secretary of State, John Kerry, bound to follow the same pattern?

The short answer is that the conflict between the two antagonists is not an ordinary dispute about territory and borders. The real answer to the question lies with the popular Muslim leaders who teach a form of violent and stealth jihad. They include Sayyid Qutb (1906-1966), Hassan Al-Banna (1906-1949) founder of the Muslim Brotherhood, and Sheikh Yusuf al-Qaradawi, who is the current spiritual leader of the Muslim Brotherhood. All three teach an ideology of hatred toward the West, especially America and Israel – the two Satans.

Listen to two authors from different perspectives who spent a lifetime studying and teaching Islam – one is a Jew, the other a Christian. Below are excerpts from Bernard Lewis's comments regarding the 2007 Annapolis peace conference about the Israel-Palestine conflict:

> What is the conflict about? There are basically two possibilities: that it is about the size of Israel, or about its existence. If the issue is about the size of Israel, then we have a straightforward border problem, like Alsace-Loraine or Texas. That is to say, not easy, but possible to solve in the long run, and to live with in the meantime.
>
> If, on the other hand, the issue is the existence of Israel, then clearly it is insoluble by negotiation. There is no compromise

---

[123] Prime Minister Stephen Harper, *Jerusalem*, January 20, 2014.

position between existing and not existing, and no conceivable government of Israel is going to negotiate on whether that country should or should not exist.

PLO and other Palestinian spokesmen have, from time to time, given formal indications of recognition of Israel in their diplomatic discourse in foreign languages. But that's not the message delivered at home in Arabic, in everything from primary school textbooks to political speeches and religious sermons. Here the terms used in Arabic denote, not the end of hostilities, but an armistice or truce, until such time that the war against Israel can be resumed with better prospects for success....

The government of Jordan granted [displaced] Palestinian Arabs a form of citizenship, but kept them in refugee camps. In other Arab countries, they were and remained stateless aliens without rights or opportunities, maintained by U.N. funding....

The reason for this has been stated by various Arab spokesmen. It is the need to preserve the Palestinians as a separate entity until the time they will return and reclaim the whole of Palestine; that is to say, all of the West Bank, the Gaza Strip and Israel. The demand for the "return" of the refugees, in other words, means the destruction of Israel. It is highly unlikely to be approved by any Israeli government....[124]

THE DIVINE RIGHT OF CONQUEST

Following are excerpts from an article by the Rev. Bassam M. Madany, "The Problem of Israel,"[125]. He reviews the events after the founding of the state of Israel in May, 1948, during which Israel repeatedly had to defend itself against the surrounding Arab countries. It often had

---

[124] Bernard Lewis, "On the Jewish Question," *The Wall Street Journal*, November 26, 2007.
[125] www.unashamedofthegospel.org.

appeared that a solution to the Arab-Israel conflict would be possible, but time and again the peace negotiations broke down. Madany suggests that the root cause of the perpetual Israeli-Palestinian conflict lies with Islam.

He explains that Islam developed an ideology that "any land that becomes a part of Daru'l Islam (House of Islam) must always remain Islamic. Islamic imperialism has distinguished itself by being totally different from European imperialisms." Madany continues:

The central drive or impulse of the Islamic Ideology is what I would like to call 'the Divine Right of Conquest.' Muslims glory in the great Futuhat (Conquest). After all, they were all done...in the Pathway of Allah. They are blest by him; more than that, they have been foreordained by the divine will! Thus, Islam cannot and would not concede to the birth of a Jewish homeland within Palestine. This land, so important to both Jews and Christians, had been 'hallowed' by Muhammad, who according to the Qur'an, paid a special 'visit' to the heavens via Jerusalem. Ipso facto, Jerusalem became the third holy city after Mecca and Medina. In fact, Islam's hegemonic penchant is seen as well in its appropriation of all the great men and prophets of antiquity, beginning with Adam, and ending with Jesus. All of them are considered as Muslims, even before the advent of Islam.

They [Western political leaders] either ignore, or are unaware of the fact that Islam is far more than a religious faith; it is a complete worldview with global aspirations and pretensions. If the West, during the last three centuries, succeeded in separating church and state, this has not happened in Daru'l Islam. The opposition to the existence of Israel is a religious matter for Muslims, and therefore cannot be negotiated.

Since its founding in 1948, Israel has needed to defend itself against on and off military attacks from nearby Arab states. It has also endured suicide bombings and thousands of rocket attacks aimed indiscriminately at villages and buildings. Survival has come at a high cost in terms of the lost lives of soldiers and unarmed citizens.

Nevertheless, Israel has been able to defend itself successfully, and continues to be a free and independent nation with a vibrant culture. How has Israel been able to survive and thrive in such a hostile environment? It has protected itself by building a strong and ready military, a defensive missile system, and a series of protective perimeter walls with checkpoints intended to prevent suicide bombers from killing innocent men, women and children. Even as the anti-Israel propagandists have vilified Israel for trying to protect its citizens, the same protections and defensive measures have been necessary for safeguarding the lives of many of its citizens.

The hard reality is that Israel is situated as a tiny speck on the map, surrounded by neighbors who have made it known that they will not rest until Israel is driven into the sea. That threat has become increasingly ominous since Iran is determined to obtain the nuclear bomb.

Charles Krauthammer has laid out Israel's perilous predicament in view of its size and location. He writes that the Holocaust led the post-WWII Jews to the conviction that their future lay in a place where they would be able to defend themselves. He agrees that the territory they chose is perilous, just a "dot on the map, a tiny patch of near desert" that can be obliterated entirely by one small battery of nuclear-tipped Scuds.

Krauthammer concludes: "The terrible irony is that in solving the problem of powerlessness, the Jews have necessarily put all their eggs in one basket, a small basket hard by the waters of the Mediterranean. And on its fate hinges everything Jewish."[126]

THE DEMONIZING OF ISRAEL

The second, and perhaps the most dangerous threat faced by Israel, is the success of the haters of Israel in spreading their vile ideology world-wide. The breeding ground for this anti-Israel ideology is the Muslim

---

[126] Charles Krauthammer, *Things that Matter: Three Decades of Passions, Pastimes and Politics* (New York: Crown Forum, 2013), 271.

madrassas and mosques in the Middle East and other parts of the world. This is where fiery imams and teachers denounce the Jews in the most diabolical terms. All too often this happens even in many mosques and Islamic schools in the free West. (A number of mostly young men have been radicalized in Western mosques and joined the Muslim jihadists in various parts of the world.)

Many university campuses in the U.S. and Canada also have become incubators of Israel-hatred. Since 2004, each year in the month of March, professors and students have organized an "Israel Apartheid Week" by calling for boycotts, divestments, and sanctions (BDS) against Israel. Their propaganda consists in picturing Israel as a pariah state that must surrender part of its territory and accept large numbers of returning Palestinian "refugees." Both measures would spell the end of Israel.

Various fraudulent documents used by the enemies of Israel have played a major role in spreading their hate-filled message. They promote the outlandish idea of the so-called blood libel, that is, the charge that the Jews kill Gentile children in order to use their blood in their religious rituals.

During the 20th century *The Protocols of the Elders of Zion,* first published in Russia in 1903, has been praised by many anti-Semites. Its major theme is that the Jews are scheming to control the world, through banking and finance. Although it has been unmasked as a fraud on the basis of comparisons with a number of books, it has been published in many countries and is especially popular in the Arab world.

The Protocols was a favorite of Hitler. It became a propaganda tool for the Nazis who ordered it to be required reading in the schools. Arab translations of Hitler's Mein Kampf were widely distributed in the Arab world, under the title My Jihad. Not surprisingly, Hitler was pleased that the Arabs were his allies in their hatred of the Jews. He established friendly relations with their leaders, including the then Grand Mufti of Jerusalem, Haj Amin al-Husseini.

The authenticity of *The Protocols* was tested in a Swiss court in 1934 - 1935. Judge Walter Meyer declared that as harmful as they are, they "are nothing but laughable nonsense."

THE UN ENABLER OF ISRAEL-HATRED

The United Nations could have and should have been a force for good among the countries of the world. After all, the UN Charter states that it is "determined to save succeeding generations from the scourge of war, which twice in our lifetime has brought untold sorrow to mankind." Its purposes and principles include the following: "To develop friendly relations among nations based on respect for the principles of equal rights and self-determination of peoples." Among those rights it mentions respect for the" fundamental freedoms for all without distinction as to race, sex, language or religion." The UN in clear violation of its own founding document and led by a coalition of 57 Arab states has consistently carried on a campaign of denouncing Israel as the worst human rights violator.

This happens despite the fact that Israel is the only law-based, democratic state in the Middle East, where some one million Arabs enjoy all the rights of citizenship, including the right to elect their own members in the Israeli parliament (Knesset).

One of the worst instances of UN bias occurred in 2001 in Durban, South Africa, at the UN World Conference Against Racism, Racial Discrimination, Xenophobia and Related Intolerance. This occasion was used to demonize the U.S. and Israel. Yasser Arafat and Fidel Castro (who was treated as a hero) gave free rein to their hatred. The South African Foreign Minister described Cuba as, "the most democratic country in the world." The blatant abuses of human rights in Arab countries were ignored, while privately the participants applauded the suicide attacks on Israel.[127]

---

[127]Cf., Arch Puddington, "The Wages of Durban," *Commentary*, November, 2001.

It is a grave error to participate in this kind of conference and thus give credence to the monstrous lies about Israel, also called the Little Satan. The Americans were correct in refusing to attend. The double-talk and outright falsehoods for which the UN is a willing carrier are far from harmless. They have a way of poisoning everything they touch. What is worse, they degrade the very basis of civility without which relations among persons and nations cannot be civilized and peaceful.

21 Israel: The Canary in the Coal Mine[128]

I have a premonition that will not leave me; as it goes with Israel so will it go with all of us. Should Israel perish, the holocaust will be upon us.[129]

Our position on the Middle East is clear. We want the root of tensions to be removed. During these 60 years what was the root of massacres, crimes and conflicts? The solution is clear and nothing has changed.[130]

The 34-day war between Israel and Hezbollah and its aftermath have spawned a wealth of commentary and reportage as contradictory and confusing as any that has come from that part of the world.

---

[128] Orig., *Christian Courier*, October 9, 2006.

[129] Eric Hoffer, "Israel's Peculiar Position," *LA Times*, May 26,1968.

[130] Mahmoud Ahmadinejad, *Tehran*, August 29, 2006.

NEWS WITHOUT CONTEXT

It should not go unnoticed that nearly all of the reporting and commentary have been preoccupied with tactics, that is, with the how of things, the details of numbers, weaponry, who is winning, or losing, and especially with the spectacular – notably the live television broadcasts of bombings, riots, massive demonstrations, those sorts of things. The more violence, the more telegenic.

The result is that the news is presented without context and a grasp of the historic background. Instead of acquiring true insight and real knowledge, many just develop opinions on the basis of the latest information provided by the most persuasive presenters, and especially by the graphic pictures shown on television and now on the Internet.

Related to the foregoing is that many tend towards opinions that are safe and uncontroversial, which is the attitude that has given rise to the current epidemic of political correctness. This outlook arises from a desire to believe what is generally accepted within the thinking elites in the academy, the media, the political Left, and the entertainment industry.

Practically, this means that belief in secularism (there is no God), moral relativism (there is no truth), and tolerance (multiculturalism) has become the new orthodoxy embraced by every right thinking, rational person. The mainstream media play a key role in fostering the worldview shaped by this mindset.

ISRAEL'S PRECARIOUS POSITION

All of this has a profound effect on the prevailing opinion about the state of Israel in the midst of a hostile Arab/Muslim world. From its very beginning, Israel's existence has been bitterly opposed and fought by its Arab neighbors. That conflict is not only a political contest over land between Israel and the Arab world, but it is also a conflict of Jews versus Muslims.

There is reason to believe that this seemingly intractable war against Israel is a microcosm of the war declared by radical Islamists on all infidels. In other words, Israel's fight is ours as well. The leading fatwa proclaimers have cast their net wide, condemning not only the two Satans, but the entire non-Muslim world. Ahmadinejad has given voice to this ambition again and again, as he did in this prediction: "Allah willing, Islam will conquer all the mountain tops of the world."

The so-called peace negotiations have gone nowhere because one side is not interested in peace but in the destruction of Israel. That became clear when Yasser Arafat walked away from an offer that gave him nearly everything he had demanded. Instead, he unleashed a reign of terror that killed hundreds of innocent Israeli (and Palestinian) men, women and children, all the while deepening the misery and hopelessness of the Palestinian people.

The mainstream world press has contributed to the idea that Israel is the cause of the ongoing violence and the bully "occupier" of a dispossessed people. The press and the schools in the Arab world are conducting an intensive campaign to poison the minds, beginning with children at a very young age, by peddling the most outlandish lies about the Jewish people. Suicide bombers of Israeli citizens are hailed as heroic martyrs assured of a privileged place in heaven.

The upshot is not only that Israel is demonized in the Arab world but that even in the free West public opinion has turned against Israel. Now there exists a widely held perception that Israel and the U.S., as the one nation that has stood with Israel, are a major threat to peace. Following are a few blatant instances of media bias that could be multiplied many times.

THE PLIANT MEDIA

The Jenin "massacre." In April 2002 the Israeli military was determined to destroy the Palestinian haven of terrorists and suicide bombers embedded in the Palestinian refugee camp in Jenin. Immediately the

British and other major news outlets were filled with horror stories of wanton destruction and the indiscriminate murder by Israeli soldiers of hundreds of innocent civilians. The Guardian's editorial on April 17, 2002 likened Israel's action in Jenin to the 9/11 attack on the U.S. The same paper carried this headline on May 6: "How the Jenin Battle Became a Massacre." The mighty BBC trumpeted the same charges. However, none of these reports were verified. When the smoke of the media's smear campaign lifted, it was revealed that 56 people had been killed, mostly in bitter house-to-house fighting, 23 of whom were Israeli soldiers. (That number included 13 who were drawn into an ambush by women who pretended to plead for help from the soldiers.) But the damage in demonizing Israel had been done.

Tuvia Grossman. His picture appeared in the *New York Times* on September 30, 2000, bloodied and scared with a club-wielding Israeli policeman hovering over him. Another young Palestinian victim of Israeli brutality. That's what the caption said below the picture that was flashed across the world. In fact, he was a 20-year old Jewish student from Chicago studying in Jerusalem. If the policeman had not intervened, Grossman would have been killed by a mob of some 40 Palestinian thugs. He spent ten days in a Jerusalem hospital, then returned to Chicago where he was confined to a wheel chair for five months. The photographer who snapped the picture obviously was not interested in the truth, nor was the photo editor of the Times. The Times apologized at the insistence of Grossman's father, but no apology can undo the harm done to Israel's reputation.

The Qana fraud. Hezbollah has been hiding its fighters and rocket launchers among the civilian population in Lebanon – which is considered a war crime. Thereby it accomplishes two things that make excellent propaganda footage. It knows that Israel seeks to minimize civilian casualties and will hold back in its efforts to destroy Hezbollah strong-holds and weaponry. But when civilians are killed, as they inevitably will, Hezbollah can accuse Israel of war crimes. This charade played itself out after Israel destroyed a complex in Qana on July 30 in which some children died. But it was found that the pictures of the dead, some of whom were imported from elsewhere, were manipulated for maximum effect. Reuters dismissed the photographer responsible for this fraud, but the haters of Israel will continue to believe the doctored photos.

Stolen Money. Israel's military response to Hezbollah's rocket attacks and the capture of two Israeli soldiers has been disastrous for the Lebanese. But Hezbollah now poses as the caring provider for the displaced victims of the war. They are distributing thousands of dollars in American currency to all whose houses and other belongings were destroyed, making sure that television photos of their "generosity" are broadcast all over the world.

Hezbollah's fighters are indeed master propagandists, and more. Some who have had a careful look at the distributed funds insist that they are counterfeit.[131] How fitting that a terrorist organization pretends to help the victims of its own recklessness by doling out fake money. How bitterly ironic that even in this sham humanitarian action Hezbollah relies on, while degrading the financial resources of the country it despises.

Funneling the News. That Hezbollah manipulates the news is bad enough. What is worse is that many Western journalists are complicit in this fraud. They report the information provided to them without asking the hard questions. Nic Robertson, a CNN correspondent, has admitted that Hezbollah controls all access to information and carefully chaperones all journalists. He said that stories about Lebanon should be read with "more than a grain of salt." But none of the journalists permitted into Hezbollah territory have accompanied their reports with that warning.

Mike Wallace's infamous interview. Wallace has earned a reputation as a hard-nosed interviewer on CBS's 60-Minutes. But when he interviewed the Iranian president Mahmoud Ahmadinejad on

---

[131]Cf., David Frum, "Counterfeit News," *National Post*, August 26, 2006.

August 8 his approach was one of deference and admiration. This is the man who wants to wipe Israel off the map and recently addressed a frenzied crowd shouting "Death to Israel" and "Death to America." He heads a country that has lied about its nuclear program, has killed and imprisoned thousands of its own people, supports the Iraqi killers of American soldiers, while funding and enabling Hezbollah to kill and terrorize Israeli citizens. None of these facts were pressed by Wallace, and the two men got along fine, even engaged in some bantering.

The tough interviewer who would have roasted his own President Bush gushed that he was much impressed by Ahmadinejad. This is despite the fact that Ahmadinejad had humiliated Wallace by keeping him waiting in a Tehran hotel for almost a week before he was allowed into the presence of this imperial president. Wallace found Ahmadinejad to be interesting and more rational than he had expected. What comes to mind is this question: Whose side is Wallace really on?

A long-standing bias. The mainstream media prides itself on its impartiality. The truth is that its bias runs deep, and it seems that an extreme form of contempt for their own country comes naturally to journalists and commentators. They have shown a special attraction to the tyrants on the Left, and more recently for those who spew their hatred of the United States and Israel in the name of radical Islam. These enablers of tyrants are following in the footsteps of Walter Duranty, an admirer of Stalin in the 1930s, and Herbert Matthews whose favorable reporting on the young Castro helped to provide a cloak of respectability for another Stalinist Gulag.

An honest admission. Dan Rather, the retired CBS anchor ended his career in embarrassment when he used a fraudulent document to reflect badly on President Bush's military service record. To his credit, Rather recently admitted to serious, systemic flaws in the way the major networks report the news. In an interview with Bill O'Reilly he conceded that what is missing in most televised war coverage is "context, perspective, background, history, and analysis." When asked whether some American networks "give moral equivalency to Hezbollah in their reporting on the war in Lebanon, he responded: "I agree it happens. And I agree it's a problem. It's a problem that those of us in journalism have been reluctant to address. I do not exclude myself from this criticism." Reluctant to address that Hezbollah is a terrorist organization.

Radical Islam has declared war on the free West, but the West is internally so divided that it cannot agree on the real meaning of that declaration. That disagreement has now reached a point where many influential shapers of public opinion treat terrorists as people who are fighting for a righteous cause.

Similarly, tyrants who cruelly enslave their own people and threaten to unleash a nuclear holocaust on the one democratic and civilized nation in the Middle East, are treated as responsible, even respectable members of the international community.

I believe that this amounts to deliberate blindness toward an ugly reality. Unless such blindness is cured, I fear that Eric Hoffer's premonition mentioned at the beginning of this article may yet be realized.

The good news is that such a cure is available. But that will require, among other things, that the press become a reliable source of information rather than a propagandist for the Stalins and Hitlers of this confused and violent age.

22 The Jew-Hatred

That Is Incurable

We shall never commit a crime against them [future generations], the crime of permitting the existence of a racialist state in the heart of the Arab world.[132]

When you think that the savagery of people against other human beings has reached its limits, then something so foul happens that sends a shock wave of revulsion through the civilized world.

On the evening of Friday, March 11, two men breached a security fence and broke into the home of a Jewish family in the West Bank village of Itamar. They massacred the parents, Ehud (Udi) and Ruth Fogel, and three of their six children, Yoav (11), Elad (4) and three-month-old Hadas.

The killers missed two other children who were asleep and unharmed, Roi (8) and Yishai (2). The eldest daughter, Tamar (12) who was at a youth event, arrived home after midnight and found her

---

[132] Yasser Arafat, quoted in *Efraim Karsh, Islamic Imperialism* (New Haven, CT: Yale University Press, 2006), 180.

father, mother and three siblings dead or dying. She ran screaming to a neighbor's house who then returned with Tamar and alerted security personnel. They found Yishai crying over his parents' bodies trying to wake them up.

WORDS FAIL

Words fail adequately to convey the true horror of this unspeakable crime. How is it possible that men can become so filled with blind hatred that sears their conscience and causes them to commit such evil? *Jerusalem Post* editor and prolific author Caroline Glick manages to convey the depth of depravity to which these murderers have sunk:

> Ruth Fogel was in the bathroom when the Palestinian terrorists pounced on her husband Udi and their three-month old daughter Hadas, slitting their throats as they lay in bed....
>
> The terrorists stabbed Ruth to death as she came out of the bathroom. With both parents and the newborn dead, they moved on to the other children, going into a bedroom where Ruth and Udi's sons Yoav (11) and Elad (4) were sleeping. They stabbed them through their hearts and slit their throats.

Glick describes the released photos of the murder scene:

> There was Hadas, dead on her parents' bed, next to her dead father Udi. There was Elad, lying on a small throw rug wearing socks. His little hands were clenched into fists. What was a four-year old to do against two grown men with knives? He clenched his fists. So did his big brother.
>
> Some claim that the Al Aqsa Martyrs Brigades, the terrorist arm of Fatah, is responsible. There was rejoicing in Gaza with carnivals and distribution of sweets. A Hamas website praised the murderers. A resident explained the celebrations as "a natural response to the harm settlers inflict on the Palestinian residents in the West Bank. The Islamic Jihad Movement in Palestine called it "a heroic attack" that proves "the Palestinians are able to go ahead

with armed resistance and overcome all difficulties to reach the targets.

(Israelnationalnews.com has reported that two teenagers, Hakem Awad and his cousin Amjad Awad, have confessed that they murdered the Fogel family members. They showed no remorse and said that if they had known that there were two more children in the house, they would have killed them, too. They saw no problem in slitting the throat of three-month-old baby Hadas, since she was a Jew.)

DOUBLESPEAK

Some Palestinian leaders condemned this attack on a defenseless family. One editor wrote, "Stabbing an infant to death is a crime against humanity." Palestinian Authority (PA) President Mahmoud Abbas telephoned Prime Minister Netanyahu to condemn the attack. On Israel radio he called it a "despicable, immoral, inhuman act...." Others chimed in.

PA Prime Minister Salam Fayyad also denounced this attack. PA Foreign Minister Riyad al-Maliki denied that any Palestinian was behind this crime. Minister of Religious Affairs Mahmoud Habbash, in a telephone interview with the Jerusalem Post, stated that the Palestinians are against such crimes, saying: "We want to see all the civilians living in peace in the Holy Land."

But deeds speak louder than words. That applies especially in a part of the world where Palestinians send a different message in Arabic than in English. Here are five salient truths that make it impossible for the Palestinian leaders to escape full responsibility for the evil done on this black Friday.

One. The three opinion-shaping institutions in Palestine, the schools, the mosques, and the media, as well as politics, are used for the systemic incitement of hatred toward the Jews. (The killers of the Fogel family are products of this brainwashing.)

Two. The so-called peace partner, Fatah (meaning victory, conquest) is constitutionally committed to the destruction of Israel within the "world-wide struggle against Zionism...." It calls Israel's existence in Palestine "a Zionist invasion with a colonial expansive base..." (Art. 8).

Its goal: "Complete liberation of Palestine and eradication of Zionist economic, political, military and cultural existence" (Art. 12). Its method: "Armed public revolution is the inevitable method to liberating Palestine" (Art. 17).

Three. The refugee camps in Gaza, under the tutelage of the UN, costing untold millions and keeping four generations in perpetual dependency and hopelessness, are a major obstacle to establishing peaceful relations with Israel.[133]

Four. Overshadowing all these and other obstacles are 1400 years of Islamic doctrine and the example of Muhammad, declaring that the enmity between Islam and the Jews is an abiding fixture of history, unless the Jews convert ("revert"), are subdued into dhimmis, or are eliminated.

Five. The Qur'an and the Hadith are full of this doctrine. When Muslims address a Western audience, they tend to stress that the struggle with Jews is over territory and borders not their Jewishness. But when they speak in Arabic, they present a different message. Sheikh Yousef Al-Qaradawi, who is the spiritual guide of the Muslim Brotherhood, engages in such doubletalk. To a Western audience he said that the ``struggle between us and the Jews is over the land and not over their Jewishness." However, addressing a Muslim audience, he said this:

Jews are the greatest enemies of the Ummah (the worldwide Muslim community). And their enmity to Islam and Muslims has been, is and will continue as long as Muslims and Jews remain on this earth. This issue has been settled without question or argument as Allah says (you will find the staunchest enemies of those that have believed are the Jews...) Sura 5: 82. So the ever ongoing Jewish

---

[133] See Michael S. Bernstam, *Commentary*, December 2010.

enmity towards the Muslims is permanent through the testimony of the Noble Qur'an and fully embedded in the mind and conscience of every Muslim who believes in the Qur'an. His faith in this sense cannot be shaken by anything in this world.[134]

THE SOURCE: A POISONED WELL

All the major Islamist leaders, throughout the centuries, including Muhammad himself, as well as the Qur'an and Hadith have left a legacy that leaves no doubt about the permanence of the Muslim-Jew hatred. What follows is a small selection from these sources, as they appear in Al-Maqdisi & Solomon Al-Yahud:[135]

Sura 2:100, Sura 5:13. "Jews are covenant breakers, full of treason, vengeful…"

Sura 2:75f, Sura 4:46, "The Jews corrupted the scriptures…"

Sura 5:62, "Jews are lovers of transgression and sin…"

Sura 2:142, "Jews are vulgar and fools…"

Sura 1:7, "Jews are people on whom is the wrath of Allah."

Sura 2:65, 5:60, 7: 166, "Jews are those who were cursed and transformed into apes and swine…"

Sura 8:55-65, 98:6, "Jews are the worst of Allah's creation…" Muhammad the messenger of Allah said, "Do not greet Jews or Christians with peace if you meet one of them in your way then push them over to a ditch or a narrow path."[136] May the curse of Allah be on the Jews and Christians who took the graves of their prophets to be as places of worship.[137] "Muhammad said that "The hour will not come until Muslims fight and kill the Jews and the Jews will hide behind trees and rocks, and these trees and rocks will

---

[134] Alias Al- Maqdisi & Sam Solomon, *AL-Yahud: Eternal Islamic Enmity & the Jews* (Afton, VA: ANM Press), 16.

[135] Cf. 34-35, 38-39, 44.

[136] Al- Muslim Hadith, number 4030.

[137] Bukhari Hadith, number 3195.

cry out saying, O Muslim, slave of Allah this Jew is hiding behind me, come and kill him."[138]

When Muslim apologists, such as Karen Armstrong, John Esposito and Tariq Ramadan try to present Islam as a religion of peace, they rely on the widespread public ignorance about the Islamic incitement of hatred toward the Jews – and toward all non-Muslims. They do not quote these teachings but the few that seem to promote peace and tolerance, including Sura 2:256, "There is no compulsion in religion...."

Maqdisi and Solomon write that this technique is totally predictable– and utterly misleading, because the verses which would offer all the good things such as forgiveness, peace and tolerance were all abrogated during Mohammad's lifetime and thus are no longer valid.[139]

The harsh reality is that the fanatics and terrorists who have declared war on the West and especially Israel, are not hijacking Islam; they are acting in obedience to the thrust of the teachings of the Qur'an and the Hadith. Those who think that peace will be assured when the conflict about land and borders is settled are living in a dreamland.

The heart of the conflict between Israel and Palestine is about the right of Israel to exist in peace. On that score the West should let the haters of Israel know that an attack on Israel will be considered an attack on the free West. Israel is once again on the front line of the battle between freedom and tyranny, truth and falsehood.

We should stand with Israel, a nation surrounded by countries that have openly declared their desire for its destruction. We ought to do so for reasons of morality and justice, and because the future of Israel is our future, too.

---

[138] Al-Muslim Hadith, number 5203.
[139] Al-Maqudisi & Solomon, 22.

23 Israel Under Threat of Another Holocaust

Islam wishes to destroy all states and governments anywhere on the face of the earth which are opposed to the ideology and program of Islam regardless of the country or the nation which rules it.... [T]he objective of Islamic Jihad is to eliminate the rule of an un-Islamic system and establish in its stead an Islamic system of state rule (Abul Ala Mawdudi, 1906-1979).

The Israel-Palestine conflict has endured ever since the founding of the State of Israel in 1948. No matter how well-intended the facilitators, including American presidents, were in their attempts to resolve the conflict between Israel and Palestine, all efforts to that end were dashed on the rock of one stubborn reality: The Palestinian leaders, whatever they state publicly to the contrary, are convinced that the state of Israel is illegitimate and must be destroyed.

NO ORDINARY DISPUTE

Efraim Karsh, in his *Islamic Imperialism*, provides this insightful explanation:

In other words, the "Question of Palestine" is neither an ordinary territorial dispute between two national movements nor a struggle by an indigenous population against a foreign occupier. It is a holy war by the worldwide Islamic umma to prevent the loss of a part of the House of Islam to the infidels. "When our enemies usurp some Islamic lands, Jihad becomes a duty binding on all Muslims."[140]

This is the reason why the 1993 Oslo Accords went nowhere, and Yasser Arafat refused to accept the Camp David offer in 2000, despite the fact that he had obtained nearly every one of the Palestinian demands. He did not sign because peace would have legitimized the existence of Israel. In his words: "We shall never commit a crime against them [future generations], the crime of permitting the existence of a racialist state in the heart of the Arab world."[141]

The Palestinian position could not be more bluntly explained than in that sentiment, repeated endlessly in all kinds of documents, sermons, on the airwaves, and even in school text books aimed at the very young. The Iranian president Mahmoud Ahmedinejad has spelled out this position so that no one can plead ignorance: "We will wipe Israel off the map."

There are many ways in which the deep-seated hatred for the Jewish people and the nation of Israel continues to thrive. Meanwhile, Western public opinion refuses to take seriously the religious fanaticism that feeds that hatred. Ironically, many blame Israel for the violence, and they want to use the unrelenting pressure of world opinion, now given added credence by President Obama, to force Israel into more concessions – including those that would result in its destruction.

The prospect of Iran becoming a nuclear power places Israel before a terrible dilemma. The West appears no longer serious about stopping Iran's nuclear ambitions. At the same time, it demands that Israel treat its declared enemies as trustworthy negotiating partners.

---

[140] Efraim Karsh, in his *Islamic Imperialism: a History* (New Haven, CT: Yale University Press, 2006), 214.

[141] Ibid., 180.

The UN, in clear violation of its own founding document and led by a coalition of the Arab states, has consistently carried on a campaign of demonizing Israel as the worst human rights violator. This is despite the fact that Israel is the only law-based, democratic state in the Middle East where more than one million Arabs enjoy all the rights of citizenship, including the right to elect their own members in the Israeli parliament (Knesset).

Regrettably, the anti-Israel forces get a great deal of help from the mainstream Western media and academic world. The leaders of radical Islam and especially the Palestinians are masters at playing the Western media and intelligentsia. This is so much so that when Israel in self-defense builds a protective wall, sets up check points, or takes military action, it invariably is accused of killing innocents and using disproportionate force. All the while Hamas and Hezbollah hide behind civilians from which they send their rockets and suicide bombers.

A FEW QUESTIONS

What should Israel do? What should we do? We, that is, people of goodwill, who pray for the peace of Jerusalem and who wish nothing more fervently than that Israelis and Palestinians would live in freedom and peace alongside and with each other.

Once before in the 1930s, the West misjudged the character of the Nazi murderers of the Jews. Had the leaders of the free world understood the truth, they might have prevented the destruction of Europe and the slaughter of six million Jews.

Unless we begin to realize that the ongoing attempts to construct the road map to peace are built on a lie, we will not make any progress in preventing a recurrence of the Holocaust.

May God have mercy on us all.

24 Tarek Fatah Takes on the Jihadists[142]

Muslims are often criticized for failing to speak up publicly against those Muslims who have turned Islam into an ideology of hatred and violence. Tarek Fatah does not belong to that silent majority. On the contrary, his new book *Chasing a Mirage: The Tragic Illusion of an Islamic State* is a courageous and eloquent testimony against those who have turned Islam into a political program of conquest and stagnation.

Tarek Fatah was born in Pakistan where he was active in the late 1960s as a left-wing student. He worked in the print and broadcast media in Pakistan and Saudi Arabia. He immigrated to Canada in 1987 where he has become well-known as an outspoken critic of Islamic extremism. Here is a sample of his unambiguous way of presenting the problem:

Islam came to free humanity from the clutches of the clergy. Instead, the religion of peace has become a prisoner of war, held

---

[142]Orig., *Christian Courier*, Aug 10, 2009. Tarek Fatah. *Chasing a Mirage: The Tragic Illusion of an Islamic State.* Hoboken, NJ: John Wiley & Sons, 2008. Pp. 432. *Reviewed by H.A.*

captive by the very priesthood it came to eliminate. Muslims have been double-duped for centuries – lied to by their leaders and clerics who supposedly hold the keys to heaven (87).

After the attacks of 9/11 Fatah founded the secular Muslim Canadian Congress. He fearlessly argues that Muslims should reject the Islamic state in favor of the state of Islam. Chasing a Mirage is a masterful exposition of what the author perceives to be the enduring clash between political Islam bent on domination and spiritual Islam that enables the free flow of ideas and beliefs. Or as he puts it: "For it is only here in Canada that I can speak out against the hijacking of my faith and the encroaching specter of a new Islamo-fascism."

Chasing a Mirage is an excellent source of information about the early, violent spread of Islam, its internal feuds and divisions, and the contemporary clash between militant Islam and the West. He describes the attempt in 2003 to introduce sharia law in the province of Ontario, which failed in part because of strong opposition by Muslim women groups and the Muslim Canadian Congress.

ISLAMIST INFILTRATION

In early 2003 Fatah attended a meeting of some 2000 young Muslims at the Toronto Convention Centre. He was unprepared for a lecture by a Kuwaiti politician and member of the Muslim Brotherhood, Tareq Al Suwaidan, who told the audience: "Western civilization is rotten from within and nearing collapse... it [the West] will continue to grow until an outside force hits it and you will be surprised at how quickly it falls."

Fatah asks the questions that should haunt everyone concerned about the future of this country, especially our political leadership: "Why were these Muslim youth, born and educated in Canada, cheering the fall of the West? Did they not consider themselves to be part of the West?"

Chasing a Mirage provides a lot of details about the many organizations in Canada active in promoting a radical Islamic agenda, including the Council on American-Islamic Relations and the Muslim

Student Association. Fatah writes that these and other Islamic organizations are far more sophisticated than naïve Westerners recognize. He explains:

> These are well-oiled, foreign inspired, politically driven machines that have their hooks in every corner of Western society. It is not a coincidence that so many Muslims who were just average American teenagers in high school get recruited by radicals and end up emerging from universities with a deep-rooted hatred for the country that has been their home all their lives (313).

A CURTAIN OF FEAR

As this book makes clear, moderate Muslims have to battle not only their radical fellow Muslims. They are also up against the gullibility and naiveté of the Western mainstream, which often responds submissively to the aggressive Islamist agenda. This servile attitude – a form of voluntary dhimmitude – motivated 11 Canadian academics with roots in Iran, Palestine, Pakistan, and Bangladesh to issue a joint statement in The *Toronto Star*. They wrote that a curtain of fear has descended on the intelligentsia of the West, including Canada. Their fear to be misunderstood as Islamophobic has silenced them.

> Canada's writers, politicians and media have imposed a frightening censorship on themselves, refusing to speak their minds, thus ensuring that the only voices being heard are that of the Muslim extremists and the racist right.

Chasing a Mirage is a compelling testimony to the bitter truth about radical Islam and the blindness of the West. It also testifies to the courage and determination of the author, who has experienced first-hand the hatred and vilification of the enemies of freedom and civility. He has been threatened with death but refuses to be silenced.

As a Christian I do not share Tarek Fatah's faith, but I deeply appreciate his decision to publish this timely wakeup call. He deserves the profound gratitude of every freedom-loving Canadian for cutting through the platitudes and double-talk that now poison the public discourse about Islam

Part III: Truth-Tellers to Be Heard

25 Solzhenitsyn:

Prophet to the World

You shall know the truth, and the truth shall set you free (Jesus).

One word of truth shall outweigh the whole world (Solzhenitsyn).

We are all, each in his own way, bound together by a common fate, by the same bands of iron. And all of us are standing on the brink of a great historical cataclysm, a flood that swallows up civilizations and changes whole epochs.[143]

On Sunday, August 3, 2008, after a day of working at his desk, Solzhenitsyn felt ill, gave some final instructions to his wife and son, and then was gone from this earth. With that one of the bravest and indomitable voices for truth and freedom of the soul was silenced.

But his life's work of witness against the lies and depravity of the communist dictatorship lives on in his voluminous and soul-stirring

---

[143] Solzhenitsyn, BBC Interview, March 1976.

writings. It is up to us, the living, to ensure that future generations will remember and honour this exceptional witness of the truth.

HARD BEGINNINGS AND IMPRISONMENT

Alexander Isayevich Solzhenitsyn was born on December 11, 1918, in Kislovodsk, Russia, closely coinciding with the birth of a regime that would bring untold misery and death to the long-suffering Russian people. No one could then have had an inkling that this baby, born to an impoverished widow would, against unbelievable odds, not only outlive that murderous tyranny but also mightily contribute to its destruction.

Shortly before his birth his father died in a hunting accident, leaving his mother and an aunt to raise Alexander in harsh circumstances. They moved to Rostov on the Don where he attended school and early felt drawn toward a literary education. Lacking an opportunity to pursue that course, he studied mathematics, a turn of events, he writes, that twice saved his life – because his skills landed him assignments during his imprisonment that helped to ease his circumstances and enabled him to begin writing.[144] (See *The First Circle*.)

During World War II he served as captain of an artillery company on the frontlines until his arrest in early 1945 when he was sentenced to eight years in a detention camp for having insulted Stalin in a letter to a friend. After serving out this sentence, he was exiled for life to southern Kazakhstan, where he taught mathematics and physics in primary schools. In 1953 he developed cancer and nearly died.[145] During his recovery he became a Christian, helped by his discussions with a Jewish doctor, who also was a Christian convert.

---

[144] Aleksandr Solzhenitsyn, *In the First Circle*, tr. Harry Willetts (New York: Harper Perennial, 2009). His first novel, orig. published in 1968.

[145] Cf. Solzhenitsyn, *Cancer Ward*, tr. Nicholas Bethell and David Burg (New York: Farrar, Straus and Giroux, 2015). His semi-autobiographical work orig. published in1966

GIVING VOICE TO THE VOICELESS

Solzhenitsyn kept writing in secret, always fearing that his manuscripts would be found and confiscated. He wrote in his autobiography:

> During all these years until 1961, not only was I convinced that I should never see a single line of mine in print in my lifetime, but, also, I scarcely dared allow any of my close acquaintances to read anything I had written because I feared that this would become known.

That changed when in 1962 Khrushchev's regime began to relax some controls, and Solzhenitsyn was allowed to publish what soon became a sensation, *One Day in the Life of Ivan Denisovich*. This book was the first of its kind to be published in Russia, detailing the mind-sapping existence in the brutal camps. Above all, it was a testimony to the strength of the human spirit in dreadful surroundings. But soon the regime tightened the screws again and Solzhenitsyn became a non-person.

Meanwhile, he secretly worked away at composing his memoirs. Although the KGB managed to seize some of his manuscripts, he continued working on the massive three-volume *Gulag Archipelago*, which he managed to smuggle out of Russia and have it published in the West, beginning in 1974.[146]

The Gulag books are a detailed look based on Solzhenitsyn's own experience, as well as on the testimony of 227 inmates of the camps, at the horrors of the Soviet system, where millions of voiceless Russians were worked, starved and beaten to death. The appearance of this first-hand testimony of the brutality at the core of the communist system exposed the bitter reality: the communist regime was built on a foundation of violence and falsehood. At the same time, Solzhenitsyn's witness against this evil was suffused with his rock-like conviction that

---

[146] Aleksandr Solzhenitsyn, *The Gulag Archipelago* (London: Vintage UK, 2002).

this regime could not withstand the power of truth and therefore would eventually disintegrate.

Finally, the lost and beaten millions perishing in the death camps had found a voice. To realize that someone had succeeded in telling their story to the whole world gave new hope to a broken and abandoned people. In contrast, to the Kremlin masters this first-person exposure of the reality they so much wanted to keep hidden was a disaster that they desperately tried to avert.

Solzhenitsyn's survival and then the widespread distribution of his shocking revelations represented a mighty blast against what President Reagan called the "evil empire" and no doubt helped to hasten the collapse of the Soviet Union.

In 1970 he was awarded the Nobel Prize in Literature. He did not attend the ceremony for fear that he would be barred from reentering his beloved homeland. In his absence, Karl Ragnar Gierow of the Swedish Academy made the presentation speech in which he recognized Solzhenitsyn as one in the company of the great Russian authors.

EXILE AND RETURN

Four years later he was stripped of his citizenship and deported to West Germany. He lived for a time in Switzerland, then moved to the United States, and in 1976 settled in Cavendish, Vermont, where he continued writing and publishing a number of novels, a history of the Russian Revolutions (1905 and 1917), his memoirs on his stay in the West, a history of Russian-Jewish relations, and many other works. In 1994 he returned to Russia where until his death he continued his arduous work schedule, ably assisted by his wife, Natalia, and other family members.

As he had used his pen to fight the ideology and practice of communism, Solzhenitsyn was no less critical of the shallow and hedonistic notion of freedom now driving the Western democracies. It is exactly on that score that Solzhenitsyn lost many of his initial admirers and supporters in the West. For he never tailored his message to what they wanted to hear. The liberal elite looked on Christianity, which Solzhenitsyn had embraced, as a relic of the past and an obstacle to progress and true freedom.

Solzhenitsyn wrote of his conversion to the Christian faith when he lay on his bed near death, utterly alone, bereft of any external source of comfort. It was then that he felt overcome by an amazing sense of God's presence that flooded his soul with a super human peace. But at the same time, he came to the realization that evil is not just out there, in the enemy, but as he put it:

> It was on rotting prison straw that I felt the first stirrings of good in myself. Gradually it became clear to me that the line separating good from evil runs not between states, not between classes, and not between parties – it runs through the heart of each and every one of us, and through all human hearts.

A HARD MESSAGE

Thirty years ago, Solzhenitsyn addressed a crowd at Harvard on "A World Split Apart." The title referred to the split between two world powers, but he meant much more than the conflict between Communism and the democratic West.

He began by reflecting on Harvard's motto "Veritas" (Truth), which easily eludes us, and that in any case often is unpleasant and even bitter. The thrust of his message to the elite Harvard audience was that the seeds of the disaster that has befallen the Russian people are also present in the free West. Solzhenitsyn said that he discerned a kind of spiritual, moral sickness in the West that has ominous implications for its future. Here is a summary of the warning signs listed in his Harvard speech.

A Decline in Courage. This may be the "most striking feature" of the West, which has lost its civil courage. Such loss is most noticeable among the ruling groups and the intellectual elite. Although there are still many courageous individuals, they have no real influence on public life. History has shown that decline in courage is often the beginning of the end.

<u>Well-Being</u>. The modern Western states were created to cater to the popular desire for happiness, which has resulted in the welfare state. Every citizen is given maximum freedom and material goods. What has been overlooked is that the desire for ever more goods and a still better life gives rise to worry and frustration. Furthermore, when generations are accustomed to seeing their happiness in the good life understood in materialistic terms, why should they risk their life in the defense of common values? ("Better Red than dead.") An extreme emphasis on safety and well-being in today's welfare state "has begun to reveal its pernicious mask."

<u>Legalistic Life</u>. Western society is organized around the letter of the law. But this has given rise to applying the law in a manipulative way so that the moral rule is trumped by the desire to win at any cost without any self-restraint. A regime, such as communism, without any legal rules is a terrible one, but a society with no other standard than a legal one is also unworthy of man. It will be impossible to stand through the trials of our threatening age with only the support of a legalistic structure, for it will give rise to "an atmosphere of moral mediocrity, paralyzing man's noblest impulses."

<u>The Direction of Freedom</u>. Freedom is now seen and experienced as freedom for good as well as for evil deeds. Statesmen who want to accomplish something important will be confronted with many traps. The emphasis on individual rights has undermined administrative power, but what now needs to be emphasized is not human rights but human obligations.

Destructive freedom has made society defenseless against human decadence and criminality. While this speech was given in 1978, Solzhenitsyn showed real foresight in saying that when a government starts to fight terrorism in earnest, it is accused of violating the terrorists' civil rights. This tilt of freedom in the direction of evil results from the humanistic belief that there is no evil inherent to human nature. Instead, evil is seen to arise from wrong social systems, which must be corrected.

The Direction of the Press. Here too the emphasis is on the letter of the law, but there is no moral responsibility for deformation or disproportion. Every day the public is exposed to hasty, immature, superficial and misleading judgments. Thus, we see terrorists treated as heroes, secret matters pertaining to a nation's security publicized, or the privacy of well-known people intruded with the false slogan: "Everyone is entitled to know everything."

Enormous freedom exists for the press, but not for the readership because newspapers mostly give enough stress and emphasis to those opinions which do not too openly contradict their own and the general trend.

A Fashion of Thinking. Without formal censorship in the West, there has nevertheless developed a trend in which certain fashionable ideas always predominate in the media and literature. "This gives birth to strong mass prejudices, blindness, which is most dangerous in our dynamic era." This self-deluding interpretation of the contemporary world becomes a "petrified armor around people's minds." (Although Solzhenitsyn did not use the term, here he is obviously referring to what is now called "political correctness.")

Socialism. Although the West has experienced unprecedented economic development and prosperity, many living in the West are dissatisfied with their own society. Some of them have turned to socialism, but it is a false and dangerous current. The Soviet mathematician Shafarevich has written a brilliant book, *The Socialist Phenomenon,* showing that socialism in any type and shade "leads to a total destruction of the human spirit and to a leveling of mankind into death."

Shortsightedness. Many in the West believe that we cannot apply moral criteria to politics. But such a position implies that we mix good and evil, right and wrong, and that we pave the way for the triumph of absolute Evil in the world. The truth is that only moral criteria can help the West against communism's well-planned strategy. Without such criteria, confusion will remain, and we will not even recognize the enemy for what it is.

This explains the ignorance about the real meaning of the Vietnam War and the betrayal of Far Eastern nations that caused untold suffering and death to millions. American pacifists thought that they had won, but their contribution was to immobilize the nation's courage. It was the same ignorance that thought the Soviet Union was an ally against Nazi Germany. In fact, Western democracies helped to nurture the Soviet Union with a large number of admirers in the West as a "fifth column."

Loss of Willpower. The current state of the West is one of psychological weakness marked by a refusal to defend itself. Hence the possibility that the next war will bury Western civilization. How has such a sad state come about?

Humanism[147] and its Consequences. Solzhenitsyn asks: "How did the West decline from its triumphal march to its present sickness?" His answer is bound to alienate most if not all of the Western elite, because he traces the problem back to the prevailing view of the Western world as it developed in the Renaissance and the Enlightenment. This is the view that humans are supreme, self-sufficient, and therefore are not subject to any authority above themselves. Solzhenitsyn refers to this as "rationalistic humanism" or "humanistic autonomy," which can also be called "anthropocentricity."

While the Middle Ages had exhausted itself in repressing man's physical nature in favor of the spiritual, the Enlightenment took the opposite turn. Then the worship of man and his happiness became the goal by means of unlimited freedom in the use and control of the

---

[147] Not to be confused with humanitarianism, that is, seeking the welfare of all others. Here it refers to a philosophy of life based on the belief that humans are not bound by the divine law (secularism).

physical world. As a result, man's sense of responsibility to God has grown dimmer and dimmer, allowing evil to have free rein.

Karl Marx could say, "communism is naturalized humanism." He was right, and that is why the communist regime in the East "could stand and grow due to the enthusiastic support of an enormous number of Western intellectuals who felt a kinship and refused to see communism's crimes."

By placing our hope in political and social reforms, we deprived ourselves of our most precious possession, our spiritual life. Both the communist East and the democratic West are facing a crisis that can only be resolved by turning away from the current, dominant materialistic ideology.

Solzhenitsyn concluded his speech by saying that we have reached a turn in the road that is similar (in impact) to the turn from the Middle Ages to the Renaissance:

> It will exact from us a spiritual upsurge; we shall have to rise to a new height of vision, to a new level of life where our physical nature will not be cursed as in the Middle Ages, but, even more importantly, our spiritual being will not be trampled upon as in the Modern era. This ascension will be similar to climbing onto the next anthropologic stage. No one on earth has any other way left but – upward.

MIXED REPONSES

The liberal establishment, well represented in the audience, never forgave Solzhenitsyn for what it perceived to be a tongue-lashing by an anti-modern and anti-Western Russophile. The *New York Times* preferred the men of the Enlightenment to the "religious enthusiasts sure of their interpretation of the divine will." James Reston wondered whether Solzhenitsyn's exaltation of Russian spirituality did not reflect "a mind split apart." The *Washington Post* found Solzhenitsyn "very

Russian" and resented his promotion of a "boundless cold war."[148] And so it went.

On the other hand, many others were overwhelmingly in favor, and Solzhenitsyn is said to have received thousands of letters filled with admiration and enthusiastic support.

Controversy, not surprisingly, has accompanied Solzhenitsyn, especially in his later years when his influence in his homeland began to wane. But he never lagged in his zeal to warn the West. In all his speeches, interviews and books directly addressed to the West he elaborated on the theme set out in his Harvard speech. He did so in his 1983 Templeton Prize address, "Men Have Forgotten God," in which he stated:

> All attempts to find a way out of the plight of today's world are fruitless unless we redirect our consciousness, in repentance, to the Creator of all; without this, no exit will be illumined, and we shall seek it in vain.

He expanded on this theme in more detail in his "Warning to the Western World," consisting of two interviews given on the BBC in March 1976. Here he gave numerous examples of Western cowardice and shortsightedness at the cost of millions of lives. He pleaded:

> We, the oppressed peoples of Russia, the oppressed peoples of Eastern Europe, watch with anguish the tragic enfeeblement of Europe. We offer you the experience of our suffering; we would like you to accept it without having to pay the monstrous price of death and slavery that we have paid. But your society refuses to heed our warning voices. I suppose we must admit, sad though it is, that experience cannot be transmitted; everyone must experience everything for himself.

---

[148] Michael Scammel, *Solzhenitsyn: A Biography* (New York: W W Norton & Co Inc., 1984), 96.

A COMPELLING QUESTION

Solzhenitsyn was a mere human with all his faults and failings. He was often wrong, as when he compared NATO with Hitler's Nazis, and he grossly misjudged the character of Vladimir Putin. But he was right about the most momentous issue now facing the world. He forced us to face this question, as phrased by his biographer Michael Scammel: "Is this [the disaster of the Soviet regime] a temporary aberration of European culture...or the beginning of the end, the start of a general collapse of our civilization into barbarism."

Solzhenitsyn's answer was clear and unequivocal. What gave his message its unassailable force is that he spoke to us from the hellish crucible of the Soviet death camps. His message to us in the West was: "Look what happened when a godless regime takes over. Let our experience teach you not to continue on your current path of trying to live without God."

Some want to turn a blind eye to the threats facing our world. Others deny that there is a problem. Then there are the pessimists who think it is hopeless anyway, so let's eat, drink and be merry, for tomorrow we die. All of them dismiss Solzhenitsyn as a nuisance who can safely be ignored.

May I suggest that the right way to assess the life and work of Solzhenitsyn is to recognize it as a sign that God has not given up on this world. This powerful voice appearing from under the rubble of a ruined civilization is a living proof that Evil cannot ultimately destroy the Good. This is so because God so loved the world that he sent his Son into the world not to condemn it but to save it.

That this former atheist was used by God to confront the whole world with this truth must be one of the great wonders of this tumultuous age. The big question is: Do we have eyes to see and ears to hear?

26 Zwemer: A Man to Remember

In this century, not many have lived who had the talent and drive of Samuel Zwemer. During his lifetime he exerted a tremendous influence on the Christian mission to Islam, as well as the worldwide advance of the Church and the Gospel.[149]

One of the defining issues in the free West is its encounter with a radical version of Islam, which is diametrically opposed to the secular spirit of our age. Instances of such encounters between two very different ways of life are everywhere.

CLASHING CULTURES

A case in point is from a letter published in the *National Post*, written by a student at the University of Toronto, who had taken a course in the history of Islam. During a break in a lecture on sharia law, she chatted with a fellow student and told him that she thought that

---

[149] Robert E. Speer, cited in J. Christy Wilson, Jr, "The Apostle to Islam…" *International Journal of Frontier Missions*, Oct.-Dec., 1996, 106.

stoning people for adultery, or any other reason, was barbarous and uncivilized. She continued:

> His response was to assure me that things weren't so bad anymore because the Qur'an permits a sentence of 80 lashes to be substituted for the stoning penalty. He apparently thought I would consider flogging to be civilized. Feeling very cold, I asked him if he thought a person who had been raped should also be lashed. He smiled and shrugged his shoulders. I felt sick.[150]

This student's experience underscores the need for knowing how we should indeed respond to radical Islam. One problem is that there is much confusion as well as denial about the real nature of Islam. Some think that radical Islam is a corruption of true Islam, which at heart, they say, is a religion of peace.

That confusion even exists within the broader Christian community, where many insist that Islam and Christianity have much in common. How to get clarity in this dilemma? How and where do we find reliable guides or mentors who can help us obtain insight into a difficult and confusing subject?

Thankfully there are many, and the Internet can provide an invaluable service. In this article I want to single out one person who spent a life-time in Christian mission to Islam, traveled widely and lived for many years in the Middle East. He mastered the Arabic language and wrote more than 50 books about Islam. He became a teacher of generations of students whom he helped to understand Islam and inspired them to take part in bringing the Gospel to the Muslim world.

REACHING OUT TO ISLAM

Samuel M. Zwemer was born into a Dutch immigrant family in 1867, in Vriesland, Michigan, where his father was pastor in the Reformed

---

[150] *National Post*, Nov. 23,

Church in America. Early in his studies at Hope College and then New Brunswick Seminary, he decided to become a missionary to the Arab world. In 1888 there were no existing American Christian mission organizations to the Muslim world. That was the year Zwemer and a few like-minded students started the Arabian Mission, which served as a springboard for a much-expanded Christian mission effort.

Zwemer completed his seminary training and was ordained in 1890, when he traveled to Beirut to begin his study of the Arabic language.

From there he traveled to Cairo, where he together with a few others explored various options open to them. They decided to start their mission work in Basra (which is in current Iraq) where he worked for six years. There he married Amy Wilkes, a trained missionary nurse from Australia.

They began a new mission station in Bahrain, which was then a British-held island in the Persian Gulf. While there, Zwemer wrote the first of his numerous books, *Arabia: The Cradle of Islam*,[151] which went through four editions between 1900 and 1912.

He became widely known as a gifted speaker and writer. While on furlough in the U.S. in 1905, he was offered the position of field secretary of the Reformed Board of Foreign Missions, as well as the traveling representative of the Student Volunteer Movement, both of which he accepted.

The next five years were occupied with traveling and speaking at many conventions and other events. He was the moving force behind the first General Conference of Missionaries to the world of Islam, held in Cairo in 1906. In 1910, Zwemer participated in the influential World Missionary Conference in Edinburgh, where plans were laid to begin a quarterly publication called *The Moslem World*.

Despite his demanding schedule of travel, speaking and writing, Zwemer served as editor of this publication without remuneration for thirty-seven years, never missing an issue. His energy and capacity for

---

[151] H. Fleming, *Arabia: Cradle of Islam* (New York: Revell Company, 1900).

work must have been enormous. (We are also told that he had a twinkle in his eyes and a great sense of humor.)

In 1912, he began teaching at the Presbyterian Seminary in Cairo, the city where the oldest and most influential Islamic Al-Azhar University is located. In the next years he traveled widely to speak at numerous venues in North Africa. In South Africa he was able to address Christians in English and Dutch, and in Arabic at meetings of Muslims. He also traveled and lectured in India and Indonesia. He even traveled to China where he was invited to speak at mosques in several cities because of his ability to speak Arabic and his understanding of Islam.

While addressing conferences in 1922 in Algiers, Tunis and Sousse, Zwemer gave addresses on "Islam as a Missionary Problem." As reported by J. Christy Wilson, Jr., quoted above, Zwemer recalled the church fathers who had been there – Tertullian, Cyprian, Augustine – when North Africa was one of the greatest centers of the Christian church. At that time it had large churches, libraries and a Christian population numbering in the millions. Then came the tidal wave of the Muslim conquest in the seventh century. The libraries were burned and the churches were either made into mosques or destroyed. Populations were blotted out and North Africa became "The Land of the Vanished Church."

In 1929, Zwemer was appointed as professor of missions at Princeton Theological Seminary where he taught until his retirement in 1938 at the age of 71. He continued teaching and speaking at training institutes, seminaries, conventions and churches where he taught and inspired large numbers. In 1946, Zwemer was a keynote speaker at the first Inter-Varsity Student Foreign Mission Fellowship Convention held in Toronto.

At age 83, Zwemer attended the 60th anniversary celebration in Kuwait of the mission to the Muslim world he had founded. In early 1952, he suffered a heart attack after he delivered three addresses at a meeting of the Inter-Varsity Christian Fellowship in New York City. He died on April 2, 1952, and after a memorial service held in the First Presbyterian Church in New York City, his body was transported to Holland, Michigan, where it was buried in the family burial plot.

A RICH LEGACY

The life of this deeply committed and gifted servant of the Lord who labored diligently in a very difficult arena of Christian service was ended. But the fruits of his work in the lives of an untold number of people are beyond measure. Zwemer left a rich legacy of wisdom and insight into the religion of Islam – a topic that has assumed a new urgency for the West in an unprecedented way.

Much of his work is still available in the form of articles, books, archived volumes stored on the Internet, and biographies by J. Christy Wilson Sr., namely: *Apostle to Islam* (1953); and *Flaming Prophet*.[152] In addition, Roger S. Greenway, professor emeritus at Calvin Theological Seminary, has edited a volume of Zwemer's writings under the title *Islam and the Cross*.[153]

Professor Lyle VanderWerff described Samuel Zwemer as "a pioneer missionary of the Reformed Church in America and mentor to many mission witnesses to Muslims," who had challenged his readers with these words:

We must become Muslims to the Muslims if we would gain them for Christ. We must do this in the Pauline sense, without compromise, but with self-sacrificing sympathy and unselfish love. The Christian missionary must first of all know the religion of the people among whom he labors; ignorance of the Qur'an, the traditions, the life of Muhammad, the Muslim concept of Christ, the

---

[152] Cf., J. Christy Wilson Sr.: *Apostle to Islam: A Biography of Samuel M. Zwemer* (Whitefish, MT: Literary Licensing, LLC, 2011); and *Flaming Prophet: The Story of Samuel Zwemer* (Chester Heights, PA: Friendship Press, 1970).

[153] Samuel Zwemer, *Islam and the Cross: Selections from "The Apostle to Islam"* Roger S. Greenway, ed. (Phillipsburg, NJ: P&R Publishing Co., 2002).

social beliefs.... ignorance of these is the chief difficulty in work among Muslims.[154]

The collection of Zwemer's writings edited by Roger S. Greenway, Islam and the Cross, introduces us to the central issue in the meeting of Islam and Christianity and a fascinating discussion of the influence of Animism on Islam.

Zwemer writes that although the Qur'an presents Christ as one of the greater prophets, it does not recognize him as the Son of God, who came into the world to take upon himself the sins of the world. On the contrary, the Qur'an denies Christ's deity and his atoning death and resurrection. It calls those who confess this central teaching of the Christian faith liars (Surah 9:30).

In the chapter "Mohammad and Christ," Zwemer shows that Mohammad becomes in fact the Muslim Christ. Islam has coined 201 titles of honour for Mohammad, including some that suggest he is more than human, such as: "The Forgiver, the Perfect, the Light, the Interceder, the Truth, the Mediator, the Holy One, the Pardoner of Sins...."

St. Paul wrote that the cross is a stumbling block to Jews and Gentiles, yet it is God's way of reconciling sinful people with a Holy God. Zwemer urges his readers never on that account to consider Muslims our enemies, "but prove to them that we are their friends by showing not by our creed only, but by our lives, the power of the cross and its glory."[155]

A COMPOSITE RELIGION

Although Islam presents itself as the latest and infallible revelation of God, Zwemer shows that the practice of many Muslims is heavily

---

[154] Lyle VanderWerff, "Christian Witness to Our Muslim Friends," IJFM, July-Sept., 1996, 112.

[155] Zwemer, 53.

influenced by pre-Islamic pagan beliefs, notably Animism. The latter is the belief that inanimate objects possess souls or spirits, which can be evil or beneficent. Such spirits, both good and evil, are believed to be present also in all people.

Interestingly, in a discussion between Mohammad and his favorite wife Ayesha about just this topic, the prophet confirmed that evil spirits exist in all Muslims and non-Muslims, including himself. But he then assured Ayesha: "Yes but my Lord Most Glorious and Powerful has assisted me against him, so that he became a Muslim." (This exchange was recorded by Abdullahesh-Shabli, in what Zwemer describes as "the most famous volume of all Muslim books on the doctrine of jinn [spirits]."[156]

This collection of essays, preserved for us by Roger Greenway, first published between 1921 and 1941, contains a compelling message for us today. It gives us a glimpse of a godly man, thoroughly committed to the historic Christian faith and filled with the desire to show in word and deed the love of Christ to the Muslim world.

May this brief overview of the life and work of Samuel Zwemer whet your appetite to learn more from this wise and effective teacher.

---

[156] Ibid., 95.

27 Bachmann vs.

Ellison

I've come here in Cairo to seek a new beginning between the United States and Muslims around the world, one based on mutual interest and mutual respect, and one based upon the truth that America and Islam are not exclusive and need not be in competition. Instead, they overlap, and show common principles – principles of justice and progress; tolerance and the dignity of all human beings.... And I consider it part of my responsibility as President of the United States to fight against negative stereotypes of Islam wherever they appear.[157]

While President Obama beavered away at fundamentally transforming America for almost four years, as he promised/ threatened to do, nearly all the focus has been on healthcare and the economy. Meanwhile, the Obama Administration's relationship with the Muslim world was undergoing a far-reaching change that has not received the attention it deserves – thanks to the lack of critical reporting in the mainstream media.

---

[157] President Barack Obama, Cairo University, June 4, 2009.

Those who want to cast some light on these changes better be prepared for strong, even vicious opposition. Why would this be, especially since Obama promised that his administration would be a model of tolerance, transparency and impartiality? The reality is that his actions are in conflict with the promises he made during the 2008 election campaign. Deeds speak louder than words.

OBAMA'S NEW PRIORITY

Obama's speech in June 2009 to the Cairo audience, which included members of the Muslim Brotherhood, provides a telling clue to the radical changes he has in mind. The key sentence in that speech is the following: "And I consider it part of my responsibility as President of the United States to fight against negative stereotypes of Islam wherever they appear."

(As of this chapter's writing), we are now three years later, and the Obama Administration has imposed radical changes in its policies toward Islam. Five Republican Members of the House Permanent Select Committee on Intelligence, led by Michele Bachmann, have initiated a discussion about that topic. They have done so by raising questions about the vetting policies of Muslim staff members in key government positions and about the relationship between government agencies and radical Islamic groups such as the Muslim Brotherhood and the Organization of Islamic Cooperation (OIC).

The five have written to the Inspectors General of the Departments of Defense, State, Justice, Homeland Security, and the Office of the Director of National Intelligence. The purpose of these letters was "to request a multi-department investigation into potential Muslim Brotherhood infiltration into the United States Government."

Word soon spread about this letter, and Michele Bachmann was met with a barrage of vitriol and character assassination. Her fellow Minnesotan and the first (of two) Muslim Congressmen, Keith Ellison, was quick to attack Bachmann and demanded that she back up her request for this investigation with relevant facts. On July 13, Bachmann answered Ellison with a 16-page letter of explanation backed by 59 footnotes. Following are just a few of the items mentioned in the Bachmann letter.

She points out that government departments and agencies are advised by organizations and individuals that "the U.S. Government itself has identified in federal court as fronts for the international Muslim Brotherhood." She finds it a matter of "genuine concern" that despite this known fact, the U.S. Government continues to associate with these groups.

FAULTY INTELLIGENCE

On February 10, 2011, Director of National Intelligence James Clapper in his testimony before the House Permanent Select Committee on Intelligence, described the Muslim Brotherhood as "largely secular." He was obviously wrong and had to retract that statement.

In contrast to Director Clapper's testimony, FBI Director Mueller had this to say: "I can say at the outset that elements of the Muslim Brotherhood both here and overseas have supported terrorism. To the extent that I can provide information, I would be happy to do so in closed session."

In fact, the largest terrorist finance trial – the Holy Land Foundation trial in 2007-08 – had introduced documents that stated that the Brotherhood is engaged in,

a civilization Jihadists process .... The Ikhwan, the Brotherhood must understand that their work in America is a kind of grand jihad in eliminating and destroying the Western civilization from within.... The 9-11 Commission Report says we must address ideologies that give rise to Islamic terrorism.

...the Deputy Chief of Staff [of Hillary Clinton], Huma Abedin, has three family members – her late father, her mother and her brother – connected to Muslim Brotherhood operatives and/or organizations. Her position provides her with routine access to the Secretary and to policy making.

Bachmann insists that asking questions about highly placed U.S. government officials with known family connections to foreign extreme organizations is not to single out Ms. Abedin, since such questions are raised by the U.S. government of anyone seeking a security clearance. She wonders what standards were used for Ms. Abedin's security clearance.

The Organization of Islamic Cooperation, an international organization of 57 countries, is determined to impose sharia worldwide. The agenda of the OIC is well known. It claims to be the "collective voice of the Muslim world," the Ummah, and promotes the spreading of sharia worldwide. It interprets sharia law according to the "Cairo Declaration on Human Rights in Islam." This Declaration states in Article 24 that "all the rights and freedoms stipulated in this Declaration are subject to the Islamic shariah."

One of the objectives of the OIC is to safeguard the rights and religious identity of Muslim communities and minorities in non-member states. The 2010 OIC Observatory Report states that Muslims living in non-Muslim countries should not attempt to be assimilated since accommodation is the best strategy for integration. Bachmann observes: "In other words, Muslims should be allowed to live in non-Muslim states without having to necessarily obey its laws."

THE OIC'S WIN AT THE UN

The close ties between the OIC and the Muslim Brotherhood is not a secret. In 2010 and in 2011, the OIC organized "Islam and Muslims in America" conferences in Chicago, which were promoted by the Council on American-Islamic Relations (CAIR) where the keynote speakers were the OIC General Secretary as well as senior leaders of the Muslim Brotherhood front groups such as the Islamic Society of North America (ISNA). Both CAIR and ISNA were identified as Muslim Brotherhood entities in the Holy Land Foundation trial.

The Bylaws of the International Muslim Brotherhood state:

… the Muslim Brotherhood is an international Muslim Body, which seeks to establish Allah's law in the land by achieving the spiritual goals of Islam and the true religion….

It continues by mentioning:

the need to work on establishing the Islamic State…. Defend the (Islamic) nation against the internal enemies…. (These quotations from the Ikhwanweb.com have since been removed.)

Bachmann writes that allowing a foreign governing entity to maintain ongoing relations with domestic front groups has security implications.

And the evidence of collaboration between the OIC and the U.S.-based Muslim Brotherhood front groups needs to be investigated if for no other reason than to rule out what may reasonably appear to be questionable behavior from a national security perspective.

Bachmann also draws attention to the attempts of the OIC to use the United Nations for imposing speech standards on non-Muslim countries. In 2005, the OIC promulgated the "Ten Year Program of Action" calling for the UN to "adopt an international resolution to counter Islamophobia, and call upon all States to enact laws to counter it, including deterrent punishments."

KILLING FREE SPEECH

What may surprise many, Hillary Clinton as Secretary of State has played a major role in participating in the "Istanbul Process" aimed at implementing the Ten-Year Program through ratifying the UN Resolution 16/18. This resolution was drafted by Pakistan on behalf of the OIC and fulfills its objectives on defamation that the West had up until that time consistently opposed.

Secretary Clinton assured the OIC Secretary General that the U.S. would use "some old-fashioned techniques of peer pressure and shaming" against those who choose not to submit to the new speech requirements. Bachmann observes that for the U.S. to commit to a sharia-friendly agenda of speech control "in violation of the U.S. Constitution raises considerable concerns about U.S. sovereignty – concerns that must be addressed by independent authorities, such as the various Inspectors General."

The Islamic Society of North America (ISNA), an umbrella organization of American Muslim groups, is the largest Muslim Brotherhood front in the United States.

> There was sufficient evidence presented at the Holy Land Foundation trial to show that ISNA has an intimate relationship with the Muslim Brotherhood, the Palestine Committee, the terrorist organization Hamas, and the defendants in this trial.

The Muslim Public Affairs Council (MPAC) and Muslim Advocates, two civil rights organizations, "exercise influence in ways that align with Muslim Brotherhood agendas." They joined several other Brotherhood front organizations by signing on to a joint letter that called for the creation of a "White House" "interagency taskforce" to conduct a "purge" of counterterrorism training materials.

These same organizations met with the Department of Justice Assistant Attorney General of the Civil Rights Division to call for "a legal declaration that U.S. citizens' criticism of Islam constitutes racial discrimination." Bachmann writes that this "call to subvert the First Amendment should have been challenged by the Department of Justice, but wasn't. That is deeply troubling."

Requests by the House Judiciary Committee from the Department of Justice and the FBI for all of the case evidence submitted during the Holy Land Foundation trial have been fruitless.

Bachmann writes that other "shocking" incidents have occurred, including the State Department's decision to give a member of an Egyptian designated terrorist group a visa to enter the country and meet with National Security Council officials at the White House. This same person used this opportunity to call for the release of the "Blind Sheikh" Omar Abdel Rahman, who is serving a life sentence for his role in the 1993 World Trade Center bombing and other planned terror plots in the U.S.

CONCLUSION

There is much more in this letter that warrants attention, not only of American citizens but also of the rest of us, because we are directly affected by America's response to treacherous Islam with a smiley face.[158]

President Obama was obviously determined to interpret his task to "fight against negative stereotypes of Islam wherever they appear" so widely that he closes his eyes to the reality of supremacist Islam that is determined to establish Allah's rule everywhere.

The American election campaign was largely a distraction, preoccupied with slinging mud and spending millions of dollars on ridiculous ads. Meanwhile, political correctness serves as a cover for the Obama Administration to transform America by teaming up with people whose agenda is fundamentally alien to what is best about this country.

Bachmann and her four colleagues are raising an issue that goes to the heart of America's existence as a free nation. The fact that this took exceptional courage and that they have to brace themselves for the worst kind of slander tells a lot about the precarious state of America. At the same time, they have done a good and honorable thing, deserving the gratitude of every person who treasures freedom and truth.

---

[158]Cf., Andrew C, McCarthy, "Questions about Huma Abedin," *National Review Online,* July 21, 2012.

28 Wilders:

Provocateur or Truth-Teller?

...free speech is a fundamental right that is the foundation of modern society. Western governments and media outlets cannot allow themselves to be bullied into giving up this precious right due to threats of violence.[159]

Geert Wilders has become famous, or infamous depending on your perspective, for using blunt language to warn that radical Islamists are bent on remaking Holland into a sharia-friendly country. This issue came to a head when the Dutch parliamentarian decided to broadcast a 15-minite film, *Fitna*, in which he warns against the threat of a jihadist invasion of the free West.

Why is this stubborn Dutchman refusing to buckle under to the prevailing opinions among his peers? He certainly has not chosen the easy way. In fact, he has been subjected to an outbreak of threats and

---

[159] Peter Hoekstra, *Wall Street Journal*, March 26, 2008.

character assassination that has caused himself and his family a great deal of grief and hardship.

Most disturbingly, he has received many death threats, and for more than three years has lived under 24-hours a day police protection. He has been greatly constrained in his freedom of movement. And that in the freedom-loving and ultra-liberal Holland! What's wrong with this picture?

APPEASEMENT OR CONFRONTATION?

Wilders has long been a thorn in the side of those peace-loving and laid-back elite in Holland who believe that they are able to handle the problem of Muslim integration with dialogue and tolerance. They believe that appeasement is good, confrontation is bad. So they reject the advice of those who, like Ayaan Hirsi Ali and Geert Wilders, argue that the radicals who preach hatred and world domination in the name of Allah should be taken at their word – and confronted to their faces.

The appeasers are turning things around and accuse the likes of Wilders of needlessly provoking the rightful anger of Muslims. We now have the topsy-turvy world in which those who warn against capitulating to threats of violence are accused of being the cause of violence. It is an ironic confirmation of their warnings against radical Islam that Wilders now must live in fear of his life.

Things have gone so far that like the Anglican Archbishop Rowan Williams in Great Britain, the former Dutch minister of justice, Piet Hein Donner, said in 2006 that in future Holland may well have to accept sharia, that is, Islamic law. Wilders will have none of such surrenderist talk.

He has pointed out that he has no problem with Muslims who respect Dutch law and language and are willing to live in peace with their neighbors. His criticism is aimed at those who on the basis of warlike passages of the Qur'an use violence and the threat of violence to bring about a radical change in Holland and other western countries.

In a hard-hitting speech in the Dutch Parliament on March 20 Wilders castigated his colleagues for ignoring the presence of Muslims in Holland who promote an extremist version of Islam. He cited a number of verses from the Qur'an, which refer to Jews as pigs and monkeys and to non-Muslims as enemies that are bound for hell and must be subjugated or destroyed.

He pointed out that such verses violate Dutch law and should therefore be declared illegal. He said that Islam is not only a religion but also a political ideology that seeks to replace political pluralism with a one-party state. Wilders said: "Islam is an ideology without any respect for others; not for Christians, not for Jews, not for non-believers and not for apostates. Islam aims to dominate, subject, kill and wage war." He concluded his speech with an appeal to Prime Minister Jan Peter Balkenende to reverse the influx of radical Muslims into the country, by among other things, closing their schools, stop the building of new mosques, ban burkas and the Qur'an and expel all criminal Muslims from the country. He told the Prime Minister: "Accept your responsibility! Stop Islamification!"

What really antagonized his detractors was his announced plan to issue a film showing the killings and destruction inflicted by Islamic terrorists. His colleagues, including members of the Dutch cabinet, warned that such a film would antagonize Muslims all over the world and might endanger Dutch society and its relations to the Muslim world, with potential damage to Holland's international trade.

The Dutch cabinet looked for ways to stop Wilders in his tracks, but could not find a legal way to do so. The Prime Minister pleaded with Wilders to cancel his film, warning that Wilders would be responsible for any violence after the film's release. He said, "We believe it serves no purpose other than to offend." Dutch government officials even took up contact with some Muslim countries to do preemptive damage control by disavowing Wilders.

MORE THREATS

The leading Egyptian Sunni cleric Sheikh Muhammad Sayyed Tantawi (who has sanctioned jihad against American forces in Iraq and suicide bombings against Israeli citizens) has demanded that the Dutch government take action against Wilders and that protecting Wilders "will negatively affect Egyptian-Dutch relations."

The Grand Mufti of Syria has warned the European Parliament that the film may result in "violence and bloodshed" for which "Wilders will be responsible." The U.N. Secretary-General Ban Ki-Moon has condemned the film, calling it "offensively anti-Islamic."

In Afghanistan, the very country where Dutch soldiers are risking their lives to liberate it from tyranny, Muslims have been burning Dutch flags and threatened to eject the Dutch. The Iranian head of the National Security and Foreign Policy Commission has promised widespread protest, and warned: "If Holland will allow the broadcast of this movie, the Iranian Parliament will request to reconsider our relationship with it." (Think oil supplies from the Middle East on which Holland and all Europe is dependent.)

It wasn't enough that many Western leaders ganged up with Muslim opponents of free speech to stop Wilders from airing his film. The prominent Dutch journalists Henk Hofland joined in condemning Wilders, but he also advised the Dutch government to withdraw state protection from Wilders, thus throwing him to the wolves. Hofland wrote: "Let him feel what it is like for those whose lives he endangers." Echoing the Prime Minister, he said that any murders committed in protest against Wilders' film would be the latter's responsibility.

Words fail to adequately describe the depth of cowardice and treachery implied in such craven advice. But it does indicate that the rot has gone deep in Dutch culture. This is not about whether Wilders is right about every point he makes. In fact, he is totally unnuanced and sometimes over the top in his analysis and recommendations. For example, he does not appear to allow for the reality that there are many

Muslims who are peace loving and civilized – though too few of them speak publicly.

DISTURBING IMAGES

It is safe to assume that no film has ever aroused the outpouring of so much vitriol and dire warnings of violence even before it was shown. The showing itself had a rocky start. Wilders had difficulty finding Web servers willing to take it on. Liveleak, a British Website, first began to post the film, then withdrew it the following day, stating that its staff and their families had received threats of a very serious nature.

That did not stop the film from becoming available. Others, including Google Video and YouTube, began posting it. And on March 30 Liveleak reposted the film. They explained that first they had no choice in canceling because of death threats against their staff, but since security had been improved, they now felt free to post the controversial film again. By now, millions have had the opportunity to see it.

It is a disturbing film in that it provides graphic pictures of horrific mass murders, such as occurred on 9/11. It includes a clip of a telephone exchange with a doomed woman hopelessly trapped in the inferno of the collapsing buildings. Her agonizing pleas for help are unforgettable. There are similarly disturbing pictures of the attacks on Madrid and London, the murder of Theo Van Gogh, and the sound of a dying man whose throat is cut.

Other pictures show a burka-clad woman being shot in the head, the hanging of homosexuals, a three-year old girl who is taught that Jews are pigs and monkeys, and crowds shouting their agreement with various ranting imams pouring out their hatred against the wicked infidels and the coming destruction of Israel and America. Demonstrators (in England) are holding signs that say: "God bless Hitler"; "Freedom go to Hell"; and "Islam will dominate the world."

There is nothing in this film that does not reflect reality. Many, if not all the pictures, have been available on the Internet and some have appeared on the Al Jezeera channel. But perhaps most offensive to Islamic fanatics is the way violent Qur'anic verses are juxtaposed with horrific scenes of death and destruction while celebrating crowds scream their praises of Allah.

If this film shows reality, what is the problem? We know why the fanatics object and try to change the subject by demonizing Wilders and declaring a fatwa against him. But why would so many leaders in the West side with his detractors? Even Dutch churches have joined the chorus of condemnation.

A coalition of Protestant churches, the Council of Churches, and two Muslim contact organizations (the CMO and CGI) in the Netherlands, even before the film had been posted, expressed their "great concern" about it. They wrote that it has "aroused unnecessary conflict for which there is no reasonable occasion whatever. Expressions that incite fear for Islam and Muslims work destructively."

In their view it is "reprehensible if the sacred (elements) in our religions are ridiculed and our faith offended. We therefore forcefully reject it if the Qur'an and the Prophet Mohammed are treated with contempt and slandered."

A COUNTRY IN TROUBLE

The mind boggles. What Wilders has done is to tell the truth about the hatred and suffering spread by the jihadists who are convinced that it is their religious duty to spread Islam by force and indoctrination. Do these Christians not know that many thousands, perhaps millions of fellow Christians living in Muslim countries, are persecuted, forbidden to practice their faith, imprisoned, and killed in the name of Allah? Do they not realize that it is Muslims who ridicule and offend their Christian faith?

How heartbreaking it must be for such persecuted Christians to hear that Christian leaders in the free West side with their oppressors. At least one Dutch academic, the Arabist Hans Jansen, has registered his objection. He found the behavior of the churches as well as the Christian Democratic party (CDA) "incomprehensibly indulgent and naïve." He asked: "Don't they even have an intern in the party who could look up what happened with the church under Islam?"

What hope is there for a country where its spiritual leaders betray their own flock by their refusal to face the ugly truth and then compound their betrayal by vilifying the one person who has the courage of his conviction to tell the truth – and to do so at great cost to his own peace of mind, even at the risk of his life?

The bitter controversy swirling around this film goes to the heart of what it means to be human and to live peaceably with one another. It is not really about the person of Geert Wilders. You may like him or not. He may be arrogant or humble, right or wrong about many things. But he is right about the core message of this film: those who love death rather than life in the cause of Allah need to be exposed for the deadly menace they are. And when a member of the government is treated as a pariah and forced to lead the life of a fugitive in his own country for simply speaking the truth, such a country is in very serious trouble.

This story is filled with numerous sad ironies and missed opportunities. Here is one more: When non-Muslims lose their critical faculties and their courage, they also make life more difficult for those Muslims who reject the jihadists and want to reform Islam from within. One such person is a Muslim member of the Dutch cabinet, Ahmed Aboutaleb, who in a recent television interview advised his fellow Muslims:

> Muslims must think about the fear generated by their religion. The majority [of Muslims] remain silent and that is not good. We have chosen for the Netherlands, precisely because of the freedom here. This has to be said. I miss the [Muslim] voice that distances itself from extremism.

Let's hope that the good sense of this Muslim will still win the day over the cowardice of the political and spiritual leadership of this troubled country.

29 The Shadow Party[160]

This book describes forces at work behind the surface of political events, which seek to remake America as a radical utopia. They are driven by the belief that American "hegemony" (as they like to describe it) is harmful and its purposes oppressive. In the name of globalism, they would deny America its nationhood, character and culture. Theirs is a party – a Shadow Party – that is subversive of the American idea itself (xv).

This is a riveting story of the behind-the-scenes manipulations in American politics. It provides a surprising – make that shocking and well-documented look at the rise of the Shadow Party and its main instigators who are determined to radically change America, as its authors explain.

PLANNING THE REVOLUTION

The leaders of this revolutionary movement are convinced that action is needed at two levels, pressures from below and from above. The latter takes place by political action in Congress and all other branches

---

[160] David Horowitz and Richard Poe. *The Shadow Party: How George Soros, Hillary Clinton, and Sixties Radicals Seized Control of the Democratic Party.* Nashville, TN: Thomas Nelson, 2006. Pp. 280. Reviewed by H.A.

of government. Getting out the "right" voters and expanding the role of government are crucial to the success of their plans.

The pressure from below is to fill the streets with rioters and protestors to create the impression that the demanded changes are popular and inevitable. (The books and articles of Frances Piven and Richard Cloward, e.g., Poor People's Movements, have taught many the fine art of persuasion by intimidation and thuggery.)

Saul Alinsky (1909 – 1972) was another expert in teaching his followers how to galvanize the poor and other minorities into action and to mobilize them for the revolution in America. He believed that radical change requires the infiltration of institutions with roots in the community, such as churches, unions, and local political machines.

But he also knew that even if all the poor people would organize, that would not be enough to get the radical changes he wanted. What is also needed is to win support among the white majority, and for that he needed middle class activists such as Hillary Clinton, whom he saw as "potential emissaries to the America heartland" and as "middle-class guerrillas"(56-57).

Hillary Clinton was much impressed by Alinsky's ideas and they kept in touch until his death in 1972. She devoted her 1969 senior thesis at Wellesley College to Alinsky, in which she praised his ideas and included excerpts from his not-yet-published Rules for Radicals. In the foreword of this book, Alinsky pays tribute to Lucifer as the first radical who won his own kingdom.

Alinsky and the Piven and Cloward team have taught their followers to manipulate left wing activists into positions of power and to overload the welfare departments in the cities. Their greatest success occurred in New York City under Mayor John Lindsay. He caved in after mass rallies and other public demonstrations. The welfare rolls expanded enormously, and New York City went effectively bankrupt in 1975. The radicals gloated about their success. But what they really accomplished was an economic disaster for American taxpayers and for millions of poor who became locked into a cycle of welfare dependency.

The Shadow Party is not widely known because it is not a party as commonly understood, but an expansive network of front groups that supposedly are independent of any party. In fact, they are used to getting around the limits imposed by the McCain-Feingold legislation on fund raising by political parties. They also claim that they are not engaged in electioneering for a particular party, but the reality is that their actions are intended to benefit only the Democratic Party.

Though the Shadow Party indeed lives in the shadow, its front organizations are well known. They include the so-called Seven Sisters: MoveOn.org, Center for American Progress, America Votes, America Coming Together, The Media Fund, Joint Victory Campaign 2004, and The Thunder Road Group LLC. There are many more, including ACORN.

WHO IS GEORGE SOROS?

Horowitz and Poe write that the founding of the Shadow Party occurred on July 17, 2003, when "a team of political strategists, wealthy donors, left-wing labor leaders and other democratic activists" met at George Soros' estate on Long Island, where a total of $23 million was pledged to rejuvenate America Coming Together (ACT).

Soros announced its founding in an interview with a Washington Post reporter in November 2003. To underscore that this organization was serious about changing America, he took direct aim at President George Bush by declaring: "America under Bush is a danger to the world. Toppling Bush is the central focus of my life... a matter of life and death. And I am willing to put my money where my mouth is."

George Soros is a Hungarian-born Jew who survived the Nazi occupation, studied and worked in England, and moved to the U.S. in 1956, where he thrived as an astute investor and financial manager. Forbes estimates Soros to be the 29th richest person in the world with a net worth of US$7.2 billion; since 1979 he has given away $5 billion in America and many other countries.

In September 1992 Soros became known as "the man who broke the Bank of England" when he forced the Bank to devalue the pound sterling. The UK Treasury estimated the cost of "Black Wednesday" to be 3.4 billion pound sterling. Horowitz and Poe write that this devaluation launched a "tsunami of financial turmoil from Tokyo to Rome." Soros "earned" an estimated US$1.1 billion on this devaluation. Later Soros had this to say in his *Crisis of Global Capitalism*,[161] published in 1998: "When I sold sterling short in 1992... I was in effect taking money out of the pockets of British taxpayers. But if I had tried to take social consequences into account, it would have thrown off my risk-reward calculation, and my profit would have been reduced.

THE NEW LENIN

Horowitz and Poe write that George Soros is one of the most powerful men on earth. They call him "the architect and guiding genius of the Shadow Party, its 'Lenin'." Like Lenin, Soros excels in manipulating "economic and political forces at the highest levels." But he also resembles Lenin in diligently cultivating the insurgent forces from below."

On the surface Soros is a well-known public figure often in the news. Yet he remains elusive, and his goals are obscured "by a smokescreen of denial and calculated misdirection." In conclusion, Horowitz and Poe issue this warning against the danger Soros represents.

He has assembled an army of radical allies who have long been at war with the American system.... Soros has constructed a party, a Shadow Party, unlike any in American history.... [It] is more like a Leninist vanguard party, fully as conspiratorial and just as unaccountable. Moreover, it is a party improbably constructed by a financial tycoon, skilled at the manipulation of money and markets.

---

[161] George Soros, *The Crisis of Global Capitalism: Open Society Endangered* (New York: PublicAffairs;1998

As only such an individual could, Soros has woven his conspiracy out of institutional elements plucked from every level of the existing social hierarchy.... It is the party of rebels but also the party of rulers – a corporate unity of capital and labor. And it has been insinuated into the heart of the American system" (242-3).

This book opens a Pandora's Box of falsehood and treachery. It is not pleasant reading. But it is essential reading for all who want to know the truth about this dangerous attempt to remake not only America but the entire world. Such revolutionary attempts have never worked, but always resulted in unspeakable evil. This revolution will be no exception. The Shadow Party was published in 2006, and the instalment of Barack Obama in the White House has put the revolution described here in overdrive. Let the readers beware.

30 Seeking Allah,
Finding Jesus[162]

The greatest concern for me, were I to accept Jesus as Lord, was that I might be wrong. What if Jesus is not God? I'd be worshiping a human. That would incur the wrath of Allah, and more than anything else, it would secure my abode in hell.

These are the costs Muslims must calculate when considering the gospel: losing the relationships they have built in this life, potentially losing this life itself, and if they are wrong, losing their afterlife in paradise. It is no understatement to say that Muslims often risk everything to embrace the cross (252-3).

"He [God] has made everything beautiful in its time. He has also set eternity in the hearts of men; yet they cannot fathom what God has done from beginning to end" (Eccl. 3: 11).

---

[162] Nabeel Qureshi. *Seeking Allah, Finding Jesus: A Devout Muslim Encounters Christianity*. Grand Rapids, MI: Zondervan, 2014. Reviewed by H.A. Nabeel Qureshi was a member of the speaking team at Ravi Zacharias International Ministries. Nabeel struggled for a time with cancer and died at age 34. More information at: RZIM.org or nabeelqureshi.com.

We are living in times of great confusion and turmoil, and often have a hard time to make sense of what is happening in the world. It seems that evil forces of hatred and violence have free play to kill and destroy. This is what is happening in many countries where the religion of Islam is supreme.

Who can forget the video showing a man totally clad in black holding a knife towering over a bound and helpless prisoner whose life he will shortly bring to a bloody end? Or the video of the Jordanian pilot, caged like an animal, and burned to death? Just yesterday I received more pictures of similar killings, all of them by ISIS terrorists. The most chilling was a picture of a toddler, perhaps one year old, with three guns pointed at his little head. Oh Lord, how long are such unspeakable barbaric crimes to go on?

It is in such a time as this that the book by Nabeel Qureshi introduces us to a very different kind of Muslim believer. He was born into a Muslim family who had immigrated to America. His father's work as an American naval officer meant that the family had to relocate to different cities, and even spend some years in Scotland.

LIVING IN TWO WORLDS

Seeking Allah, Finding Jesus is a page-turner book about the challenge of living in two different cultures, secular America and devout Pakistan-rooted Islam of the peace-loving Ahmadi kind.

Nabeel's father (Abba) and mother (Ammi) took their faith seriously and taught him and his sister to love the Muslim way of life. They were a loving family, but that came crashing down when Nabeel decided, after much honest soul searching and intense study of the Bible and the Qur'an, to leave Islam and embrace the Christian faith. His parents felt betrayed and were heart broken. This was the hardest thing that also broke Nabeel's own heart.

This book gives us an inside look into his heart-rending struggle with conflicting forces that almost destroyed him. Yet it is above all a story of the victory of the love of Christ in the life of a gifted and humble servant of the Lord. Nabeel has a threefold purpose in writing this book.

One, to tear down walls by giving non-Muslim readers an "insider's perspective into a Muslim's heart and mind." Two, to equip you "with facts and knowledge, showing the strength of the case for the gospel in contrast with the case for Islam." Three, "to portray the immense inner struggle of Muslims grappling with the gospel, including sacrifices and doubts.... It is in the midst of this struggle that God is known to reach people directly through visions and dreams" (17-18).

Nabeel writes that there is a stark difference between the first generation of immigrants from the Eastern Islamic cultures and those born in the West, especially during the teenage years. He points out that this difference is amplified because of the difference between Western and Eastern notions of authority and truth. People from Eastern Islamic cultures generally depend on authority, not individual reasoning, to arrive at truth. Critically examining data to arrive at the truth is left to specialists, not the unlearned (80).

Nabeel's inquiring mind could not accept the requirement to depend on authority, especially when he befriended David Wood, a fellow student who was a thoughtful Christian. The two students began to discuss and debate each other's faith. That's how a new phase in Nabeel's life began with consequences that would fundamentally change his life forever.

BEGINNING DOUBTS

The discussion started when they were both staying in a hotel during a forensics tournament. Nabeel noticed that David was reading the Bible and that's how they began talking about the reliability of the Bible. As a Muslim, Nabeel had learned that the Bible was changed over time and therefore corrupted. But this first discussion with David caused him to reexamine what he had been taught about that topic. He was still convinced that the Bible was corrupt but he realized that he must go beyond the arguments he had previously heard (128).

After many discussions about the Bible and the Qur'an, they agreed that the truth of Christianity hinges on the crucifixion and the resurrection of Jesus. They agreed to meet with a few other Christians and Nabeel's father to discuss the crucifixion of Jesus. Such a meeting took place, but instead of confirming Nabeel's faith in Islam, it caused him to feel less secure about his faith. He began to suspect that he no longer was able to trust what his parents had taught him.

It was as if a veil of certainty was lifted from him and he was beginning to see the world in a new light. He writes: "Maybe, just maybe, I should start considering it a remote possibility that the Christian message could possibly be true" (154).

When Nabeel read the opening of John's Gospel he was struck by the inevitability that Jesus is God. Yet he could not believe that, because if that were true, then his family and everyone he loved were caught in a lie. "If Jesus truly did claim to be God, then the Qur'an is wrong and Islam is a false religion." He prayed to Allah to show him that Jesus is not God (179).

Another bone of contention between Nabeel and David was the Trinity, and the belief that Jesus is able to take upon himself and forgive the sins of man (substitutionary atonement). Yet gradually he was overcome with the reality of a loving God who forgives sinful people who are unable to bridge the gulf that separates them from a holy God.

Such a notion of forgiveness and grace is totally different from the Muslim belief that salvation is obtainable by doing more good deeds than bad ones. After another intense discussion with David about divine forgiveness, Nabeel began to grasp something of the power of God's grace who teaches us to call him "Father." He writes: "It was as if I was meeting my Heavenly Father for the first time. After having just confronted the depravity of my sins, His forgiveness and love was that much sweeter. This God, the God of the gospel, was beautiful. I was spellbound by this message. My heart and my mind were caught in the beginnings of a revolution (202).

TESTING MUHAMMAD AND THE QUR'AN

Nabeel was not yet ready to break with his Muslim faith. He agreed to further examine the role of Muhammad and the Qur'an in a meeting with his close friends and a few others. There he presented the story of Muhammad as he was taught by his parents and Muslim teachers, which is that Muhammad was a peace-loving, righteous and exemplary leader. But he was questioned about the reliability of the Muslim sources about Muhammad and the Qur'an that left him feeling that his presentation was unconvincing. He decided to take a closer look at the life of Muhammad and the reliability of the Qur'an.

On both counts, he was disappointed. He found that the Qur'an, instead of being from eternity and unchanged, had a much less solid foundation. Muhammad's first biography by Ibn Ishaq is based on a later biographer, Ibn Hisham, who altered the story of Muhammad's life as follows: "Things which it is disgraceful to discuss, matters which would distress certain people, and such reports as [my teacher] told me he could not accept as trustworthy – all these things I have omitted" (215).

Reading further in the Bukhary hadith 1.24, Nabeel discovers Muhammad's own statement that he had been ordered by Allah to fight against people and force them to worship Allah, "then they will save their lives and property from me." He also read that the greatest thing a Muslim can do is to engage in jihad. Bukhari explains that this is "religious fighting."

Nabeel is shocked to discover that the list of Muhammad's cruel deeds is long and cannot be justified or ignored. Especially after reading in the Qur'an and the Hadith that Muhammad had justified the raping of women whose husbands had been killed or taken prisoner, he comes to this conclusion: "That was more than enough. I was done. I could not think about it any longer. It was revolting, and thinking about it would cause me to despise my prophet and my faith. I would not allow myself to despise them, but I could find no way to excuse them either. So I was done. I was done fighting. I was finally broken" (245).

Yet his future was filled with doubt and fears. He did not know who he was or what he should do, now that he was bereft of the Muslim faith that had sustained him all his life. He is flailing for something to hold on to, but what? This is when his friend David told him to ask God directly, for if you ask Him to reveal the truth, He will (249).

A COSTLY DECISION

Nabeel knew the tremendous cost of a Muslim's decision to follow Jesus. It would mean immediate ostracism from the Muslim community and the forfeiture of friendships and social connections that had been built from childhood forward. It would mean dishonor to the family, as well as condemnation to hell!

In Islam, there is only one unforgivable sin, shirk, the belief that someone other than Allah is God. Shirk is specifically discussed in the context of Jesus in 5:72. He who believes that Jesus is God, "Allah has forbidden Heaven for him, and his abode will be the Hellfire" (252-3).

Nearing the end of the book Nabeel writes that the edifice of his worldview, all he had ever known, had slowly been dismantled over the past three years. This is part of his prayer to God:

Please God Almighty, tell me who You are! I beseech You and only You. Only You can rescue me. At Your feet, I lay down everything I have learned, and I give my entire life to You. Take away what You will, be it my joy, my friends, my family, or even my life. But let me have You, O God.

Nabeel prayed urgently for confirmation by a vision or dream that he had made the right decision by following Jesus. The Lord gave him one vision and three dreams, which he interpreted as a direct answer to his questions. In addition, his Bible reading about surrendering and trusting God gave him the certitude and the faith that leaving Islam and following Jesus was right.

The hardest thing Nabeel had to do was tell his parents of his decision. His father's eyes welled up with tears.... "To be the cause of the only tears I had ever seen those eyes shed, I could not bear it. Why, God...?" His father did not say much. "Nabeel, this day, I feel as if my backbone has been ripped out from inside me." These words tore through Nabeel and haunted him ever since.

His mother spoke even fewer words, but her eyes said more:

You are my only son. You came from my womb. Since you were born, I have called you my *jaan kay tuqray*, a physical piece of my life and heart. I cradled you, sang to you, taught you the ways of God. Every day since you came into the world, I have loved you with all of me in a way I have loved no one else. Why have you betrayed me, Billoo?

Nabeel writes that his mother's eyes "seared my soul and remain branded in my memory" (280-1).

I think that the author has succeeded in his three-fold purpose to provide insight into a Muslim's heart and mind; to bring facts and knowledge to show that the case for the Gospel is stronger than that for Islam; and to portray the immense inner struggle, sacrifices and doubts of Muslims grappling with the Gospel, while God sometimes reaches people directly through visions and dreams.

Readers will come away with a better understanding of the relationship between Christians and Muslims. It takes real courage, honesty, and above all love, to open up one's heart and soul to other people, as Nabeel Qurashi has done. Every Christian will be enriched and encouraged by reading this fine and heart-stirring book.

31 The Devil We Don't Know[163]

It isn't easy to figure out what is really happening in the turmoil of the Middle East. Is the Arab Spring really taking hold, or is it a case of one kind of dictatorship being replaced by another, perhaps a worse one? It's hard to know amid the conflicting claims of the various contestants. That's why this book by Nonie Darwish should be read eagerly by all who look for clarity about one of the most consequential and controversial issues of our time.

The author leaves no doubt about her position by beginning her book with this blunt statement: "Revolutions across the Middle East are rapidly unravelling before our eyes, telling us the sad truth that Islamic uprisings eventually crawl back to where they came from – back to tyranny." She then spends 225 pages providing the evidence for her position. Why should we believe her?

---

[163] None Darwish. *The Devil We Don't Know: The Dark Side of Revolutions in the Middle East.* Hoboken, NJ: Wiley, 2012. Reviewed by H.A. Orig., *Christian Renewal*, June 2012, "Arab Spring or Islamic Winter?"

Nonie Darwish speaks from experience, having lived her first 30 years in Egypt as a Muslim. Since 1978 she has lived in America, where she embraced Christianity. You might say that she has had a front row seat on the world-scale struggle between freedom and tyranny.

ESCAPE FROM TYRANNY

Darwish was born into a Muslim family in Egypt where her father was a military officer. He was killed when she was eight years old. She was able to obtain a good education, and became increasingly disconnected from Islam – which she began to see as a fear-driven religion that stifled all true cultural development. She and her husband immigrated to America in 1978, a move she described in her previous book, *Now They Call Me Infidel*,[164] as follows:

> During my first two years in America, my sudden exposure to the freedom of religion and social and racial equality in America made me realize to what degree Muslim society oppressed, shamed and manipulated its citizens.... Moving to America was like being catapulted to another time in history. America was not just a place for making money... it was a place for becoming a human being.

Especially after 9/11, Darwish began to speak out publicly about what lies behind that horrendous crime against America. The purpose of *The Devil We Don't Know*, she writes, is not "simply … to point out Islam's failures in order to tear it down." First of all, she wants to explain the revolutions in the Middle East and to expose the real Islam for what it is: "a belief system that will inevitably doom those revolutions. Islam and its sharia cannot coexist with freedom and democracy."

Darwish writes with candor about growing up in Egypt where she experienced the destructive impact of Islam on every aspect of life, including the most intimate aspects of marriage and family. She explains how and why the Islamic notion of sharia law, which seeks to

---

[164]Nonie Darwish, *Now They Call Me Infidel: Why I Renounced Jihad for America, Israel, and the War on Terror* (New York: Sentinel, 2006).

combine religion and politics, destroys all privacy, individual initiative and trust among people.

CRIES FOR HELP

Recently, the purging of Christians, Jews and Hindus all over the Middle East has been stepped up, though very few Jews are left. This is not the Arab Spring. Instead, Darwish calls it a "shameful ethnic cleansing" that is now hitting the Coptic Christians with full force. The elimination of these Christians is in keeping with the commandment given by Muhammad on his deathbed: "Let there not be two religions in Arabia." The goal is to turn Egypt into a pure Islamic state like that of Saudi Arabia.

Darwish points out that many are fearful of the future and would leave the Middle East if they could. Yet the support for Islam is still widespread, as indicated at the time of Osama bin Laden's death. There was no rejoicing about the death of this mass murderer. On the contrary, there were many eulogies to bin Laden on the Internet at that time. We should not underestimate the support that Islamic leaders enjoy because they are often seen as heroes in the vanguard of Islam. The most popular Arab TV station, Al Jazeera aired a program that was a tribute to bin Laden's life.

There is much talk about moderate Muslims' forming a peaceful alternative to the Islamists. Darwish is not so sure, because she says that there is no such thing as moderate Islamic scriptures that support peace, tolerance, respect for other religions, or loving one's neighbour. The very few verses of tolerance In the Qur'an have been annulled by the concept of abrogation.

Darwish writes that moderation is only in the minds of peaceful Muslims but not in their scriptures, and that is why their position is weak over against the Islamists. She believes that moderates are in denial by creating an image of Islam that does not exist. She writes: "That is why they expect a positive outcome, and every time a revolution occurs, their hopes are built up, only to be dashed by great disappointment."

The Egyptians who understand the real problem do not dare to speak up. Some of them are no longer Muslim believers, and now lead a double life of fear that they would be killed if their apostasy were discovered. Darwish receives many desperate appeals for help. One friend wrote:

> I feel extremely anxious at the out-of-control situation, the reckless violence that many are fooled into believing is justified. They are asking for renewal of hostilities and war with Israel. I do not believe they even understand the meaning of peace or war or the power of those they want to fight. They do not understand that their true enemy is Islam. Nonie, do you think I have time to escape this mess? I fear I will not leave this country alive.

Another apostate told Darwish:

> The situation is borderline mass insanity.... I want out but cannot get a visa to a Western nation. What can I do?" Here is another appeal in which the sense of helplessness and despair comes through very clearly: "Please help me. I've got to get out! I'm a Muslim and I left Islam and please, brothers, help me out from the prison of Pakistan.

A HOUSE OF CARDS?

In the chapter "A Muslim's Burden," Darwish lists a number of demands and duties that include the following: vengeance, reforming others rather than oneself, the sin of admitting sin, redemption in Islam, distrust of novelty and the other, criminalization of love and beauty, the duty of protecting Muhammad's honour.

Darwish points out that Islam has a built-in tendency of self-destruction, which it tries to prevent by making apostasy (leaving Islam) a crime worthy of death. To expose the misery and suffering, especially of girls and women, under such a system is to invite hatred and being demonized even in the free West.

Darwish is convinced that Islam cannot stand the light of truth about its violent history nor about its current efforts to establish a sharia beachhead by Muslim immigrants in the West. To succeed in doing so they must manage to persuade people that it is a good thing to forbid anyone from leaving Islam, and that those who do so are committing a crime punishable by death. Or they must hide the truth by deception and doublespeak (taqiyya).

This is why the Islamic leadership is sending jihadists and Islamists to work among the Muslim immigrants in the West to keep them from assimilating. They push the envelope to see how far the Western countries will bend to meet Muslim demands. The Western leadership is weak and divided with the result that Muslims have been successful in infiltrating all the vital institutions of society, including education and politics, even in the U.S.

Darwish believes that without expanding into the West, Islam is doomed to die as Muhammad himself feared. She predicts that unless Islam is able to conquer new territories, it will turn in on itself with revolutions, counterrevolutions and assassinations, which is what is happening now. It is like a Ponzi scheme which must expand to survive.

Western democracies have helped to extend the life of jihadist Islam by giving it an enormous degree of tolerance and respect. Will that goodwill prolong the life of Jihadist Islam? That is the question the West must face. Darwish is convinced that the right choice is to reject Islam as it is practiced today by containing and discrediting it. But for that to happen, "the West must undo many of its policies toward Islam and Muslim countries." How likely is that to happen?

WESTERN VULNERABILITY

Many in the West are confused about the Arab Spring because they do not understand that in Islam "freedom from oppression" means something quite different than what it means in the West. To many Muslims, especially among its leadership, it means life in the ideal Islamic state under sharia law.

The same problem of understanding key concepts in fundamentally different ways applies to all the other terms such as peace, justice, trust, tolerance, fairness and kindness. They mean something different in Islam than in our Western way of thinking, because our frame of reference is totally different. In the West there are still traces of Judeo-Christian influence, although that is in serious decline. When a Muslim says that Islam is the solution to all problems, he means what he says in absolute terms.

To put that negatively: There is no peace, justice, etc. outside of Islam where everything is regulated by what is written in the Qur'an and the other scriptures of Islam, including the sayings and actions of Muhammad. This conviction is the basis for the merger of religion and politics (mosque and state). In other words, the outcome is a totalitarian state sanctioned by religion.

Shortly after 9/11, Sheikh Raid Sallah, head of the Islamic movement in Israel, had this to say: "Oh, Peoples of the West… we say to you: We are the masters of the world and we are the repository of all good [in the world], because we are 'the best people, delivered for mankind'" [Qur'an 3:111].

This kind of Islamic supremacism is what feeds all the Islamic revolutions, including the Iranian in 1979 and the Arab Spring of 2011. Begun in high hopes, ending up, as Darwish puts it, "in the same mold of Islamic sharia." She thinks that by now people in the West should understand the dynamics of revolutions in the Middle East and the danger that Islam presents to the free world. However, the opposite is true, and she provides a raft of instances in America where the harsh reality of sharia is ignored or whitewashed.

ISLAM VERSUS TRUTH

Darwish is convinced that the biggest enemy of Islam is the truth. In fact, in sharia law lying and slander are encouraged if that is needed to advance the cause of Islam. That is why those who are considered enemies of Islam are portrayed as evil, such as the little and great Satans (Israel and America).

She herself has experienced the raw hatred of Islamists for speaking up about the truth of sharia, by being demonized, shouted at, and prevented from speaking at certain venues in America. She writes that America's freedom has given her the opportunity to discover and publicly proclaim the truth about Islam. Her greatest disappointment is that many Americans are blind to the truth and serve as enablers of those who want to expand the influence of Islam in America.

The road to discovering the truth has been hard for Darwish. It led her family in Egypt to completely cut all their ties with her. They broke with her not only because she left Islam, but even more so because she loves the Jewish people and supports the State of Israel. The ultimate act of apostasy in Islam is to "regard Jews as equally human and worthy of love" and to believe "that their culture, their Jerusalem, and their small nation deserve to be preserved."

Darwish thinks that the ingrained Jew-hatred in the Muslim world can be traced back to Muhammad's anger about the Jews' refusal to become his followers. One of his final instructions before his death was "kill the Jews." That's why sharia and ingrained Jew-hatred are inseparable. This will not change as long as jihad is one of the foundation blocks of Islam.

This is an extraordinarily fine book, written not in anger against all the evil done in the name of Islam but out of love for the author's estranged family and for those still in bondage to a cruel ideology of power and control. It lets the light of truth shine on a very dark subject that many would rather ignore or cover up with lies.

32 Nomad¹⁶⁵

This is an incredible, often heartbreaking, story of a noble and courageous woman who escaped the misery and abuse suffered by millions of women in the Muslim world.

Ayaan Hirsi Ali previously published The Caged Virgin and Infidel in which she explained why and how she escaped a life of virtual slavery under Islam. Nomad is her answer to a question she is often asked: "Is your experience typical and representative of life under Islam?" She responds:

> It is not only about my own life as a wanderer in the West; it is also about the lives of many immigrants to the West, the philosophical and very real difficulties of people, especially women, who live in a tightly closed traditional Muslim culture within a broadly open culture. It is about how Islamic ideals clash with Western ideals. It is about the clash of civilizations that I and millions of others have lived and continue to live (XIII).

Nomad is devoted to a discussion of her family members, explaining how most of them who immigrated to the West came to grief; her move from Holland to America in 2006 amidst political turmoil; the three most difficult areas confronting Muslim immigrants

---

¹⁶⁵ Ayaan Hirsi Ali. *Nomad: From Islam to America: A Personal Journey Through the Clash of Civilizations*. New York: Free Press, 2010. Reviewed by H. A. Orig., Christian Courier, Aug 9, 2010.

(sex, money, violence); and how to navigate the gap between a closed clan-based society and an open Western democracy.

ESCAPE FROM BONDAGE

Born in Somalia in 1969, she was destined, similar to her grandmother and mother, to marry someone selected by her father. When she was 22 years old, her father arranged her marriage to a distant relative who was a stranger to her. In "a kind of instinctive desperation" she decided to defy her father and flee to Holland where she applied for and received refugee status.

In Holland she was overwhelmed with the kindness and freedom she had never experienced before. She quickly learned the language, studied political science at the University of Leiden and worked as an interpreter for the Dutch social services. In 2003 she became a member of the Dutch Parliament where she specialized in immigration policies.

Ali is an outspoken critic of radical Islam and of Muslim immigrants who refuse to integrate and to respect the culture of their host countries. She cooperated with Theo van Gogh in producing a short film, Submission, about the oppression of Muslim women. On November 2, 2004, Dutch-born Muslim Mohammed Bouyeri murdered van Gogh. He left a letter on van Gogh's body in which he warned Ali that she too would be killed. (At his trial Bouyeri was unrepentant and said: "I was motivated by the law that commands me to cut off the head of anyone who insults Allah and his prophet.")

In 2006 the Dutch minister of immigration told Ali that she would be stripped of her Dutch citizenship, although that threat was shortly withdrawn. She resigned from Parliament, and moved to the U.S., where she joined the Washington-based American Enterprise Institute.

The largest section of the book is about her agonizing struggle to overcome a sense of fear, guilt and loss she experienced when she renounced her Muslim faith and brought shame to her family. Via telephone she kept in touch with her mother and father, though listening to their pleadings to return to Allah left her feeling empty and alone. Her father died in a London hospital where she visited him a few times when he was near death.

Ali has spent a lot of time addressing audiences all over the U.S., while being forced to live under 24 hour-a-day bodyguard protection. She discovered that many of her listeners were incredulous when told about the number of child brides, honour killings, and female excisions in Islamic countries, but also in the West. Most of her audiences have been receptive. But not at university campuses where she met well-organized and hostile opposition by members of the Muslim student organizations.

CHALLENGING THE CHRISTIAN CHURCH

In June 2007 she met in Rome with a Dutch priest, telling him that she was not a Christian and did not want his help in becoming one. But then she said something that should resonate within the entire Christian church:

> ... I think the Christian churches should begin dawa [proselytizing] exactly as Islam does. You need to compete, because you can be a powerful tool to reverse Islamization. You should start with Muslim neighborhoods in Rome. Europe is sleepwalking into disaster – cultural, ideological, and political disaster – because the authorities of the church have neglected the immigrant ghettoes (238).

In the last chapter, "Seeking God but Finding Allah," she speculates that many Muslims are seeking a God who meets the description of the Christian God, but they find Allah. She thinks that Christian leaders are wasting precious time in futile dialogues with self-appointed leaders of Islam. Her advice to them: "Redirect your efforts and seek to convert as many Muslims as possible to Christianity, "introducing them to a God who rejects Holy War and who has sent his son to die for all sinners out of love for mankind" (247).

Though she now is an atheist, she has high regard for Christian churches and believers who are reaching out to Muslim immigrants in

Holland – as she herself experienced. This book is filled with insight about one of the biggest challenges facing the free West. It should be required reading for every politician and public servant involved with immigration policies.

Nomad should become a must-read in every Christian church and family. You will be moved to tears at times. Above all, you will be moved to a profound respect for the fortitude and honesty of this lady who overcame hardship and obstacles that most of us cannot even imagine in our worst nightmares.

33 After America[166]

Europe climbed out of the stream [of the natural order of things]. You don't need to make material sacrifices: the state takes care of all that. You don't need to have children. And you certainly don't need to die for king and country. But a society that has nothing to die for has nothing to live for: it's no longer a stream, but a stagnant pool (123).

The ominous-sounding title of this book may steer some away from Mark Steyn's description of the grave dangers facing America and the rest of the still-free world. But if they are prepared for an honest encounter with what is eating away at the very foundations of American society (and our own), readers will be well rewarded.

Steyn has the knack of blasting away the sugar-coated cover of the fact that powerful forces are busy dismantling America. This is the same country that for more than two centuries – though not without its failures – has stood out as a beacon of freedom and opportunities for millions of people. Now it's not so sure.

---

[166] Mark Steyn, *After America: Get Ready for Armageddon*, Washington DC: Regnery Publishing, 2011. Reviewed by H.A. Orig., *Christian Courier*, April 9, 2019.

The author's previous book, written in 2006, bears the title *America Alone*, by which he meant to say that America was indeed an exceptional nation. It still had the opportunity to avoid what he called the "civilizational exhaustion" that is afflicting the West. However, five years later, the title After America suggests that America, too, has capitulated to the same destructive forces and beliefs.[167]

In the prologue, "The Stupidity of Broke," the author reviews the various phases of being insolvent, in addition to running out of money. He points out that it starts with the money; last year's debt had risen to $13 trillion, which is more debt than all the Congresses from 1789 till 1989 accumulated. A fundamental change of course is needed, but it will be extremely difficult to do.

THE WRITING ON THE WALL

Steyn believes that America is in danger of following on Europe's path to becoming an ever-expanding state that will drown itself in a sea of indebtedness. Now is the time for America to get serious about drastic cutbacks, though that will hit many people very hard. At the same time Steyn is convinced that the financial mismanagement is much more than a problem that can be neatly isolated and treated by itself. He writes:

> Increasing dependency, disincentivizing self-reliance, absolving the citizenry from responsibility for their actions; the multitrillion-dollar debt catastrophe is not the problem but merely the symptom. It's not just about balancing the books, but about balancing the most basic impulses of society. These are structural and, ultimately, moral questions (14).

Interestingly, Steyn draws an analogy between our time and a story told in the book of Daniel. King Belshazzar of the Babylonians threw a

---

[167] Mark Steyn, *America Alone: The End of the World As We Know It* (Washington DC: Regnery Publishing, 2008).

party where they toasted the gods of gold, silver, and other materials. Suddenly in the midst of the drunken revelry there mysteriously appeared a hand that wrote these words on the wall: "*mene, mene, tekel, upharsin*," which means: counted, weighed, and found wanting. The same night Belshazzar was killed and Darius the Mede became the new king.

Steyn has a list of words beginning with all the letters of the word Armageddon as in:

Addiction. We spend too much, borrowing from the future to such an extent it's no longer clear we've got one.

Redistribution. Day by day, an unprecedented transfer of wealth from the productive class to the obstructive class is delivering a self-governing republic into rule by regulators, bureaucrats, and social engineers.

Global Retreat. As Britain and other great powers quickly learned, the price of Big Government at home is an ever-smaller presence abroad. An America turned inward will make for a more dangerous world.

Steyn sets out the two possibilities in stark terms. If America continues on its current course, he predicts that there will be nothing to unite it. It will no longer be a nation with a limited government the first generation of Americans built. "And life, liberty, and the pursuit of happiness will be conspicuous by their absence."

Steyn points out that America is still different. In other countries, including France and Britain, rioters took to the streets demanding more from the government. America was the only nation in the developed world where millions took to the streets to tell their government to stay out of their lives and their pockets. The America that "stands for economic dynamism" for "self-reliance ... not the security state in which Britons are second only to North Koreans in the number of times they are photographed by government cameras," that America, Steyn wants to believe, still has a fighting chance.

UNDREAMING AMERICA

The bulk of his book is devoted to describing how far America has already gone in the wrong direction. The notion of multiculturalism is a major contributor to that wrong turn. If you really believe that no culture is better than another, you will do very poorly in defending your own. As Steyn puts it: "There is a fine line between civilization and the abyss."

Steyn traces the current problems afflicting America not in the first place to this or that policy. Instead, he takes a critical look at the underlying popular mindset that has given rise to the current and impending dangers facing America.

In the chapter," Undreaming America," Steyn refers to the writings of Alexis de Tocqueville (1805-59), who praised the American sense of self-reliance and cooperation, but he also had a warning for the seductions of the all-providing state. He envisioned a herd mentality that surely would undo the dream of America as the land of the free and the home of the brave. De Tocqueville's premonition has proved to be close to the mark and is worth pondering:

> I see an innumerable crowd of like and equal men who revolve on themselves without repose, procuring the small and vulgar pleasures with which they fill their souls.... The sovereign extends its arms about the society as a whole; it covers its surface with a network of petty regulations – complicated, minute, and uniform – through which even the most original minds and the most vigorous souls know not how to make their way...it does not break wills; it softens them, bends them, and directs them; rarely does it force one to act, but it constantly opposes itself to one's acting on one's own... it does not tyrannize, it gets in the way: it curtails, it enervates, it extinguishes, it stupefies, and finally reduces each nation to being nothing more than a herd of timid and industrious animals, of which the government is the shepherd (45-46)

This grim picture of herd-like behavior all too realistically reflects the behavior of a large and growing segment of the America population. Steyn piles example on example of cases where indeed the state hinders people in their entrepreneurial endeavors by means of complicated and costly regulations, as well as by silly rules that make a child's lemonade stand and serving customers a cup of coffee in a neighborhood hardware store illegal and punishable acts.

During the frantic campaign to force through the gigantic ObamaCare legislation, it became obvious that the more than the 2000-page bill had not been carefully read by the lawmakers themselves. In response to a question, Nancy Pelosi, then House Leader, said that they should first pass the bill so that they then can find out what it contains.

REGULATORY NIGHTMARES

It gets worse. The 2000-plus page bill will be accompanied by many more thousands of pages of regulations. Who writes the regulations? Not the lawmakers but the thousands of bureaucrats led by the various cabinet secretaries. This will call for an untold number of oversight management agencies and committees that are bound to get bogged down in the complexity and the vastness of this bureaucracy. The American health sector covers 16 per cent of the American economy and involves doctor-patient relations that are often accompanied by deep emotional feelings. No bureaucracy can "manage" such a monstrosity.

Kathleen Sebelius, as Secretary of Health and Human Services is required to oversee the application of the ObamaCare bill. This law contains 700 references to the Secretary "shall," another 200 to the Secretary "may," and 139 to the secretary "determines." If you were tasked with such a huge responsibility, what would you do? Would you be able to sleep at all? Of course the Secretary passes those tasks on to an army of regulators. But the point that Steyn makes is that she can pretty well do anything she wants. Here is a sample plucked at random: "The secretary shall develop oral healthcare components that shall include tooth-level surveillance." Steyn remarks: "Tooth-level surveillance: From colonial subjects to indentured servants in a quarter-millennium."

While Steyn is on the subject of regulations, he points out that to open a restaurant in NYC you need to deal with at least 11 municipal agencies, plus submit to 23 city inspections, and apply for 30 different permits and certificates. The city realized that this could all become quite complicated, so they created a new bureaucratic body to help you navigate through all the other bureaucratic bodies. "Great," says Steyn, "an agency of Bureaucratic Expeditiousness Regulation to keep it up to snuff."

Now you know why bureaucracies keep growing – at least until they self-destruct and leave only wreckage. A current case is the meltdown of Greece, a disaster that other countries are now desperately trying to avoid. The prospects do not look promising.

THE SEXUAL REVOLUTION

Steyn is convinced that the family is an essential building block for a healthy society. Here the picture is bleak, and possibly more devastating than in any other sector of society. The sexual revolution of the 1960s is based on the Big Lie that to live free is to have sex whenever and with whomever you want without consequences, now that the normal results of sexual relations can be prevented, or can be undone by abortion.

Steyn writes that the traditional notions of chastity, fidelity, monogamy, are now considered mere social constructs. In other words, the traditional bonds of marriage between a man and a woman calling for responsibility and self-denial in the raising of children, have been destroyed in the revolution. What has been the result?

He reports that 40 percent of American children are now born out of wedlock, a majority of Hispanic children are born to unmarried mothers; so are 70 percent of black children. New categories of crime have sprung up in the wake of familial collapse. Millions of American children are raised in dysfunctional households where even elemental character formation is near impossible. Steyn predicts: "In an America of fewer jobs, more poverty, more crime, more drugs, more disease, and growing ethno-cultural resentments, the shattering of the indispensable social building block will have catastrophic consequences" (234).

Steyn writes that the sexual revolution was well-named because its consequences are everywhere. It was not only a revolt against sexual norms but against all norms. Its underlying normlessness, or nihilism, eats away at all the other social structures too. Many now look to the government as the only source of support and stability, which is the reason that the government is expanding and everything else is diminishing.

THOUGHT CONTROL IN ACADEMIA

The American educational system is another significant building block of society – for good or ill. Steyn thinks it is the latter. In fact, he bluntly states that education is "the biggest single structural defect in the United States," though he acknowledges that America has world-class academic institutions in science and engineering.

America spends more per pupil on education than any other major industrial democracy, but the results do not reflect that. Nearly 60 percent of U.S. high school graduates entering college require remedial education. In New York, it's 75 percent.

Steyn argues that the educational system has been hard hit by the experiment with affirmative action and diversity. He believes that it has corrupted the integrity of American education, so that it now "affirmatively acts in favor of ideological and cultural homogeneity." He writes that American education is now in the "grip of a ruthless and destructive conformity," also referred to as political correctness.

One might think that the academy would be a place where conformity of thought would be shunned like the plague. Should it not be a place where all ideas can be openly stated and debated in an atmosphere of freedom and intellectual curiosity?

Yes, but the reality is very different, because political correctness and intolerance now rule the Academy, where only the liberal, far Left ideology is acceptable. Hence conservative academics are rarely invited to address a university audience, and if they are, they often need body-guards. Even then they are sometimes shouted down and unable to complete their presentation. Just ask David Horowitz, Nonie Darwish, Pamela Geller, Robert Spencer, and others on the "wrong" side of the ideological divide.

POLITICAL CORRECTNESS KILLS

This is not a minor issue. In fact, political correctness kills. As Steyn reminds us, 13 men and women and an unborn baby died on November 5, 2009, gunned down, of all places, at a military base at Fort Hood, Texas. They died because the military authorities did nothing although they knew that the killer, Major Nidal Malik Hasan, was a Muslim fanatic who hated America. They knew that he was in contact with the late Anwar al-Awlaki, the American-born radical cleric who advocated all-out holy war against the United States.

Yet they did not dismiss Hasan from the army. Instead, they promoted him, and 14 people died. Nobody got fired or court martialed. Subsequent investigations mentioned nothing about Hasan's Islamic fanaticism, but this crime was categorized as a case of "workplace violence." Why such negligence that borders on the criminal? The Associated Press reported that "a fear of appearing discriminatory against a Muslim student kept officers from filing a formal written complaint."

To put it bluntly, political correctness has reached the highest levels of the American military and the Obama administration. As Steyn put it: "The craven submission to political correctness...the wish for a quiet life leads to death, and not that quietly. When the chief of staff of the United States Army has got the disease, you're in big (and probably) terminal trouble."

Here is Steyn's summation of the choice before America – and the rest of us:

> Americans face a choice: you can rediscover the animating principles of the American idea – of limited government, a self-reliant citizenry, and the opportunities to exploit your talents to the fullest – or you can join most of the rest of the western world in terminal decline. To rekindle the spark of liberty once it dies is very difficult. The inertia, the ennui, the fatalism is even more pathetic than the demographic decline and fiscal profligacy of the social democratic state, and, because it's subtler and less tangible, even harder to rally against (348).

After America is easy to read but hard to absorb. In good Steyn fashion there are some funny stories and deft wordplays. But if you are looking for an honest, straightforward – though painful – diagnosis that is essential for the proper treatment of the disease that is afflicting America, this is the book for you.

34 Good News in a World of Bad News[168]

When life is full of despair, it is only the glory of God that truly sustains. There have been times when everything has gone wrong, when friends and colleagues have been killed and there has seemed to be no hope. It is at times like this when I ask God to show me his glory. He always does so, though I do not always see it immediately.[169]

The Bible speaks in language that rivets our attention on the power of God in the affairs of nations:

Why do the nations conspire and the peoples plot in vain? The kings of the earth take their stand and the rulers gather together against the Lord and against his Anointed One. Let us break their chains, they say, and throw off their fetters. (Ps. 2: 1-3)

Nations are in uproar, kingdoms fall; he lifts his voice, the earth melts. The Lord Almighty is with us; the God of Jacob is our fortress. Come and see the works of the Lord, the desolations he has brought

[168] Orig., *Christian Courier* (Jan 9, 2012).

[169] Andrew White, *The Vicar of Baghdad: Fighting for Peace in the Middle East* (Mansfield, TX: Monarch Books, 2009), 171

on the earth. He makes wars cease to the ends of the earth; he breaks the bow and shatters the spear; he burns the shields with fire (Ps. 46:6-9).

The purpose of this book is to investigate whether it is still possible to find our way in a world where many believe that there is no absolute truth, only different versions of what we decide to be true for ourselves. Pilate's mocking question to Jesus, "What is truth?" has resounded through the ages, and in our time has become ensconced in our Western culture.

THE BAD NEWS

One thing is sure, we are living in times of momentous, even revolutionary changes on a world scale. Instead of creating a peaceful and humane world as intended in the U.N. Charter, we can only watch with helpless frustration that millions are still living in conditions of slavery and terror that we in the free West cannot even imagine. The Soviet Union has collapsed, but the specter of Communism is still hovering over China, Cuba, North Korea, Venezuela and Vietnam where men without a conscience rule with unspeakable cruelty. (Another place where Communism still holds sway is at the universities in the West, though they now call it progressivism or liberalism.)

Most of the Sharia-law ruled countries are mired in poverty and hatred toward the infidels. Christians and other non-Muslim people are viciously persecuted. Every day, we hear of torture, murder, imprisonment of Christians, and destruction of their churches, houses and businesses in Pakistan, Nigeria, Somalia, Sudan, Egypt, Iran, Iraq, Afghanistan, Kenya and many other countries.

The ongoing war fought by the radical ISIS in Syria and Iraq has forced many to flee with nothing but the clothes on their backs. The refugees, now numbering in the hundreds of thousands are living in camps where the conditions are dismal.

Hundreds of young girls have been kidnapped in Nigeria by Boko Haram whose spokesmen have said that these girls would be "sold" to the ISIS fighters. Amnesty International has released a publication called Escape from Hell: Torture, Sexual Slavery in Islamic State Captivity in Iraq. It reports that possibly thousands of Yezidi women and girls have suffered horrifying abuse by the terrorists in Northern Iraq. Survivors who escaped have told how some of the women tried to kill each other by strangulation in an attempt to avoid the suffering at the hands of the ISIS murderers.

The Christians who were not able to flee before the ISIS terrorists arrived were given the choice of converting to Islam, paying a heavy tax, or be killed. Some refused and were killed. Others "converted" to Islam and were spared, but lived with a terrible sense of having betrayed their Lord. No one can forget the pictures of the helpless kidnapped Westerners standing next to a man totally clad in black holding the knife used to behead his victims. This is the face of evil from the depth of human depravity that is impossible to fathom.

In a recent interview on CBN News the Anglican priest Andrew White, also called the "Vicar of Baghdad," told about the Christians fleeing from Baghdad to Nineveh when Islamic militants began to terrorize them. He said:

Then one day, ISIS, the Islamic State, the Islamic caliphate came [to Nineveh] and they hounded all of them [Christians] out. Not some, all of them. And they killed huge numbers. They chopped their children in half; they chopped their heads off.... Today's pictures are too awful to show. You know I love to show photos but the photo I was sent today was the most awful I have ever seen. A family of eight all shot through the face lying in a pool of blood with their Bible open on the couch. They would not convert [and] it cost them their life.[170]

---

[170] Raymond Ibrahim, "Islam: Built on the Blood of (Christian (Child) Martyrs," frontpagemag.com, December 8, 2014.

In the same interview White told the story of four Christian children, all under 15, who were told by ISIS terrorists that they must convert to Islam, but they refused and said: "No, we love Jesus (Yeshua). We have always loved Jesus. We have always followed Jesus. Jesus has always been with us." The ISIS men repeated their order to say the words "Shehada, convert to Islam." The children said, "No, we can't." [White starts sobbing] "They chopped all their heads off. How do you respond to that? You just cry. They're my children. That is what we have been going through. That is what we are going through."

CHRISTIANITY DISLODGED FROM ITS CRADLE

Nina Shea, director of Hudson Institute's Center for Religious Freedom, and co-author (with Paul Marshall) of *Persecuted,*[171] is a tireless defender of freedom of religion for all people. She pays special attention to Christians who now again are severely persecuted in all countries headed by fanatic tyrants. On December 24, 2014, she began an article posted on *National Review Online* with these compelling and sad words:

> For the first time in 1,400 years there will be no Christmas celebrations in Nineveh province, home to Iraq's largest remaining Christian community and largest non-Muslim minority, and site of great biblical significance. This Northern Province, whose area is over three times larger than that of Lebanon, is now part of the Islamic State's caliphate, and its Christians and churches are no longer tolerated. What has become of Nineveh's Christians? What will be their fate?

These questions should haunt us who (still) live in freedom and generally in prosperous circumstances of the West. But the secular media has paid little attention to the destruction of Christianity in the Middle East, which in many ways was the cradle of Christianity 2000 years ago, more than 600 years before the birth of Islam. Thousands of

---

[171] Paul Marshall, Lela Gilbert and Nina Shea, *Persecuted: The Global Assault on Christians* (Nashville: Thomas Nelson Publishers, 2013).

years before that it was the location where God made a covenant, going back to Adam and Eve, and later with Abraham from whom the people of Israel, the Jewish nation, came into being. God promised Abraham that he and his descendants would be a blessing to the whole world. (See Gen. 12: 2-3)

Shea writes that the events in Iraq should be of interest to America with its 247 million Christians. Yet the mainstream media pays little attention. A *New York Times* reporter explained in a recent e-mail that the events in Iraq are of limited interest to most of their readers for they have only a vague notion about Iraq's relevance to America.

What is worse is that, with few exceptions, the Christian churches in the West have shown little interest in the plight of their fellow believers who are now going through the fire of unimaginable suffering and heartbreak. For them it is a matter of life or death. The blood of small children, young girls, women and men in the thousands is again crying out to the heavens. Religious leaders in church and government ought to double down on protesting the evil done to Christians – and other non-Muslims. (Here the voice of the most powerful political office on the world scene should be heard loud and clear. But all we got from the Obama White House are a few banalities that safely can be ignored by the evildoers.)

Christians and their ancestors who have lived for time stretching back to the beginning of the Christian Church are now forced from their homes, tortured, raped, imprisoned and murdered, which is drastically changing the population patterns. Before 2003 there were an estimated 1.5 million Christians in Iraq; now there are only about 200,000 left. Where did more than a million Christians go? Some perished by starvation, cold, and murder, a few emigrated, many, perhaps the majority, ended up in refugee camps, desperately clinging to life under horrifying conditions.

NOW THE GOOD NEWS

How is it possible to talk about Good News in this world of injustice, persecution, torture, murder, and wars and rumor of wars, not to mention the deadly epidemics or the calamities that can occur in the natural world of floods, drought, earthquakes and tsunamis? Where to find the source of goodness, except in the Creator who made the heavens and the earth and then saw that it was very good.

Something went dreadfully wrong with the entry of sin into the world. But God did not abandon his creation and mankind made in his image. By his death and resurrection Christ secured salvation for his own. That is the Good News for the whole world. Jesus is the One who is making all things new and he told us: "I have told you these things, so that in me you may have peace. In this world you will have trouble. But take heart! I have overcome the world" (John 16: 33). St. Paul, in his letter to the Christians in Corinth, writes:

> We are hard pressed on every side, but not crushed; perplexed, but not in despair; persecuted, but not abandoned; struck down, but not destroyed…. Therefore, we do not lose heart. Though outwardly we are wasting away, yet inwardly we are being renewed day by day…. So we fix our eyes not on what is seen, but what is unseen. For what is seen is temporary, but what is unseen is eternal (2 Cor. 4: 8-9; 16, 18).

Where now is the Good News? Where is God in these dreadful circumstances? I hardly dare to go on. What can I say? What can we Christians say? What would I do in facing the choice of life or death for my family? The amazing reality is that many who are going through heartbreaking suffering and losses testify to their steadfast faith in God who has not abandoned them. The best we can do is listen to their testimony that in the midst of a terrifying darkness, the light of the Gospel still shines. That's a miracle beyond our understanding. We should pay a lot of attention to the voices that tell us about that miracle and to beg us not to forget them. So what can we do? What should we do?[172]

We can begin by contacting and supporting persons and organizations that are in the midst of these suffering people, doing what they can to help them. We should get to know people such as pastor Andrew White and his team, helping with immediate needs for food, water, and medical care, but above all in providing spiritual sustenance and comfort in what seem hopeless situations. Here are few more comments from Pastor White that testify to his faith that amidst the darkness the light of God's presence still breaks through.

In his 2011 book called *Faith Under Fire* White writes that the Bible text "Perfect love drives out fear" (1 John 4 :18) has become important to him because it sustains him and his people. When they are afraid, he tells them that they are loved, loved by God. The knowledge that love sustains them is more than book knowledge. In Iraq it is a matter of life or death. He writes that they experience the reality of that love "that surrounds us, enables us, and sustains us through the heat of the fire."[173]

Pastor White realizes that some people in the Baghdad church suffer a severe degree of despair, depression and loss. For such, he writes that all they can do is what anyone else would do, that is to pray for them, be there for them, and surround them with love.[174] At the same time White writes that when you undergo severe persecution, the reality of God's presence is of great comfort.

That presence is what gives the leadership team at St George's the strength that prevents them from slipping into despair. They are surrounded by brokenness, uncertainty and tragedy. Although they suffer

---

[172] The magazine, *The Voice of the Martyrs Canada*, is an excellent source of information and support of the persecuted churches.

[173] Andrew White, *Faith Under Fire: What the Middle East Conflict Has Taught Me about God* (Mansfield, TX: Monarch Books, 2011), 98.

[174] Ibid., 100.

for their faith in the Lord, and many people would view their circumstances as terrifying and somber, White has often said that far from being miserable, the congregation of St. George's are the most joyful people he has ever served.[175]

Pastor White is often asked why he spends so much time in a dangerous place such as Baghdad. He answers:

The more I have done this type of work, and the more I have struggled with the reality of death and destruction, the more I have had to put my trust simply in my Lord and my God.... However dreadful the tragedy, my Lord is there. Amidst the greatest havoc I have witnessed in post-war Iraq or in Gaza, or in Bethlehem during the siege, I have still seen his glory.[176]

Pastor White's fearless and unselfish dedication to the spiritual and physical wellbeing of the beleaguered Iraqi people is powerful evidence that God is at work in the most unlikely and desperate circumstances. He concludes his book with a hymn that he composed and that sums up his experience in Iraq. Here are two verses:

The bullets fly, the rockets thud.
I long, O Lord, to see you here,
To see your peace breaking through.
Oh, reconcile me now to you!

I see your glory shining through.
The darkness fades at your command.
The glory heals the brokenness.
Oh, reconcile me now to you!

---

[175] Ibid., 101-2.

[176] White, *The Vicar of Baghdad*, 170-1.

Afterword

We should have no illusions about the significance of the conflict of world views behind the 34 chapters. The popular story charts the major divisions between the left and right, between social-centered government versus a government that protects individual rights and freedoms. More fundamentally, the rift between God and Satan, good and evil, go back to the real story that begins right at the dawn of creation, with the first human created in the image of God.

At first, creation was very good, but soon Satan appeared on the scene and tempted man and woman to become like God. If they only disobeyed God, they would become like him in all his splendor and power. They accepted the deceptive message, they disobeyed God, and the rest is a history of sin and its creeping catastrophic consequences.

While the harmony and the beauty of the creation was destroyed, and even as we find ourselves in a constant battle with the forces of deceit and evil, the good news is that God does not let Satan extinguish the truth, nor have the last word.

Made in the USA
Monee, IL
15 February 2020